THE PHENOMENAL BASIS OF INTENTIONALITY

PHILOSOPHY OF MIND

SERIES EDITOR: David J. Chalmers, Australian National University
and New York University

The Phenomenal Basis of
Intentionality

Angela Mendelovici

OXFORD
UNIVERSITY PRESS

OXFORD
UNIVERSITY PRESS

Oxford University Press is a department of the University of Oxford. It furthers
the University's objective of excellence in research, scholarship, and education
by publishing worldwide. Oxford is a registered trade mark of Oxford University
Press in the UK and certain other countries.

Published in the United States of America by Oxford University Press
198 Madison Avenue, New York, NY 10016, United States of America.

© Oxford University Press 2018

CIP data is on file at the Library of Congress
ISBN 978-0-19-086380-7

9 8 7 6 5 4 3 2 1
Printed by Sheridan Books, Inc., United States of America

To David, Eleni, and Vera

Contents

Preface

THIS PROJECT BEGAN 15 years ago when, as an undergraduate at McGill, I set out to write my undergraduate thesis on phenomenal consciousness. After reading David Chalmers' *The Conscious Mind*, I decided that there wasn't much more for me to say on phenomenal consciousness and resolved to steer clear of the topic. So I turned to the problem of intentionality. But I soon came to realize that attempts to understand intentionality independently of phenomenal consciousness ultimately fail. What's more, I came to believe that intentionality is in fact one and the same thing as phenomenal consciousness. I wrote my undergraduate thesis on precisely this topic (and the idealist consequences I took to ensue), and then my PhD thesis on this same topic again (minus the idealism). This book is the culmination of these efforts.

The ideas presented here have benefited from practically every philosophical interaction I have ever had with friends, colleagues, students, and mentors at McGill University, Princeton University, the Australian National University, the University of Western Ontario, and elsewhere. I was especially lucky to benefit from the exceptionally rich intellectual environment at the Australian National University, where I spent time as a postdoctoral fellow at the Centre for Consciousness and as a visitor.

Many of the ideas in this book have been presented in talks I have given at the Australasian Association of Philosophy Conference (2008 and 2011), the European Congress of Analytic Philosophy (2011), the 23rd World Congress of Philosophy at the University of Athens, the Canadian Philosophical Association Meeting (2013, 2014, and 2017), the Pacific American Association of Philosophy Meeting (2013), Princeton University, the Australian National University, the University of Toronto, the University of Melbourne, the University of Western Australia, the Central European University, the University of Crete, Oakland University, Victoria University at Wellington, Tulane University, the University of Texas at Austin, the University of Waterloo, Cornell University, the University of Washington at St. Louis, the University of Minnesota, CUNY, the University of Wisconsin–Madison, Yeshiva University, Wellesley College, Wayne State University, Charles Sturt University, Ruhr-Universität Bochum, and the University of Western Ontario. I thank the audiences at those talks, and especially my commentators Mike Collins, Tim Crane, Janette Dinishak, Mark Herr, David Ivy, Charles Siewert, and Brad Thompson for their helpful and incisive commentaries and our subsequent discussions.

I am especially indebted to the Phenomenal Intentionality Reading Group— Tim Bayne, David Bourget, Rob Stainton, and Chris Viger—for reading an early version of this manuscript and providing valuable criticisms and concrete suggestions on both content and presentation. The final version grew out of our many discussions. I am also extremely thankful to Charles Siewert, Declan Smithies, Laura Gow, and Adam Pautz for reading this manuscript in its entirety and providing extremely helpful and incisive feedback. Thanks also to Daniel Stoljar and the ANU Philosophy of Mind Work-in-Progress Group for reading and discussing several chapters of this work and providing extremely helpful feedback. I am also thankful to those who read and provided helpful comments on ancestors of various chapters, especially Frank Jackson, Gilbert Harman, Jack Woods, Adam Pautz, Uriah Kriegel, David Pitt, Philipp Koralus, Jimmy Martin, Paul Benacerraf, Anthony Appiah, Gideon Rosen, Jeff Speaks, and David Davies.

This book has also benefited from numerous discussions that have helped me see many issues in a new light. Thank you to Derek Baker, Sam Baker, John Bengson, Mark Budolfson, David Chalmers, Tim Crane, Kati Farkas, Bill Fish, Tamar Gendler, Terry Horgan, Josh Knobe, Dan Korman, Uriah Kriegel, John Maier, Carla Merino, Matthew Moss, Daniel Nolan, Gurpreet Rattan, Susanna Schellenberg, Vanessa Schouten, Daniel Stoljar, Jackie Sullivan, and Bas van Fraassen.

I am especially grateful to my dissertation supervisors, Frank Jackson and Gil Harman, for encouraging me to write the dissertation I wanted to write, which formed the basis of this book, and to my undergraduate thesis supervisor, David Davies, for encouraging me to write the undergraduate thesis I wanted to write, which formed the basis of my dissertation. I owe special thanks to Jeff Speaks, who raised an objection to my undergraduate thesis in 2004 that inspired the views defended in Chapter 7, and to David Chalmers, who suggested that my ideas might work well as a book.

I owe special gratitude to my parents, Lina and Marius, for exemplifying both insight and rigor in academic work and for their love, support, and confidence in me. I am especially grateful to my mother and my family in Greece—especially Giagia, Maria, and Tryphon—for creating a near utopian work environment for me at our summer house. Most of this book (as well as the theses it is based on) was written there.

The editors and production team at OUP have been tremendously helpful throughout the publication process. Thanks especially to Peter Ohlin, David Chalmers, Isla Ng, Raj Suthan, Thomas McCarthy, and Sangeetha Vishwanthan.

My greatest debt by far is to David Bourget, my partner, frequent co-author, and (near) doppelgänger. When I first met David in 2008, I was surprised to find someone with almost exactly the same philosophical views as me. This book has been heavily influenced by all our discussions throughout the years, due to which our views have almost entirely converged (some residual disagreements remain concerning the material of Chapter 9). David has read every chapter of this book multiple times and discussed every single idea in it with me, providing helpful criticisms and even more helpful constructive suggestions, and in many cases spending hours and days helping me work through key ideas. I am immensely thankful for all his help, as well as for his unwavering moral support and encouragement.

Overview

THE AIM OF this book is to defend a radically internalist theory of intentionality, the aboutness or directedness of mental states, on which intentionality is simply identical to phenomenal consciousness, which is an intrinsic, non-relational feature of mental life. This view has been described to me as obviously false, unfashionable, and flying in the face of everyday intuition and cognitive science. It has also been described to me as trivially true and uninteresting. I aim to defend a version of this view that is true but not trivial, interesting but not false, and surprisingly conciliatory with our intuitive and scientific understanding of the mind.

My target, intentionality, can be understood as the observed "aboutness" or "directedness" of mental states. We introspectively notice that many mental states in some way or other seem to "present," "represent," or be "about" things. For example, you might notice that your current visual experiences represent a page before you, some marks of various shapes and colors, and perhaps the words that these marks form. You might also notice that your current thoughts represent that there is a page with marks and words before you, something to do with your own mental states, or a need for a cup of coffee. Intentionality, roughly, is this phenomenon of aboutness or directedness that we notice in these and other everyday cases.

My aim is to offer a theory of intentionality, a theory that describes the deep nature of intentionality, or, in other words, that tells us what intentionality really *is*, metaphysically speaking. Examples of theories of intentionality include tracking theories, on which the most basic kind of intentionality is a causal or other kind of tracking relation between internal representations and items in the world (see, e.g., Dretske 1986 and Fodor 1987), and functional role theories, on which the most basic kind of intentionality is a matter of internal states' functional dispositions with respect to other internal states and perhaps also with respect to items in the environment (see, e.g., Harman 1987 and Block 1986).

This book proposes a very different kind of theory of intentionality, the phenomenal intentionality theory (PIT), which takes the most basic kind of intentionality to arise from a conceptually distinct mental feature, phenomenal consciousness, the felt, subjective, or "what it's like" (Nagel 1974) aspect of mental life. This and related views have recently been defended by various authors, including Horgan and Tienson (2002), Loar (2003), Farkas (2008b, 2008a), Strawson (2008), Siewert (1998), Montague (2010), Bourget (2010a), Mendelovici (2010), Kriegel (2011), Pitt (2004, 2009), Pautz (2013a), and Mendelovici and Bourget (2014), and have historical roots in the works of Brentano (1874) and Husserl (1900). This book proposes a version of PIT that is not only motivated on in-principle grounds but also empirically adequate in that it can accommodate all cases of intentionality, including those that are commonly thought to pose problems for PIT.

I proceed as follows: Chapter 1 of Part I fixes reference on our target, intentionality. I argue that while the notions of aboutness and directedness gesture toward this target, they are too fuzzy to provide us with a firm grip on it. I propose to replace these notions with an ostensive reference-fixing definition, which can be contrasted with other candidate definitions that take intentionality to be whatever plays certain roles, such as roles in folk psychological or scientific theories of behavior, roles in securing truth and reference, or simply roles in explaining how we get around in the world. On my approach, intentionality is a phenomenon we observe and want to explain, rather than a posit in a theory primarily aimed at explaining something else.

Chapter 2 of Part I specifies the kind of theory of intentionality we are after and describes two theory-independent ways of knowing about our intentional states: introspection and consideration of psychological role.

Part II considers and argues against what I take to be the two main competitors to my favored approach to intentionality, tracking and functional role theories. Chapter 3 of Part II argues that tracking theories face a mismatch problem: there are cases in which we represent a content that does not match anything we can plausibly be said to track. The tracking theory, then, is empirically inadequate, since it cannot accommodate all the required cases. Chapter 4 of Part II argues that the mismatch problem also afflicts the best versions of the functional role theory. Now, while the mismatch problem shows *that* the tracking theory and the best versions of the functional role theory are false, it does not pinpoint the precise reasons for their failure. Chapter 4 further argues that the fundamental problem with these theories is that tracking relations and functional roles simply do not have what it takes to give rise to intentionality.

Part III turns to my favored approach to intentionality, the phenomenal intentionality theory (PIT), on which the most basic kind of intentionality arises from phenomenal consciousness. Chapter 5 of Part III presents and motivates PIT. I argue that, unlike tracking theories and functional role theories, PIT provides the right kinds of ingredients to account for intentionality and is not clearly empirically inadequate. I distinguish between different versions of PIT, focusing especially on my favored version, strong identity PIT, which, roughly, takes every intentional property to be identical to some phenomenal property. Chapter 6 of Part III considers and responds to some theoretical worries with PIT, such as that it is not naturalistic.

Part IV further supports PIT by considering certain challenging cases for the view. In doing so, it fleshes out my favored version of strong identity PIT and shows that it is both interesting and tenable. Chapter 7 of Part IV considers the challenge raised by the case of thoughts, which appear to be rich in intentional content but poor in phenomenal character. I argue that thoughts have a kind of content that does indeed arise from their fairly impoverished phenomenal characters, though this content is correspondingly impoverished. I further argue that, although thoughts do not phenomenally represent many of their alleged contents, they do the next best thing: they *derivatively* represent them. I propose self-ascriptivism, a view on which we derivatively represent various contents by ascribing them to ourselves, which is a matter of being disposed to have thoughts accepting ourselves or our phenomenal contents as representing these further contents. Although, as I argue, the resulting kind of derived mental representation does not qualify as a kind of *intentionality*, it qualifies as a kind of representation on a broad sense of the term.

Another important challenge for PIT is that of accounting for mental states that we take to be intentional but that appear to have no phenomenal character. Such states include standing states, like beliefs and desires that we are not currently entertaining, as well as occurrent states that we are not aware of, such as nonconscious states involved in language processing, blindsight, and early visual processing. Chapter 8 of Part IV addresses these challenges. I argue that standing states are not genuinely intentional states. However, I also suggest that self-ascriptivism can be extended to accommodate standing state contents and perhaps even standing states in their entirety.

Chapter 8 also argues that many nonconscious occurrent states, such as states involved in early visual processing, are neither intentional nor derivatively representational. While this position might seem fairly extreme, even "flying in the face of cognitive science," it is arguably very much in line with the standard view on the matter. It agrees with the standard view that such occurrent states track or carry information about various items in the environment and play various functional roles, and it also agrees that they represent various items, if all we mean by "representation" is something that boils down to tracking, carrying information, or having a functional role. The key disagreement with the standard view does not concern nonconscious occurrent states, but rather *conscious* occurrent states.

Part V, which consists in only one chapter, Chapter 9, turns to the question of whether intentionality is a relation to distinctly existing entities that play the role of content or whether, instead, intentionality is simply an aspect of intentional states or subjects. I argue in favor of the latter aspect view of intentionality. While it might be thought that the alternative relation view has various virtues that the aspect view lacks, such as according with common sense, allowing for public contents, helping us make sense of structured intentional states, and accounting for conditions of truth and reference, I argue that the aspect view fares no worse than the relation view when it comes to these alleged virtues.

The main goal of this book is to offer, flesh out, and defend a theory of intentionality, but it also has a secondary aim. As I mentioned above, Chapter 1 will argue that it is possible to get a good grip on the phenomenon of intentionality without defining it in terms of truth and reference, our abilities to get around in the world, folk psychology, or the scientific study of the mind. Throughout this book, I return to these alleged roles of intentionality and argue that it turns out that most of them are not in fact played by intentionality itself but by various closely related phenomena: The relevant ability to get around in the world is explained by a combination of factors, including intentionality and tracking relations; the notions of representation implicit in folk psychology don't correspond to intentionality but to some combination of intentionality and derived representation; conditions of truth and reference might end up requiring something more than merely having intentional states, like a primitive correspondence relation or our specifications of how we'd like to be interpreted; and the notions of representation invoked in the mind-brain sciences are often a matter of tracking relations and functional roles. The concluding chapter, Chapter 10, returns to the alleged roles of intentionality and summarizes these findings. The end result is a picture on which intentionality, as picked out ostensively, is a matter of phenomenal consciousness, and the various other roles intentionality is sometimes thought to play are in fact often played by distinct, although sometimes closely related, phenomena.

I Introduction

MY AIM IS to provide a theory of intentionality. Before comparing competing theories of intentionality, it is important to fix firmly on our target and to get clear on what kind of theory we are after. Chapter 1 proposes an ostensive way of fixing reference on intentionality, while Chapter 2 specifies what kind of theory we want and overviews two sources of theory-independent knowledge of intentionality that we can use to test our theories: introspection and considerations of psychological role.

1 Fixing Reference on Intentionality

THE AIM OF this book is to provide a theory of intentionality. The aim of this chapter is to clarify just what a theory of intentionality is a theory *of*. It is important to get clear on this before we start. A theory of intentionality is a theory that tells us that intentionality has a particular nature, but if it is unclear just what "intentionality" refers to, then it is unclear what it is that such a theory says has that nature.

I propose to get clear on our target by defining it ostensively using introspectively accessible paradigm cases. My ostensive definition can be contrasted with alternative definitions that may or may not end up picking out the same thing. I will suggest that the ostensive definition does a better job of capturing the core notion we are interested in. But first, I will say something about why common characterizations of intentionality in terms of "aboutness" and "directedness," though they succeed in gesturing toward our target, do not provide a satisfactory way of fixing firmly upon it.

1.1 Aboutness and Directedness

Intentionality is sometimes characterized, at least as a first pass, as the "aboutness" or "directedness" of mental states (and perhaps other items) to things that may or may not exist. We might say that a perceptual experience of a cup is "directed" at a cup, that a thought that it is raining is "about" the putative fact that it is raining, and that a belief in Santa Claus is "about" Santa Claus or the putative fact that Santa Claus exists.

This characterization of intentionality has roots in an oft-cited passage from Brentano, who is often credited with introducing the notion of intentionality to contemporary discussions:

> Every mental phenomenon is characterized by what the Scholastics of the Middle Ages called the intentional (or mental) inexistence of an object, and what we might call, though not wholly unambiguously, reference to a content, direction toward an object (which is not to be understood here as meaning a thing), or immanent objectivity. Every mental phenomenon includes something as object within itself, although they do not do so in the same way. In presentation, something is presented, in judgment something is affirmed or denied, in love loved, in hate hated, in desire desired and so on. (Brentano 1874, p. 88)

There are many examples of contemporary characterizations of intentionality in terms of "aboutness" and "directedness." For instance, Siewert (2006) writes: "Intentionality has to do with the directedness or aboutness of mental states—the fact that, for example, one's thinking is *of* or *about* something" (p. 1). Similarly, Speaks (2010b) writes: "The closest thing to a synonym for intentionality is 'aboutness'; something exhibits intentionality if and only if it is about something" (p. 398).[1]

In light of the widespread acceptance of such characterizations of intentionality in terms of aboutness and related notions, I will take it as given that such characterizations at least *gesture* toward the phenomenon of interest. However, despite this, the characterization of intentionality in terms of aboutness or directedness would not make a good definition, not even a good reference-fixing definition, of "intentionality." As a definition of "intentionality," it is too fuzzy and metaphorical to give us a firm grip on our target. It is simply not clear what is being said when we say that a mental state is "directed at" or "about" something, especially if this thing need not exist. An experience of a cup is not literally pointed in the direction of a cup (which may not even exist), in the way that a finger or an arrow might point to a cup, and a thought is not literally pointed in the direction of a proposition, which might be an abstract entity having no spatial location at all. If we take "aboutness"

---

[1]   For additional representative examples of this way of characterizing intentionality, see Jacob 2003, Byrne 2006, Kim 1998, p. 21, Searle 2004, p. 112, and O'Madagain 2014.

and "directedness" talk to supply a definition of "intentionality," it is simply not clear what this definition says.[2]

1.2 The Ostensive Way of Fixing Reference

Although "aboutness" and "directedness" talk do not provide us with a satisfactory definition of "intentionality," they do gesture toward the phenomenon of interest. I want to suggest that what is doing the work when we use "aboutness" and "direct-edness" talk to fix on intentionality is a prior grasp we have on the phenomenon. My suggestion for defining "intentionality," then, is to look past our descriptions of this phenomenon in terms of aboutness and related notions and focus instead on the phenomenon thus described. This is possible because we have a special access to this mental feature independent of any fuzzy or metaphorical descriptions: We can directly notice it through introspection, at least in some cases. This allows us to ostensively define "intentionality" as this feature, whatever it is, that we at least sometimes notice in ourselves and are tempted to describe using representational terms like "aboutness" and "directedness."

In order to flesh out this suggestion, let us begin by considering some cases of mental states that we are tempted to describe using representational terms like "aboutness" and "directedness." Take your present perceptual experiences: You might be visually experiencing some marks on a page, pens on your desk, or parts of your body. Likewise, you might be enjoying auditory experiences of voices, music, or various noises. These experiences have a certain feature, a feature we are tempted to describe using representational terms like "aboutness," "directedness," "ofness," or "saying something." We might describe these experiences as being "of" or "about" things or ways things are or might be, or as "saying" that things are a particular way. We might say they are "about" some marks on a page, that they "say" that these marks are in front of you, and so on.

Now consider the thoughts you are currently having. You might be thinking about your experiences, desiring another cup of coffee, or judging that I am pointing out the obvious. Like perceptual experiences, these thoughts have a feature that it is tempting to describe using representational terms. We might describe these thoughts as being "about" things or as "saying" that things are a certain way. We might say that

---

[2] Chisholm (1957a) criticizes Brentano's definition as being too fuzzy and suggests instead a linguistic criterion of intentionality. Speaks (2010b) also argues that we should not *define* "intentionality" in terms of aboutness; see also n. 5.

they are "about" our experiences, that they "say" that I am pointing out the obvious, etc.[3]

The above examples show that we have mental states that have a certain feature that we at least sometimes introspectively notice and are tempted to describe using representational terms, such as "about," "of," "represent," "present," and "saying something." *That* feature, whatever it is, is intentionality.

We can put things more precisely as follows: Call the mundane, everyday cases such as those described above our **paradigm cases** of intentionality. These are the cases that will form our initial sample of cases of intentionality for the purposes of our ostensive definition. Then we can fix reference on our target as follows:

Intentionality The feature that in paradigm cases we sometimes both (i) notice introspectively in ourselves and (ii) are tempted to describe using representational terms, such as "about," "of," "represent," "present," or "saying something."[4]

It is important to emphasize that the feature picked out by my definition is the feature of paradigm cases that we at least sometimes *both* introspectively notice *and* are tempted to describe representationally. This allows that there are features of paradigm cases that we *either* introspectively notice *or* are tempted to describe representationally, but not both, and that do not qualify as intentional. For example, the definition does not by itself rule out the view that paradigm cases have introspectively accessible phenomenal features that are distinct from intentionality.

It is also important to emphasize that, although we are using introspection to fix reference on intentionality, the ostensive definition does not rule out the possibility of instances of intentionality that are not introspectively accessible, or even instances of intentionality that are not mental. Such cases would not be paradigm cases of intentionality, but they would nonetheless be cases of intentionality so long as they had the relevant feature exemplified by paradigm cases. For example, as far as my definition is concerned, it could turn out that nonconscious beliefs and the nonconscious states posited by cognitive science, which, presumably, are not introspectively accessible, are instances of intentionality. For the same reasons, the ostensive definition does not rule out the possibility of instances of intentionality that we are not tempted to describe representationally. For example, it does not rule out the possibility of moods and afterimages being instances of intentionality, even though we (arguably) are not tempted to describe them representationally.

---

[3] I take the category of thoughts to include occurrent beliefs, occurrent desires, and other occurrent "cognitive" states but not standing beliefs, standing desires, or other standing states. See §1.4.2.

[4] Definitions of key terms can be found in the glossary on p. 249.

The ostensive definition arguably both does justice to the intuition behind the characterization of intentionality in terms of "aboutness" and "directedness" and is an improvement over a definition of "intentionality" in terms of this characterization. If I am right, "aboutness" talk aims to characterize a phenomenon that we have an antecedent grasp on. My ostensive definition picks out precisely that phenomenon, so it does justice to the intuition behind characterizations of intentionality in terms of "aboutness" and "directedness." It offers an improvement over a definition of "intentionality" in terms of such characterizations, since it fixes firmly on our target. Unlike a definition of "intentionality" simply as aboutness or directedness, it avoids being fuzzy or metaphorical, since it merely *mentions* our fuzzy and metaphorical representational terms rather than *use* them. (Of course, it uses the term "representational term," but this is a term picking out a class of terms rather than a representational term itself.)[5]

We can use this ostensive definition of "intentionality" to define some related notions: **Intentional properties** are ways things are or might be with respect to their intentionality, or intentional ways things are or might be, and **intentional states** are instantiations of intentional properties. As I am using the terms, intentional states are not the same thing as **intentional mental states**, which are mental states that include, but may not be exhausted by, the instantiation of intentional properties. For example, a judgment that grass is green might involve the instantiation of the intentional property of representing that grass is green together with a particular non-intentional "judgment" component. So, it is an intentional mental state but not an intentional state.[6]

What intentional properties and intentional states "say" or are "directed at" are their intentional contents. More precisely, we can think of intentional content as

---

[5] One might object that "aboutness" talk gestures at reference rather than at the ostensively defined phenomenon (but see Crane 2013, pp. 8–9, for a convincing argument against this). After all, one might argue, we sometimes say that mental states that fail to refer, like a thought that Santa Claus exists, are not really about anything at all.

  Now, we might agree that "aboutness" talk is sometimes used to pick out reference but disagree that this means that "aboutness" talk, *when used to characterize intentionality*, gestures at reference, since whatever "aboutness" talk is supposed to gesture at is normally taken to include mental states in which there is a failure of reference, such as the thought that Santa Claus exists. In any case, if "aboutness" talk is normally used to pick out reference, this only further supports my claim that characterizations of intentionality in terms of "aboutness" would not provide an adequate definition of intentionality. Speaks (2010b) makes a similar point, arguing that for such reasons the "characterization of intentionality as aboutness is only true to a first approximation" (p. 398).

[6] The term "intentional state" is often used to mean what I mean by "intentional mental state." I deviate from this usage because my discussion focuses on instantiations of intentional properties, so it is useful for me to reserve the term "intentional state" for them.

follows: When we introspectively notice intentional states, we notice the general phenomenon that we are tempted to describe as "directedness" or "saying something." But we also notice something we are tempted to describe as *what* our mental states are "directed at" or what they "say"; this is their **(intentional) content**.[7] When a state, property, or other item has a certain intentional content, we can say that it **(intentionally) represents** that content.[8] For example, the judgment that grass is green represents the content <grass is green>.[9]

It is worth emphasizing that my starting point is fairly noncommittal in that my definition of "intentionality" and the introspective observations it is based on do not prejudge questions concerning the nature of intentionality. As far as they are concerned, intentionality might end up being a causal or other tracking relation, a matter of the functional roles of internal states, or a matter of phenomenal consciousness. My starting point is neutral on these and other possible views of intentionality. Likewise, my starting point does not prejudge questions concerning the nature of contents. Contents might turn out to be ordinary objects and properties, propositions, facts, sense data, ideas in a world of forms, ways of representing, properties of intentional states, or even intentional states or properties themselves.

Relatedly, my starting point does not prejudge any issues regarding the **vehicles of intentionality**, which are the bearers of intentional properties. The vehicles of intentionality could turn out to be, for example, subjects, symbols in a language of thought, brain states, internal states, or immaterial souls.

For simplicity, however, I will assume that the vehicles of intentionality are internal items that I will call **(mental) representations**. Since different intentional states involve different vehicles of representation, this way of speaking allows us to talk about intentional states while remaining noncommittal on their contents, which is useful when the content of a particular intentional state is under dispute.[10]

---

[7] When we introspectively notice intentionality, we do so at least in part by introspectively noticing our contents. Indeed, it might be that there is nothing more to notice when we notice intentionality than these intentional contents.

[8] I sometimes use "represent" more broadly to describe representation-like phenomena that are not instances of intentionality, but context should disambiguate. The alternative would be to use a special term, like "intend," for having an intentional content, but this would be too awkward.

[9] Contents might include propositional contents, like <grass is green>, but might also include proprietal or objectual contents, like <green> and <George> (see Montague 2007, Grzankowski 2013, and Mendelovici 2018, MS). (The notions of objectual and proprietal contents are something like Crane's (2013) notions of contents and objects, respectively, though not equivalent.)

[10] In what follows, I will also sometimes assume something like a language of thought view (Fodor 1975), on which there are subpropositional vehicles of representation, like RED and CAT, which come together to constitute complex vehicles of representation representing complex contents. Apart from, I think, being largely correct, this assumption provides a useful way of talking about our particular representa-

1.3 Other Ways of Fixing Reference

I have recommended an ostensive way of fixing firmly upon the phenomenon that the fuzzy and metaphorical notions of aboutness and directedness merely gesture toward. This section considers some alternative ways of defining "intentionality" and shows that they might not pick out the same thing as the ostensive definition (§§1.3.1–1.3.4). It then argues that if what we are interested in is the phenomenon that "aboutness" talk gestures at, the ostensive definition is preferable to these alternatives (§1.3.5).

1.3.1 FOLK PSYCHOLOGY

One approach to intentionality defines it in terms of its role in a third-personal folk psychological, or common sense, theory of mind and behavior. We attribute beliefs, desires, and other mental states to each other, and we take these states to be related to one another in various ways and to have various other features. A definition of "intentionality" in terms of folk psychology takes intentionality to be whatever plays a particular role in such a folk psychological theory.[11]

Such a definition might not pick out the same thing as the ostensive definition. For instance, it could turn out that what the ostensive definition picks out lacks some of the extra features attributed to it by folk psychology. If these features are considered crucial by folk psychology, then the folk psychological notion will not pick out the ostensively defined phenomenon. For example, it could turn out that the ostensively defined phenomenon does not play certain causal roles considered crucial by folk psychology.

The folk psychological definition and the ostensive definition might also pick out different things if the folk psychological definition fails to pick out anything at all. Suppose that folk psychology is hopelessly false. Then its theoretical terms, including those putatively referring to intentional states, will fail to refer, and it will turn out that what it calls "intentionality" does not exist.[12] But the ostensively defined

---

tional capacities via their alleged vehicles. However, this assumption, along with the assumption that vehicles are internal items, can be discharged by replacing talk of mental representations with the more awkward talk of intentional capacities and amending my discussion appropriately. See Ryder 2009 for a useful overview of different views of the structure of representations.

[11] See Sellars 1956, Lewis 1974, Braddon-Mitchell and Jackson 1996, and Fodor 1987 for this way of fixing reference on intentionality.

[12] Paul and Patricia Churchland argue that folk psychology is false and hence that its posits fail to refer (see, e.g., Churchland 1981). If they are right, and if we take intentionality to be merely a posit in folk

phenomenon might still exist. So, the folk psychological notion might fail to pick out the same thing as the ostensive definition.

1.3.2 THE MIND-BRAIN SCIENCES

Another approach to intentionality takes it to be a posit in scientific approaches to the mind and brain. For instance, some approaches in cognitive science aim to explain mental processes and behavior in terms of operations over internal states that are described as carrying information or "representing" various contents, and it is not uncommon for neuroscientific theories to speak of neural structures as carrying information about or "representing" their causes. A suggestion for an alternative way of picking out our target, then, takes intentionality to be a posit in the mind-brain sciences.[13]

There are interesting questions in the philosophy of science surrounding the notions of representation operative in various disciplines and research programs. What are these notions of representation? What roles do they play? Do different research programs use the same notion of representation? Some philosophers explicitly claim to be trying to answer these types of questions and not the types of questions I'm concerned with.[14]

It could turn out that this approach picks out the same thing as the phenomenon we noticed introspectively in ourselves. But it also might turn out that the best elucidations of the notions implicit in the mind-brain sciences pick out different features of internal states than the one we ostensively picked out through introspective observation. One prima facie reason to think this might be the case is that it makes sense to ascribe at least some of the kinds of representational states operative in the mind-brain sciences to artifacts that we might not really believe to have genuine intentional powers, such as calculators and computers. This suggests that, at best, the ostensively defined phenomenon is a species of whatever representational phenomenon is picked out by the mind-brain sciences. At worst, it is something else entirely.

---

psychology, then it will turn out that there is no intentionality. (Note that the Churchlands do not think there are no intentional states of any sort; see Churchland 1989b.)

[13] See, e.g., Fodor 1987, Millikan 1984, and Cummins 1994. Note that Fodor takes intentionality to be a posit in computational cognitive science, as well as a posit in folk psychology; on his view, cognitive science and folk psychology point to the same thing.

[14] Cummins (1994, pp. 278–279), for instance, specifically claims to be describing a notion of representation that is useful for computational theories of cognition but not necessarily for the kinds of representation implicit in folk psychology.

It could also turn out that the two ways of defining "intentionality" do not pick out the same thing because the definition based on the mind-brain sciences does not pick out anything at all. Perhaps the best understanding of talk of representation in the mind-brain sciences takes representational notions to be merely a dispensable fiction (see Egan 2010). Then the mind-brain sciences do not really posit representational states after all. Another possibility is that they do posit representational states, but nothing plays the roles they are defined in terms of, so the notions of intentionality based on the mind-brain sciences fail to refer. Again, this shows that this way of defining "intentionality" might not pick out the same thing as the ostensive way.

1.3.3 GETTING AROUND IN THE WORLD

For the most part, we manage to acquire the things we need, avoid the things that are harmful to us, perform sophisticated actions involving multiple steps, and, more generally, get around in the world fairly successfully. It is quite plausible that we do this by means of internal representations of the world. Inspired by this way of thinking, we might take intentionality to be whatever explains successful behavior in the relevant way.[15]

Behavioral phenomena such as those listed above call out for explanation, and it may very well be that the phenomenon we fixed on with our ostensive definition is a crucial part of this explanation. What is less clear is exactly what role the ostensively defined phenomenon plays. Vehicles of intentionality might have properties apart from intentional properties, such as syntactic, neural, or other broadly physical or functional properties.[16] It could turn out, then, that intentionality itself is causally impotent and it's these other properties of vehicles of intentionality—say, their syntactic properties—that are responsible for their usefulness in helping us get around in the world. If this (unhappy) situation were the case, an explanation of successful behavior might not involve the ostensively defined phenomenon, and so the approach to defining "intentionality" based on getting around in the world might fix reference on something other than what the ostensive definition picks out.

The two definitions might also fail to pick out the same thing in skeptical scenarios in which we do not in fact manage to acquire the things we need, avoid the things that are harmful to us, or generally manage to get around in the world successfully, perhaps because we are brains in vats or dreaming, disembodied souls. In such

---

[15] Versions of this approach might also be versions of the approaches based on folk psychology or the mind-brain sciences described earlier.

[16] See also Dretske's distinction between representational facts and mere facts about representations (1995, p. 3).

scenarios, the definition based on getting around in the world would fail to fix reference on anything, since nothing in fact helps us get by in the world in the way required, but the ostensive definition would not fail to refer.

1.3.4 TRUTH AND REFERENCE

If mental states "say something," then it seems to follow that what they say can be either true or false, and if mental states are "of" or "about" something, then it seems to follow that they can either refer or fail to refer to whatever they're "of" or "about." So, perhaps we can use the notions of truth and reference to fix on our target. One such approach takes intentionality to be the having of conditions of truth or reference, while another takes intentionality to be that which gives rise to the having of conditions of truth and reference.[17]

This approach is certainly attractive. It promises to provide a substantive characterization of intentionality, defining it in terms of one of its apparently key features, and it does justice to the intuitive idea that intentionality serves to connect us to the external world, the world outside the mind. It also does justice to the idea that, at least when they are successful, there is some existing thing that intentional states are in some sense directed at or about. The approach also seems fairly unobjectionable. It certainly seems that intentional states have conditions of truth and reference, that what we think can be true or false, and that an object we represent can exist or fail to exist. The claim that intentional states have conditions of truth and reference is quite uncontroversial.

But, like the other alternative definitions of "intentionality" considered above, definitions in terms of truth and reference might fail to pick out the phenomenon picked out by the ostensive definition. They would fail to pick out the ostensively defined phenomenon if intentionality did not automatically connect us to the world without the help of additional ingredients. Consider, for the sake of illustration, a sense data theory of perceptual intentionality (a view, of course, which has few contemporary adherents[18]). On one way of characterizing such a theory, it can be divided into two main claims: First, perceptual intentionality is a relation of awareness to sense data. Second, sense data refer to whatever external items cause them (or bear some other special relation to them). The first claim offers a story of perceptual intentionality in terms of sense data, while the second claim offers a story

---

[17] See, e.g., Siewert 1998, Chalmers 2004, Siegel 2010, and Byrne 2009 for understandings of intentionality based on truth, reference, or the closely related notion of accuracy.

[18] In the 2009 PhilPapers Surveys, only 3.1% of respondents at leading English-speaking universities reported holding a sense data theory (Bourget and Chalmers 2014).

of truth and reference in terms of causation (or other relations). It could turn out that the second part of the story is secured by the first part, that the nature of sense data and our relation to them makes it the case that intentional states refer to certain items in certain conditions. But it could also turn out that the first part of the story leaves open whether and how sense data, and hence intentionality, is connected to the world through reference. On such a theory, perceptual intentionality *alone* might not automatically give rise to conditions of reference.

Something similar might be true of other pictures of intentionality. Consider a Frege-inspired picture on which intentionality is a matter of being appropriately related to abstract senses, while truth and reference are a matter of how senses connect with the world. Depending on how we characterize senses, their connecting with the world might not occur automatically but might instead require an extra in-gredient, a "satisfaction" relation or some such. So, if truth and reference require the ostensively defined phenomenon in combination with something else, a definition of "intentionality" in terms of conditions of truth and reference or what gives rise to them will pick out this combined phenomenon rather than the ostensively defined phenomenon alone.

Relatedly, the definition in terms of truth and reference would fail to pick out the ostensively defined phenomenon if it fails to refer because having conditions of truth and reference requires something in addition to the ostensively defined phenomenon and our mental states exhibit the ostensively defined phenomenon but lack the additional ingredients. In such a case, there would be no such things as conditions of truth and reference, and so there would be nothing answering to the definition of "intentionality" in terms of truth and reference. But there would still be something answering to the ostensive definition.

1.3.5 WHY WE SHOULD PREFER THE OSTENSIVE DEFINITION

I have outlined various alternatives to the ostensive definition of "intentionality" and argued that these alternative definitions might pick out something other than the ostensively defined phenomenon. Now, of course, there is no arguing over definitions. Different definitions of "intentionality" might pick out different things, and we are free to theorize about any of them. However, I want to suggest that if we are interested in the phenomenon gestured at by "aboutness" and "directedness" talk, we should prefer my fairly minimal ostensive definition. As we've seen, alternative definitions of "intentionality" build in assumptions about their target that are not present in the ostensive definition. This leaves someone who adopts these alternative definitions vulnerable to eliminativist threats: If there is nothing that satisfies the additional assumptions, then there is no intentionality, in their sense. But, I want to suggest, the phenomenon gestured at by "aboutness" and "directedness" talk is not vulnerable to eliminativism in the same way, which suggests that the extra assumptions that are built into the alternative definitions are substantive claims about, rather than defining features of, the phenomenon we gesture at with "aboutness" and "directedness" talk. If this is right, then there is reason to prefer my fairly noncommittal ostensive definition.

Here is a thought experiment that supports this point: Suppose that folk psychology is horribly mistaken, the mind-brain sciences have no need for a notion of content at all, and, relatedly, our best account of how we successfully get by in the world doesn't either. Suppose further that there is no determinate fact about how mental states are supposed to correspond to the world, and so there are no such things as truth and reference. On this scenario, none of the alternative ways of defining "intentionality" manage to pick out anything at all. Still, on this scenario, we might introspect and notice paradigm cases of intentionality. We might notice perceptual experiences and thoughts that seem to be "about" or "directed" at something or that seem to "say something." And we might want to know how this "aboutness" arises. This curiosity would not be misdirected, a mere result of our ignorance that the alternative definitions fail to refer. Even if we knew that nothing, not even paradigm cases, had the features invoked by the alternative definitions, we would still be left with the question of how thoughts and experiences get to have the features we are tempted to describe using representational vocabulary like "aboutness" and "directedness." What this shows is that observation of paradigm cases by itself gives rise to curiosity about "aboutness" and "directedness," which suggests that my ostensive definition best captures the notion of intentionality that such talk gestures at.

1.4 Worries with the Ostensive Definition

I now turn to some potential worries one might have with the ostensive definition of intentionality.

1.4.1 ARE WE TALKING PAST EACH OTHER?

When different theorists pick out their topic of interest in different ways, there is a danger that they end up talking past one another. Suppose that the folk psychologically defined phenomenon is distinct from the ostensively defined phenomenon. It seems that there is no real disagreement to be had between someone who takes the nature of the folk psychological phenomenon to be N and someone who takes the nature of the ostensively defined phenomenon to be M. The two theorists take different phenomena to have different natures.

However, it seems to me that in the case of many debates on intentionality, there often is a real disagreement between competing theories that employ different definitions of "intentionality." Many theorists who define "intentionality" in alternative ways still intend their theories to account for the phenomenon that we introspectively observe and are tempted to describe representationally, the phenomenon gestured at by "aboutness" talk. For example, although Dretske (1995) does not employ an ostensive definition of his target, he states that his tracking theory covers anything answering to the term "intentionality":

> Brentano (1874) conjectured that a mark of the mental was intentionality. Whatever, exactly, Brentano meant by intentionality, and whether or not he was right about its being a feature of all, and only, mental events, most philosophers take intentional characteristics (variously understood) to be distinctive of a great many mental phenomena. What follows is a brief catalog of those aspects of intentionality that have figured most prominently in the recent literature. In each case we find that a representational account of the mind provides a satisfying explanation of intentionality. (Dretske 1995, p. 28)

The aspects of intentionality that Dretske claims to accommodate are the power to misrepresent, aboutness, aspectual shape (roughly, our ability to represent things in different ways), and directedness (pp. 28–34). In effect, Dretske claims that all there is to any kind of intentionality-like phenomenon we have any reason to believe in is captured by his account. So, even though he does not define "intentionality" in my ostensive way, at least part of what he aims to account for is the ostensively defined phenomenon, the phenomenon gestured at by "aboutness" talk.[19]

Further reason to think that many theorists who define "intentionality" in one of the ways I reject aim to be targeting a phenomenon that at least includes the ostensively defined phenomenon is that they often use what appear to be introspectively accessible paradigm cases to illustrate their claims, such as judgments concerning barnyard animals and hallucinations of pink rats and daggers. Although there could be intentional states that are not introspectively accessible with such contents, the examples are usually supposed to be of the kinds of states that are or at least could be introspectively accessible.[20] This appeal to introspectible cases suggests

---

[19] Similarly, Fodor (1990) explicitly states that his theory solves "Brentano's problem" (pp. 127–128).

[20] This is especially clear in discussions of the disjunction problem, which partly rely on intuitions about what is represented in possible cases (e.g., Baker 1989 and Fodor 1990). If these intuitions aren't

that whatever else theorists who fix reference on their target in ways other than my own are trying to do, they are also often trying to explain intentionality in my sense.

1.4.2 STANDING STATES

One might agree with my suggestion of defining "intentionality" ostensively but find my choice of paradigms overly restrictive. All my paradigm cases are **occurrent states**, mental states that are used, entertained, or otherwise active at the time at which they are had, such as judgments and perceptual states. But we might also want to include in our stock of paradigms some **standing states**, mental states that need not be used, entertained, or otherwise active at the time at which they are had, such as beliefs and desires that one is not currently entertaining. For example, the belief you had five minutes ago that the Acropolis is in Athens is a standing state, and one might suggest that it is a prime example of intentionality.[21]

My reason for not including standing states in my stock of paradigm cases is that we do not have the same kind of introspective access to them as we do to introspectively accessible occurrent states. While we can simply observe the intentionality of my preferred paradigm cases, we cannot observe our standing states or their features. Instead, we *infer* that we have standing states, perhaps on the basis of our noticing that we sometimes have corresponding occurrent states or on the basis of a folk psychological theory of mind and behavior. These ways of knowing about standing states are relatively indirect compared to our ways of accessing my preferred paradigm cases, and, relatedly, their existence is less certain for us than that of my introspectively accessible paradigm cases. In short, then, we have an especially secure epistemic access to introspectively accessible cases of intentionality, one that we do not have to standing states, which is why I do not include standing states in my paradigm cases.

Notice also that if, as the objector is likely to hold, the proposed additional paradigms have the feature that we notice in my paradigm cases, then my choice to not include them has no effect: My ostensive definition will cover them as well, and including them in our initial stock is unnecessary. We end up picking out the same thing either way.

Excluding standing states only has an effect on what we end up picking out if the proposed additional paradigms either do not exist or do not have the feature picked out by my ostensive definition. But, in such cases, it is arguably a virtue of

---

supposed to be intuitions about the kinds of contents that a subject might notice in herself, then it's not clear where they are supposed to come from and why we should put any weight on them.

[21] Thanks to David Bourget and Tim Bayne for pressing me on this worry.

my ostensive definition that it keeps the clearly intentional introspectively accessible feature of mental states separate from whatever it is that the proposed additional paradigms have. In any case, the terminological difference between me and someone who adopts an ostensive definition including standing states as paradigms does not make a substantive difference in what follows: Although my target is intentionality, in my sense, I also offer an account of standing states, as well as other alleged instances of intentionality (see Part IV). The overall story offered would be the same whether or not we include standing states in our paradigm cases, though it would be stated differently.

1.4.3 PERCEPTION AND THOUGHT

The ostensive definition fixes on our target by pointing to several of its instances, including instances in perception and instances in thought. But one might worry that these instances do not belong to a unified natural kind. Perhaps we end up picking out a disjunctive kind, consisting of two distinct natural kinds. This might be the case if perceptual states are importantly different from "cognitive" states such as thoughts, and so what we might call "perceptual intentionality" is not the same kind of thing as what we might call "cognitive intentionality." If this is the case, then my paradigm cases are actually instances of two different kinds of phenomena, which I am mistakenly lumping together.

Of course, when we use multiple examples in an ostensive definition, there is always a risk that they are very different in their natures and we end up picking out a disjunctive kind. One response to this sort of worry is that this scenario is unlikely. While it remains a possibility that I've picked out a disjunctive kind, it at least initially seems that the observations concerning thought and those concerning perception are similar in important ways. Both thought and perception are readily described as "saying something" or being "directed at" something. And both intentionality in perception and intentionality in thought seem fairly distant from other kinds of phenomena, such as reflexive behaviors and the automatic control of vital functions. Their similarity to one another and distance from other phenomena suggest that there is an interesting natural kind that they both belong to.[22]

A second response to this worry is that even if it turns out that perceptual intentionality and cognitive intentionality are very different phenomena that do

---

[22] Of course, even if intentionality is a unified natural kind, perceptual representation and representation in thought might end up forming two more specific distinct natural kinds. This does not affect my claims here, since the issue is over whether intentionality is a unified natural kind, not whether it has various distinct subkinds.

not form a unified natural kind, this is not a problem, since my starting point will not steer us too far in the wrong direction. Assuming our target is whatever "aboutness" and "directedness" talk gesture toward, the problem with approaches to fixing reference on our target that I want to reject is that they risk missing our target entirely. For example, defining our target as an explanatory posit in a theory of behavior risks missing our target if intentionality does not play the requisite role in generating behavior. If nothing plays the requisite role (say, because the relevant parts of the theory are false), then it will turn out that there is no intentionality. If something plays this role, but it is not whatever "aboutness" and "directedness" talk gesture toward, then it will turn out that there is intentionality, but that it's not the same thing as our targeted phenomenon. In contrast, picking out a disjunctive kind does not carry with it the risk of missing our target. Perhaps perceptual intentionality and cognitive intentionality are two entirely different kinds of things. Then we would need two distinct, and perhaps unrelated, theories to explain them, and if we start off thinking of perceptual intentionality and cognitive intentionality as relevantly similar, then it might take longer to reach such a conclusion. However, such a conclusion has not been ruled out from the start because nothing in the way we fixed on intentionality requires that it be a unified phenomenon.[23]

1.4.4 PERCEPTUAL STATES DON'T HAVE CONTENTS

One might object that perceptual states don't have contents, at least not prior to an act of "interpretation." For example, one might argue that the visual experience one enjoys when one views a red ball is neutral between multiple external-world possibilities, such as that there is a red ball in normal lighting conditions, that there is a white ball lit by red light, etc. The experience does not by itself "say" which of these possibilities is the case, so it does not represent the ball as being any particular color at all. Instead, a further state, such as a judgment, interprets the perceptual state and commits us to one or another possibility. On this view, there is a distinction between non-intentional mental features of some perceptual experiences, which we might call their "raw matter," and further states that interpret them, or "interpretations." Interpretations are intentional, but mere raw matter is not. One might object that if this view is correct, then my ostensive definition is too permissive: it

---

[23] Of course, whatever their apparent similarities, perceptual intentionality and cognitive intentionality also seem quite different in certain respects. For instance, perceptual intentionality is more vivid, detailed, and closely related to phenomenology than is cognitive intentionality. Eventually, I will offer a view of intentionality that begins to explain both the similarities and differences between intentionality in perception and in thought (see especially Chapter 7).

includes both raw matter and interpretations, whereas we should only include interpretations.[24]

However, if the above view is correct, then it is not in fact the case that my approach is too permissive. My observations pick out *intentional states*, states that "say" something, not non-intentional components or contributors to those states. And so, my way of picking out the phenomenon of intentionality isn't meant to and wouldn't in fact pick out uninterpreted raw matter, if there were such a thing. Instead, my method would pick out interpreted raw matter, or interpretations. It might then turn out that some of our allegedly perceptual paradigm states are not mere perceptual states but instead thoughts or combinations of perceptual states and thoughts. If the above view is in fact correct, then, ultimately, a complete theory of intentionality should isolate the components of interpreted raw matter and distinguish their contributions to intentionality. Note that nothing in my ostensive definition rules out such a view from the get-go.

1.5 Conclusion

The central aim of this book is to offer a theory of intentionality, the phenomenon we at least sometimes notice introspectively in ourselves and are tempted to describe using representational terms, and which, I've suggested, is the phenomenon that "aboutness" talk gestures at. This book develops a theory of this ostensively defined phenomenon in terms of a conceptually distinct mental feature, phenomenal consciousness, the "what it's like" of mental states.

This book also has a secondary aim. This chapter considered and rejected alternative ways of fixing reference on intentionality via some of its alleged additional roles. Thus far, I have argued that intentionality *might not* play these roles. A secondary line of argument in this book argues that intentionality alone in fact *does not* play many of these roles. Many of them are played by something else. In Chapter 3, I argue that a crucial part of a story of how representations contribute to successful behavior must invoke non-intentional features of representations, namely, their tracking relations to external items. In Chapter 8, I argue that folk psychological notions of content most closely correspond to a combination of intentional content and derived mental representational content. In Chapter 8, I also argue that the kinds of representation implicit in the mind-brain sciences are distinct from intentionality and that nonconscious occurrent states might satisfy these notions of

---

[24] Travis (2004) presents a view along these lines.

representation but lack intentionality. Chapter 9 argues that it is not even clear that intentionality gives us conditions of truth and reference without the help of further ingredients.

On the resulting picture, then, intentionality is a matter of phenomenal consciousness, and many of the other roles that are sometimes used to pick it out are in fact played by something else.

2   Goals and Methodology

THE PREVIOUS CHAPTER fixed on our target, intentionality. This chapter considers what exactly we want to know about intentionality and some methods that can help us come to know it. In §2.1, I consider what it would take to provide a theory of intentionality and the goals around which I will structure most of my discussion. In §2.2, I suggest two theory-independent ways in which we can know about our intentional states, which can be used to test competing theories of intentionality: introspection and considerations of psychological role.

2.1 What is a Theory of Intentionality?

A **theory of intentionality** is a theory that describes the deep nature of intentionality, where intentionality's **(deep) nature** is what it really *is*, metaphysically speaking. For example, a theory of intentionality might tell us that intentionality is a tracking relation, a relation of isomorphism between a functionally defined system of representations and abstract propositions, a primitive relation to properties, objects, and facts, or an adverbial modification of subjects.

My aim is to provide a theory of intentionality that specifies the nature of all actual and possible intentional states. But I will structure much of my discussion around a less ambitious goal, that of providing a theory that specifies what *gives rise* to *actual* instances of *original* intentionality. Let me explain these three italicized terms:

Arising

A **gives rise** to B (or, equivalently, B **arises from** A) when B is nothing over and above A, e.g., because B is identical to, fully grounded in, constituted by, or realized by A. A theory that tells us what gives rise to intentionality tells us what exactly intentionality amounts to, though it might remain neutral on how exactly that thing gets to amount to intentionality. For example, a theory of intentionality might claim that intentionality arises from tracking relations obtaining between internal states and items in the environment, though it might remain neutral on whether intentionality is identical to this tracking relation, grounded in it, or arises from it in some other way.

Actual and Possible Instances of Intentionality

Actual, as opposed to merely possible, intentional states are intentional states existing in the actual world. A theory of intentionality might account for all actual intentional states while allowing for the possibility of intentional states that it cannot account for. For example, a theory of intentionality in terms of tracking might allow that there are non-actual possible worlds in which intentionality is a primitive phenomenon.[1]

Original and Derived Intentionality

Original intentionality is intentionality that does not derive from other instances of intentionality. Original intentionality can be contrasted with **derived intentionality**, which is intentionality that derives from other instances of intentionality. For example, one might think that linguistic expressions have derived intentionality that is derived from the original intentionality of mental states, e.g., from our thoughts, beliefs, interpretations, or communicative intentions (Grice 1989).

A few more definitions are in order: **Originally intentional properties** are ways things are or might be with respect to their original intentionality, or originally intentional ways things are or might be, and an **originally intentional state** is an instantiation of an originally intentional property. We can say that something **originally (intentionally) represents** a content when it instantiates an originally intentional property representing that content. Correspondingly, **derivatively intentional properties** are ways things are or might be with respect to their derived

---

[1] Compare: A physicalist theory of mental states can be neutral on the question of whether nonphysical mental states are possible.

intentionality, or derivatively intentional ways things are or might be. A **derivatively intentional state** is an instantiation of a derivatively intentional property, and we can say that something **derivatively (intentionally) represents** a content when it instantiates a derivatively intentional property representing that content.

Note that although it is often thought that the line between original and derived intentionality is to be drawn between mental instances of intentionality and non-mental instances, there can also be mental cases of derived intentionality. Bourget (2010a) offers one important early development of this idea, providing a wide range of examples of derived mental intentionality. We will soon see that derived mental intentionality plays a role in most versions of the phenomenal intentionality theory, the view that I will eventually defend. But it is also true of many alternative views that accept a language of thought-like picture on which internally unstructured representations, representations that do not contain other representations as proper parts, come together to form internally structured representations whose contents are determined by their constituent representations and the ways they are combined. As Bourget (2010a) notes, one natural way of understanding this idea takes the intentionality of internally structured representations to be derived from their constituent internally unstructured representations and their mode of combination.

Although I will eventually propose a theory of intentionality that specifies the nature of all actual and possible intentional states, I will structure much of my discussion around the more modest goal of providing a theory of intentionality that specifies what gives rise to actual instances of original intentionality. My reason for this is that it allows us to classify theories of intentionality in terms of their most general common factors: what they take actual-world instances of original intentionality to amount to, or, in other words, what they take to be the actual-world "source" (Kriegel 2011, 2013b) of intentionality. As we will see, this method of classifying theories ends up classifying them along familiar lines. Once we have settled on the source of actual-world instances of intentionality, we will then turn to providing a more complete theory of intentionality, one that settles other questions about intentionality, including those of how exactly intentionality arises from whatever it arises from, how it might arise in other possible worlds, and whether and how original intentionality can yield derived intentionality.

2.2 Theory-Independent Access to Intentionality

As we will see in Chapters 3–5, many theories of intentionality make predictions as to the contents of particular mental states. So, in order to assess these theories, it is useful to have a theory-independent way of testing these predictions, i.e., a way that is independent of our theories of intentionality. If we cannot test a theory's predictions in a theory-independent way, then (except in cases where theories make inconsistent predictions), we cannot use a theory's predictions to help us decide whether or not to accept it.

This section describes two theory-independent ways of finding out which contents we represent: introspection and considerations of psychological roles. Importantly, my claim is only that these methods allow us to discern *which* contents we represent, not that they can fully reveal to us the nature of our intentional states and contents. As I will put it, they can tell us about an intentional state or content's "superficial character," but not its deep nature. Before describing our theory-independent ways of knowing about intentional states and contents, then, it is helpful to first clarify the distinction between deep nature and superficial character.

2.2.1 DEEP NATURE AND SUPERFICIAL CHARACTER

Let us first consider an analogy: There is a distinction between two different kinds of questions we might ask about furniture. We might ask deep, metaphysical questions about the nature of furniture. For example, we might ask if being a piece of furniture is a physical or functional state, if an item's status as a piece of furniture is dependent on minds or societies, if being a piece of furniture is an intrinsic or extrinsic property, and how pieces of furniture are related to the matter that constitutes them. These questions are questions about the "deep nature" of furniture, about what furniture really *is*, metaphysically speaking.

There is a different set of questions we might ask about furniture: We might ask what kind of furniture some piece of furniture belongs to, e.g., whether it is a couch, a chair, or a futon. We might ask questions about the shapes, colors, material, or textures of various pieces of furniture, such as whether a particular table has a square or a rectangular top or whether a particular couch is made of leather or pleather. And we might ask questions about the uses or functions of certain kinds of furniture, such as whether futons are used for sleeping, sitting, or both. These are all questions about what we might call the "superficial" features of furniture.

I want to suggest that we can draw a parallel distinction between the "deep" and "superficial" features of intentionality. We have already defined the deep nature of intentionality as what it really *is*, metaphysically speaking (§2.1). We can similarly take the (deep) nature of intentional states and contents to be what they really *are*, metaphysically speaking. Views of the deep nature of intentional states include views on which they are states of bearing tracking relations to worldly objects and properties, states of bearing primitive relations to abstract sets of possible worlds, or intrinsic states of subjects. Views of the deep nature of contents include views on which contents are concrete combinations of worldly objects and properties, sets of possible worlds, or properties of intentional states.

The **superficial character** of an intentional state or content is the set of superficial features that characterize it as the intentional state or content that it is. Claims about the particular contents of particular intentional states are usually best interpreted as claims about their superficial characters. For example, the claim that Justin Trudeau is currently thinking that grass is green is a claim about the superficial character of his present intentional states, not their deep natures. Similarly, the claim that Putnam's (1975) Oscar and his Twin Earth duplicate, Toscar, have watery-stuff-related thoughts with different contents is best understood as a claim about the superficial characters of Oscar and Toscar's intentional states. Some generalizations about intentional states are also best understood as claims about their superficial characters. For example, the claims that most people can visually represent 10 million colors, that perceptual states have more fine-grained contents than thoughts, and that nonconscious intentional states have vague or indeterminate contents are all best understood as claims about the superficial characters of the relevant states.[2]

Theories of intentionality can make predictions about both the deep natures and the superficial characters of the contents we represent. For example, a theory of intentionality that predicts that the content of the concept CAT is the universal *cat* makes predictions about both this content's deep nature and its superficial character. With respect to its deep nature, it predicts that the content of CAT is, at bottom, a universal. With respect to its superficial character, it predicts that the content has a cat-ish, rather than dog-ish or octopus-ish, superficial character, i.e., that CAT has the content <cat>, rather than <dog> or <octopus>.[3]

While I think it is possible to assess a theory's predictions about both the superficial characters and the deep natures of intentional states or contents, many of my central arguments will focus specifically on predictions about superficial characters. This is because, as we will soon see, it is quite plausible that we can know

---

[2] I introduce the distinction between the deep nature and the superficial character of contents in Mendelovici 2018, where I also argue that propositionalism and objectualism are best construed as views about the superficial characters of intentional states.

[3] I use angle brackets to name contents in a way that roughly reflects our intuitive way of naming them, which is by their superficial characters. For example, the content <grass is green> is the content we would express with "that grass is green," which is a content with a grass-is-green-ish superficial character.

  I take a C-ish superficial character to be a superficial character that at least includes C-ish-ness as a part or aspect. This way of talking about superficial characters allows us to talk about an intentional state or content's superficial character without fully specifying it. For example, we can say that a perceptual state representing a red square has a red-square-ish superficial character, but also that it has a red-ish superficial character and that it has a square-ish superficial character.

about the superficial characters of our intentional states and contents prior to having a theory of intentionality and, indeed, prior to doing much philosophy at all. The next two subsections outline two ways in which we can do this.

2.2.2 INTROSPECTION

One theory-independent way in which we can know the superficial character of our intentional states and contents is through introspection.

In §1.2, we saw that we can introspectively notice that we have intentional states. I want to suggest that introspection can tell us a bit more than that. At least sometimes and at least to a certain extent, introspection informs us as to *which* intentional states we have. For example, introspection can tell me that I am presently thinking <a cat is in my lap>, rather than, say, <an octopus is wrapped around my arm>. Further, the way that introspection tells me that I am thinking <a cat is in my lap> is not by providing me with a number, symbol, or other marker that I have come to associate with my thinking this content. Instead, introspection provides me with some sort of access to some of the features of the content that characterize it as the particular content that it is and that distinguish it from other contents. In other words, introspection provides me with some access to its superficial character. More generally, introspection, at least sometimes and at least to a certain extent, can inform us as to the superficial characters of our intentional states and contents.

In contrast, introspection does not reveal to us the deep natures of intentional states and contents. In the above example, introspection tells me that I represent <a cat is in my lap>, but it arguably[4] does not tell me whether this content is a set of possible worlds, a structured proposition, a way of representing, or an idea in the mind of God. Similarly, introspection does not reveal to me the nature of my intentional state; it does not tell me that my intentional state is a tracking relation to cats and other things in the world, a complex set of functional roles, or a primitive relation to sets of possible worlds. Since a theory of intentionality is a theory that specifies the deep nature of intentionality, this means that, as suggested in Chapter 1, introspection does not reveal to us the correct theory of intentionality. Of course, this is not to say that introspective evidence cannot form the basis of arguments for claims about the deep nature of intentionality, but only that introspection does not simply tell us what it is.[5]

---

[4] See §9.3.1 for an argument.

[5] Similarly, much of the debate on the hard problem of consciousness presupposes that we can at least sometimes introspectively tell *which* phenomenal states we have, even if introspection does not reveal to us the nature of phenomenal states. For example, introspection might tell us that a phenomenal

In short, introspection can, at least sometimes and at least to a certain extent, inform us as to the superficial characters of our intentional states, though it does not reveal to us their deep natures. Before moving on, let me make two clarifications.

First, my claim that introspection can at least sometimes provide at least partial access to the superficial characters of our intentional states and contents is compatible with the claim that there are intentional states and contents to which we have no introspective access or only partial introspective access. For example, we presumably have no introspective access to the superficial characters of unconscious intentional states, and we arguably have no or only partial introspective access to the superficial characters of states with broad contents, contents the representation of which depends on relations to the environment. However, it is natural to suppose that we have at least partial access to the superficial characters of the contents we represent in paradigm cases of intentionality (see §1.2), since these are cases we notice introspectively in ourselves. This is all I will need in order to make many of my arguments.

The second caveat is that the claim that introspection does not reveal to us the nature of intentionality does not imply that what we are presented with in introspection is not our contents in their entirety. It could be that introspection presents us with our contents in their entirety but does not specifically tell us the deep natures of those contents, i.e., what they are at bottom, metaphysically speaking. For example, introspection might present us with structured propositions consisting of instantiated properties and existing objects but might not be able to tease apart and identify those components, for whatever reason. What is meant by the claim that introspection does not reveal the nature of intentionality is simply that we cannot simply tell, from introspection alone, what is the nature of intentionality.[6]

2.2.3 PSYCHOLOGICAL ROLES

A second theory-independent way of finding out about the superficial characters of our intentional states and contents is through their psychological roles. Our intentional states generally play various psychological roles, and these psychological roles are appropriate to which contents they represent. These roles might be roles in the inferences we are disposed to make, the behaviors we are disposed to engage in,

---

experience of a ripe tomato has a red-round-ish phenomenal character, even if it does not reveal to us whether its nature is that of being a brain state, a functional state, a representational state, a higher-order thought, or a primitive mental state. This is to deny what is sometimes called "revelation" (see, e.g., Goff 2017).

[6] See Mendelovici 2018 for discussion along the lines of this section of what introspection can and cannot tell us about intentionality. See also Bayne and Spener 2010 for a congenial discussion of the limits of introspection.

or the higher-order thoughts or introspective judgments about our intentional states we are able or likely to have. These roles might also be roles in contributing to our overall phenomenology, which might include our phenomenal experiences or our "grasped" representational perspectives on the world.

While it might be an open question precisely which roles any given intentional state plays, I will assume that intentional states play a psychological role appropriate to their contents. In some way or other, intentional states behave as if they're there. I will also assume that these psychological roles can often be detected by us, either through introspection or through third-person observation. If this is right, then intentional states often leave some detectable traces in our minds or behaviors, and these traces can be used to help us find out which intentional states we have.[7]

Like introspective evidence, evidence from psychological role most clearly tells us about an intentional state's superficial character, not its deep nature. For example, Maria's bringing an umbrella to work is evidence that she believes it might rain and desires to stay dry, but it is not clearly evidence for or against the view that her intentional state is a primitive relation to a set of possible worlds. Of course, this is not to say that facts about psychological roles cannot form the basis of arguments for claims about the deep nature of intentionality, but only that an intentional state's psychological roles do not clearly reveal this nature to us. Accordingly, I will say that an intentional state is **psychologically involved** when it plays a psychological role appropriate to its superficial character.

Importantly, the claim that considerations of psychological involvement most clearly tell us about an intentional state's superficial character does not imply that it is not intentional states in their entirety that play the relevant psychological roles. It might be that it is intentional states in their entirety that play various roles, but *which* specific roles they play most clearly and uncontroversially tells us about their superficial characters, not their deep natures.

2.3 Conclusion

In summary, a theory of intentionality is a theory that describes the deep nature of intentionality. Though the theory of intentionality that I will propose is much more

---

[7] Even if intentional states are causally impotent, our inferences and behaviors should still *respect* their contents, so considerations of psychological role can still provide evidence as to what they represent. For example, someone who believes that it is raining and desires to stay dry will display appropriate rain-avoiding behavior, even if the contents of her beliefs and desires do not play a causal role in generating this behavior.

ambitious, I will structure much of my initial discussion around the question of what gives rise to all actual instances of original intentionality. As we will see, by providing us with theory-independent access to the contents of at least some intentional states, introspection and considerations of psychological involvement can help us settle this question.

With these preliminaries under our belt, it's time to begin our search for a true theory of intentionality! Part II considers approaches to intentionality that take it to arise from tracking or functional roles and argues that they fail. Part III turns to my favored approach, the phenomenal intentionality theory, and together with Part IV, argues that it succeeds.

II Alternative Theories of Intentionality

THE TRACKING THEORY and the functional role theory are arguably the two main competitors to my preferred theory of intentionality. This part argues that both theories face unforgivable problems: Chapter 3 argues that tracking theories make false predictions about certain paradigm cases of intentionality, while Chapter 4 argues that this problem also afflicts the best versions of the functional role theory. I return to the tracking theory again at the end of Chapter 4, where I argue that the underlying reason that both tracking and functional role theories fail is that tracking relations and functional roles are simply not the kinds of things that can give rise to intentionality.

Part III develops my preferred theory of intentionality, the phenomenal intentionality theory, which, we will see, succeeds precisely where tracking and functional role theories fail.

3   The Mismatch Problem for Tracking Theories

TRACKING THEORIES TAKE intentionality to arise from tracking relations that internal states bear to items in the environment. This chapter argues that while tracking theories have various attractions, including that of providing an account of intentionality in terms of perfectly respectable natural phenomena, they are unable to account for certain paradigm cases of intentionality. In these cases, there is a mismatch between the contents attributed by tracking theories and the contents we have theory-independent reason to think we represent. This chapter overviews tracking theories (§3.1) and presents this mismatch problem (§§3.2–3.5), arguing that it cannot be avoided using sophisticated maneuvers involving modes of presentation, nonconceptual contents, and other devices (§3.6). I close with a discussion of the significance of tracking (§3.7).

3.1 Tracking Theories

According to the tracking theory, original intentionality arises from tracking, where **tracking** is detecting, carrying information about or having the function of carrying information about, or otherwise appropriately corresponding to items in the environment, such as particular objects, properties, or states of affairs. We can state the core commitment of the tracking theory as follows:

The tracking theory All actual originally intentional states arise from tracking.

Recall that B arises from A when B is nothing over and above A, perhaps because B is identical to, fully grounded in, constituted by, or realized by A (§2.1). Recall also that original intentionality is intentionality that does not derive from other instances of intentionality (§2.1). According to the tracking theory, then, tracking relations give rise to the most basic kind of intentionality, and all other kinds of intentionality (if there are any) are derived from it.[1]

There are different versions of the tracking theory. **Optimal-functioning tracking theories** take the relevant tracking relation to be the causal relation that holds between a mental representation and some item in conditions in which the representation helps its bearer survive, flourish, or otherwise function appropriately (see Tye 2000).[2] **Teleological tracking theories** take the relevant tracking relation to be at least partly determined by an organism's biological functions, which might be a matter of its evolutionary history (Millikan 1984, 1989, Papineau 1987, Dretske 1995, and Neander 2013).[3] Another approach is the **asymmetric dependence tracking theory**, on which, simplifying significantly, a mental representation originally represents whatever causes it via a causal relation that does not depend on any other causal relations (Fodor 1987, 1990).[4]

One alleged virtue of the tracking theory is that it is a **naturalistic theory** of intentionality, a theory that appeals only to **naturalistic items**, which are

---

[1] Note that no particular token mental representation need be caused by, carry information about, or bear any other such relation to any concrete existing thing in order for it to represent. What is generally required for a token mental representation r of type R to represent a content C is, roughly, for tokens of R occurring in particular circumstances to be caused by, carry information about, correspond to, or bear some other such relation to C (or instances of C).

[2] Tye (2000) holds something like an optimal functioning theory, though he also invokes teleological elements.

[3] Millikan's view states, roughly, that a representation R originally represents content C just in case the systems that make use of R (R's "consumers") need the occurrence of tokens of R to correspond to C in order to perform the functions they were naturally selected for performing (their "proper functions").

[4] Slightly more precisely, and slightly more in line with Fodor's own characterization, the asymmetric dependence theory states that an internally unstructured representation R represents content C if C (or instances of C) cause tokens of R (in a law-like way) and for anything else, D, that causes tokens of R, the D-to-R connection is asymmetrically dependent on the C-to-R connection. The D-to-R connection is asymmetrically dependent on the C-to-R connection just in case the D-to-R connection is dependent on the C-to-R connection and the C-to-R connection is not dependent on the D-to-R connection. Dependence is cashed out counterfactually: The D-to-R connection is dependent on the C-to-R connection just in case if the C-to-R connection were to break, then the D-to-R connection would break as well.

fundamental physical items lacking mentality or items arising from them. Dretske, for example, describes his project as "an exercise in naturalism—or, if you prefer, materialistic metaphysics. Can you bake a mental cake using only physical yeast and flour?" (Dretske 1981, p. xi). Millikan (1984) similarly expresses a firm commitment to naturalism: "That our theory of the world has to be a totally naturalist theory I am not prepared to argue" (p. 87).[5]

3.2 Overview of the Mismatch Problem for Tracking Theories

When combined with information about what particular mental representations track, tracking theories make predictions as to what they represent. In the remainder of this chapter, I argue that there is a certain class of cases, which I call "mismatch cases," in which tracking theories make the wrong predictions about *which* contents we represent. The existence of mismatch cases means that the tracking theory is empirically inadequate and hence false.

My main example of a mismatch case is that of perceptual color representations, the representations of colors involved in perceptual color states, though I briefly consider other mismatch cases in §3.5. In a nutshell, my argument for the claim that perceptual color representations are a mismatch case for tracking theories goes like this: Perceptual color representations track something like surface reflectance profiles, molecular properties of objects, or dispositions to cause certain internal states in us. But this is not what they represent; instead, they represent something like primitive colors. These claims about what perceptual color representations do and do not represent are prima facie obvious, but they are also supported by

---

[5] While Dretske takes naturalism about intentionality to require that a theory only appeal to non-mental ingredients, Fodor's oft-cited passage expressing his commitment to naturalism only takes naturalism to require that a theory only appeal to non-*intentional* ingredients. He writes:

I suppose that sooner or later the physicists will complete the catalogue they've been compiling of the ultimate and irreducible properties of things. When they do, the likes of *spin*, *charm*, and *charge*, will perhaps appear upon their list. But *aboutness* surely won't; intentionality simply doesn't go that deep. It's hard to see, in face of this consideration, how one can be a Realist about intentionality without also being, to some extent or other, a Reductionist. If the semantic and the intentional are real properties of things, it must be in virtue of their identity with (or maybe of their supervenience on?) properties that are themselves *neither* intentional *nor* semantic. If aboutness is real, it must be really something else. (Fodor 1987, p. 97; emphasis in original)

Even though, for Fodor, naturalism amounts to reductionism, he seems to assume that the ingredients that a naturalistic project can appeal to are primarily uncontroversially physical and functional ingredients, since he does not consider possible views that invoke ingredients whose status as physical is controversial, such as phenomenal consciousness. So, in practice, his commitment to naturalism amounts to much the same as Dretske's.

theory-independent considerations from introspection and observed psychological role: First, we can introspect on perceptual color states, and when we do, we discover something like primitive colors rather than any of the items perceptual color representations can be said to track. Second, the psychological roles of perceptual color representations also suggest that they represent primitive colors rather than anything they happen to track. For instance, they are inferentially related to beliefs about primitive colors rather than beliefs about surface reflectance profiles or the like. If all this is right, then the tracking theory makes the wrong predictions in the case of perceptual color representations, and we have a mismatch case.

The argument is simple and obvious: Perceptual color representations track one thing but represent another, so the tracking theory delivers the wrong answer. But there are many methodological assumptions working in the background of this argument, and it is open to various sophisticated replies. The next few sections unpack the argument, clarify some of the assumptions at work, and overview the most compelling lines of response (Appendix A considers more).[6]

3.3 Background and Assumptions

When combined with information about what a representation tracks, tracking theories yield predictions as to what it represents. For example, suppose that, on a given tracking relation, the representation HORSE tracks the property of being a horse. Then a tracking theory taking this tracking relation to give rise to intentionality predicts that HORSE represents the property *horse*.

Section 2.2.1 distinguished between the deep nature and the superficial character of contents, where the deep nature of a content is what it *is*, metaphysically speaking,

---

[6] Pautz (2006, 2013b), Hardin (1988), Akins (1996), and others have argued that there is a "structural" mismatch between the contents of representations and what they track: There is a mismatch in the relations of similarity and difference between what a set of representations represent and the relations of similarity and difference between the items that they track. For example, the contents of color representations have a certain structure (e.g., $<red_5>$ is more similar to $<purple_{28}>$ than it is to $<green_{35}>$), which fails to match the structure of the surface reflectance profiles that color representations track (e.g., what RED_5 tracks is not more similar to what $PURPLE_{28}$ tracks than to what $GREEN_{35}$ tracks). If this is right, then what color representations track is not what they represent. See Ivanowich 2015 for a lucid overview and defense of this line of argument.

My argument based on mismatch cases is more committal on some controversial issues—it invokes premises concerning the specific contents of representations in mismatch cases rather than just premises involving less controversial claims about the relations between those contents—but the problem it points to is more blatant: We don't need to examine the structural relations between what we track and what we represent to see that they are different when, as I will argue, we can conclude they are different from our theory-independent knowledge of the superficial characters of the represented contents alone.

while its superficial character is the set of superficial features that characterize it as the particular content that it is. In the above example, the tracking theory in question is naturally understood as making predictions about both the deep nature and the superficial character of the content of HORSE. It tells us that the content of HORSE has the deep nature of being a particular property, rather than an object, state of affairs, or other item, though it remains neutral on what exactly properties are. It also tells us that the content of HORSE has a horse-ish superficial character, by which I mean a superficial character that at least includes horse-ish-ness as a part or aspect. More simply, we can say that the tracking theory predicts that HORSE represents <horse>, where <horse> is a content with a horse-ish superficial character.[7]

In §2.2, we saw that it is possible to test a theory of intentionality's predictions using two theory-independent methods, methods that do not presuppose any particular theory of intentionality: introspection and consideration of psychological role. These methods most clearly tell us about a content's superficial character, not its deep nature. They most clearly tell us *which* contents we represent without telling us what those contents really are, at bottom. Accordingly, the predictions of the tracking theory that I am concerned with are its predictions about the superficial characters of represented contents, not its predictions about their deep natures.

Let us consider these two theory-independent methods of testing a theory of intentionality's predictions in more detail. In §2.2.2, we saw that introspection can help tell us *which* intentional contents we represent by at least partially revealing their superficial characters. For example, we can introspectively tell that we are representing <grass is green>, rather than <snow is white> or <there is an elephant sulking in the corner>. While introspection may not *fully* reveal the superficial characters of *all* contents, it arguably provides some access to paradigm cases of intentionality, the introspectively accessible cases that we used to fix reference on intentionality in §1.2.

Since at least some intentional states involving the representation HORSE are paradigm cases of intentionality, introspection can speak to the question of which content HORSE represents. Introspection arguably suggests that it represents <horse>, a content with a horse-ish superficial character. In this way, introspection confirms the tracking theory's prediction that HORSE represents <horse>.

The second way of finding out about an intentional state's superficial character is by considering its psychological role. As suggested in §2.2.3, intentional states are

---

[7] Recall that a C-ish superficial character is a superficial character that at least includes C-ish-ness as a part or aspect, and angle bracket notation names contents in a way that is reflective of their superficial characters. See n. 3 of Chapter 2.

psychologically involved, where an intentional state is psychologically involved when it plays a psychological role that is appropriate to its content's superficial character. Psychological involvement might involve playing a role in the drawing of inferences and the generation of behavior, being available to introspection, or simply being part of a subject's representational phenomenology, such as the phenomenology of "grasping" a content. We might not always be able to discern an intentional state's psychological roles, but when we are, this can help inform us of its content.

Intentional states involving the concept HORSE arguably play psychological roles appropriate to having the content <horse>. They are appropriately connected to intentional states representing horse-related activities, perceptual states representing the perceptual features of horses, higher-order thoughts about representing horses, horse-appropriate behaviors, and an experienced "grasp" of horses. In short, intentional states involving the concept HORSE play a psychological role that is appropriate to representing the content <horse>, which suggests that HORSE represents <horse>, a content with a horse-ish superficial character. So, considerations of psychological role confirm the tracking theory's prediction that HORSE represents <horse>.

As we've seen, our theory-independent ways of finding out about the contents of intentional states arguably confirm the tracking theory's predictions about the content of HORSE. Another "good case" for the tracking theory is that of perceptual representations of shapes. The tracking theory might predict that perceptual shape representations track particular shape properties and hence that they represent particular shape contents. Our theory-independent considerations arguably support such content attributions and thus confirm the tracking theory's predictions.

I will say that two contents **match** when they are exactly alike in superficial character. In the case of HORSE and perceptual shape representations, the contents ascribed by the tracking theory arguably match the contents those representations in fact represent. In what follows, I argue that there are cases in which the contents ascribed by the tracking theory do not match the contents that are in fact represented. Such cases are **mismatch cases** for the tracking theory, cases in which it makes false predictions about a represented content's superficial character. The tracking theory, then, has a **mismatch problem**.

3.4 A Mismatch Case: Perceptual Color Representations

In this section, I focus on what I take to be one of the most obvious mismatch cases for the tracking theory, that of perceptual color representations, which are representations of color involved in visual states representing surfaces or objects as colored, such as a visual state representing a blue mug.[8] Section 3.5 considers other candidate mismatch cases.

When combined with information about what perceptual color representations track, the tracking theory makes predictions about what they represent. Perceptual color representations arguably track physical properties of objects such as their surface reflectance profiles (dispositions to reflect, transmit, or emit such-and-such proportions of such-and-such wavelengths of light), the categorical bases of surface reflectance profiles, or the disposition to cause certain physical or functional states in organisms like us.[9] For ease of exposition, I will focus on the view that, on the relevant tracking relations, perceptual color representations track surface reflectance profiles, though the general form of argument applies with few modifications to alternative views.[10,11]

---

[8] I assume, as is plausible, that perceptual color representations are **subpropositional representations**, representations with contents that do not have a propositional form but that sometimes form parts of propositional contents, and that they originally represent the relevant color contents. These assumptions are congenial to views on which there is a language of thought; see §2.1. Alternative views might deny that there are subpropositional representations or take subpropositional representations to derive their contents from the propositional representations of which they form parts (see, e.g., Millikan 1984 for this latter view). For those who hold these alternative views, my examples of subpropositional representations representing colors can be substituted with examples of propositional representations representing contents involving colors, such as representations representing that a particular object has a particular color, and the discussion can be amended accordingly. See also n. 10 of Chapter 1. For those resistant to the idea that perceptual states are intentional, some nonperceptual mismatch cases are described in §3.5.

[9] These options for what perceptual color representations track map onto well-known views of what they represent: Dretske (1995), Tye (1995b, 2000), and Byrne and Hilbert (2003) take perceptual color representations to represent surface reflectance profiles; Armstrong (1968), Jackson and Pargetter (1987), Jackson (1998a), Lewis (1997), and Smart (1975) take them to represent the categorical bases of surface reflectance profiles; and Cohen (2009) and Averill (1992) take them to represent relations between putatively colored objects and subjects. See Gow 2014 for an excellent overview.

[10] However, see Hardin 1988 for extensive discussion of the difficulties involved in isolating the precise external causes of color experience.

[11] Another option is to take perceptual color representations to track qualia or dispositions to cause qualia in subjects, where **qualia** are felt, subjective, sensational, qualitative, or phenomenal mental items that are not intentional contents (see Peacocke 1984, Levin 2000, and Shoemaker 2003 for the view that perceptual color representations represent dispositions to cause qualia). I set views on which perceptual color representations track something involving qualia aside for two reasons: First, the view that there are qualia is largely, and I think correctly, rejected. One reason to reject qualia is the so-called transparency of experience: Introspection simply does not reveal such non-content mental qualities (see Harman 1990, Dretske 1995, Tye 2000, and Mendelovici 2013a). Second, it is unlikely that the tracking theorist will be attracted to such a view, since appeal to qualia is in tension with a commitment to naturalism: Either qualia are naturalistic items or they are not. If they are, then the view that perceptual color representations track qualia or dispositions to cause qualia boils down to one of the physicalist alternatives listed in the main text or something similar. If they are not, then appealing to qualia is incompatible with a commitment to naturalism.

Combined, then, with the view that perceptual color representations track surface reflectance profiles, the tracking theory predicts that perceptual color representations represent surface reflectance profiles. This prediction is a prediction about the deep nature of the contents of perceptual color representations, i.e., that they are properties of a certain type. It is also a prediction about *which* contents perceptual color representations represent, i.e., that they represent contents with surface-reflectance-profile-ish superficial characters. For example, it might predict that a particular perceptual color representation, SKY-BLUE, has as its content a particular surface reflectance profile, *SRP* (pronounced "surp"). This is not only a prediction about the deep nature of SKY-BLUE's content, but also a prediction about *which* content SKY-BLUE represents, i.e., that it represents <SRP>, which is a content that has a SRP-ish superficial character.

The problem is that our theory-independent methods of finding out which contents we represent suggest against the tracking theory's predictions and in favor of alternative content attributions that the tracking theory cannot accommodate. Let us first see how our two theory-independent methods suggest against the tracking theory's content attributions.

At least some perceptual states involving perceptual color representations are paradigm cases of intentionality, so they are introspectively accessible. But when we introspect on these states, we notice nothing to do with specific surface reflectance profiles. For example, when we introspect upon intentional states involving SKY-BLUE, we do not notice <SRP> or any aspect or component of such a content. Whatever content we do notice does not have a SRP-ish superficial character. So, introspection fails to support the tracking theory's predictions.[12]

Considerations of psychological role also fail to support the tracking theory's predictions. Our perceptual intentional states representing colors do not behave as if they represented surface reflectance profiles. They are not causally, inferentially, or otherwise interestingly related to beliefs about surface reflectance profiles or higher-order thoughts stating that we perceptually represent surface reflectance profiles. And they in no sense allow us to "grasp" such contents or have any other related phenomenological effects. These states' psychological roles in no way suggest that they represent surface reflectance properties. For example, intentional states involving SKY-BLUE do not behave as if they represented <SRP>: They do not allow us to draw inferences about SRP or to have higher-order thoughts saying that we represent <SRP>, and they do not have a SRP-ish phenomenology. These

---

[12] The related claim that colors don't look dispositional is a well-known complaint against views of the content of perceptual color representations on which they represent dispositions to affect subjects in various ways; see Boghossian and Velleman 1989 and McGinn 1996.

states' psychological roles in no way suggest that SKY-BLUE's content has a SRP-ish superficial character. So, considerations of psychological role also fail to support the tracking theory's predictions.

So far, I have argued that our theory-independent ways of knowing about the contents of intentional states do not support the tracking theory's content attributions. Of course, absence of evidence does not imply evidence of absence. However, when combined with some further facts about the case, it does: While some representations might only be involved in intentional states that are not introspectively accessible and whose psychological roles we cannot discern, it turns out that many intentional states involving perceptual color representations *are* introspectively accessible and have psychological roles that we *can* discern. Indeed, intentional states involving perceptual color representations are arguably amongst the intentional states to which we have the best theory-independent access. We are constantly confronted with them, we can easily notice them introspectively, and we are often in a position to notice them play a role in guiding our reasoning and behavior, forming the targets of higher-order thoughts, and affecting our overall representational phenomenology. So, if perceptual color representations represented surface reflectance profiles, we should expect this to be supported by our theory-independent considerations. Indeed, if *any* of the tracking theory's content attributions can be supported by theory-independent considerations, these ones should. Since they are not, this means not only that theory-independent considerations fail to support the tracking theory's predictions but also that they positively suggest against them.

The tracking theory, then, wrongly predicts that perceptual color representations represent contents with surface-reflectance-profile-ish superficial characters. For example, it wrongly predicts that SKY-BLUE represents <SRP>, a content with a SRP-ish superficial character. We can call this kind of error an **error of commission**, since it includes unwanted material in the superficial character of SKY-BLUE's content. Similar claims hold for other perceptual color representations. Since the tracking theory makes false predictions about the superficial character of the contents of perceptual color representations, the case of perceptual color representations is a mismatch case for the tracking theory, and the tracking theory faces the mismatch problem. It is empirically inadequate and hence false.

We can summarize this line of reasoning in the case of SKY-BLUE in the following **argument from commission**:

(C1) If the tracking theory is true, then SKY-BLUE has the content <SRP>.
(C2) SKY-BLUE does not have the content <SRP>.
(C3) Therefore, the tracking theory is false.

In other words, the tracking theory predicts that SKY-BLUE represents a content with a SRP-ish superficial character, but in fact, it does not, so the tracking theory is false. (C1), which expresses the tracking theory's (false) prediction, follows from the specification of the tracking theory together with facts about what SKY-BLUE tracks, while (C2) is supported by our theory-independent considerations that inform us as to which contents we represent.

So far, I have argued that theory-independent considerations suggest against the tracking theory's predictions about the superficial characters of perceptual color representations. This gives us the argument from commission. I will now argue that theory-independent considerations support alternative content attributions, which cannot be accommodated by the tracking theory. This will lead to another argument against the tracking theory, the argument from omission.

We've noted that perceptual color representations are involved in intentional states that are introspectively accessible and have discernible psychological roles. So, our theory-independent ways of finding out about intentional states give us some hint as to what they represent. Which content attributions, then, do they support?

Introspection suggests that perceptual color representations represent qualitative, simple (not having constituent parts), primitive (not made up of other items), sui generis (in a category all of their own), non-dispositional, non-relational, and non-mental color properties. In short, introspection suggests that perceptual color representations represent contents that are, or at least involve, what Chalmers (2006) calls **edenic colors**. For example, introspection upon intentional states involving SKY-BLUE reveals a content with a qualitative, simple, primitive, sui generis, non-dispositional, non-relational edenic-sky-blue-ish superficial character, i.e., <edenic sky-blue>. In sum, introspective considerations suggest that SKY-BLUE and other perceptual color representations represent edenic colors.[13,14]

Considerations of psychological involvement also suggest that perceptual color representations represent edenic colors. Intentional states involving perceptual color representations are inferentially related to beliefs about edenic colors, they are available to form the basis of higher-order thoughts about representing edenic colors, and they allow us to in some sense "grasp" contents involving edenic colors. For example,

---

[13] Chalmers (2006) describes edenic color properties using the allegory of the garden of Eden: "In the Garden of Eden, we had unmediated contact with the world. We were directly acquainted with objects in the world and with their properties. Objects were simply presented to us without causal mediation, and properties were revealed to us in their true intrinsic glory" (p. 49). In Eden, an apparently red apple was "gloriously, perfectly, and primitively red" (p. 49).

[14] Contemporary defenders of such a view include Mackie (1976), Holman (2002), Maund (1995), Chalmers (2006), Campbell (1993), Pautz (MS), and Gow (2014). Historically, such a view was notably held by Democritus, Descartes, Galileo, and others.

absent countervailing theoretical beliefs, a perceptual intentional state representing that an object is sky-blue might lead to the judgment that the object is some shade of edenic blue, i.e., that it has a sui generis, primitive, non-dispositional, non-relational, and non-mental property of blueness. So, considerations of psychological role also suggest that perceptual color representations represent edenic colors.

The problem is that it is quite implausible that perceptual color representations track edenic colors. Edenic colors are qualitative, simple, primitive, sui generis, non-dispositional, and non-relational color-like features. But neither surface re-flectance profiles nor their categorical bases nor other properties of objects involve any such features. If there are no instantiated edenic color properties, then it is hard to see how any tracking relation can single them out. What tracking relations relate us to are surface reflectance profiles, their categorical bases, and other related properties of objects, none of which are or involve edenic colors. Perceptual color representations do not track edenic colors, and so the tracking theory cannot say that they represent them.

In short, the tracking theory falsely predicts that SKY-BLUE's content is not <edenic sky-blue>, a content with an edenic-sky-blue-ish superficial character. The tracking theory, then, makes an **error of omission**, since it wrongly omits certain material from the superficial character of SKY-BLUE's content. The same holds for other perceptual color representations. From this, we can conclude that the case of perceptual color representations is a mismatch case for the tracking theory, that the tracking theory faces the mismatch problem, and that it is empirically inadequate and hence false.

We can summarize this line of reasoning in the case of SKY-BLUE in the following **argument from omission**:

(O1) If the tracking theory is true, then SKY-BLUE does not have the content <edenic sky-blue>.

(O2) SKY-BLUE has the content <edenic sky-blue>.

(O3) Therefore, the tracking theory is false.

In other words, the tracking theory predicts that SKY-BLUE does not represent a content with an edenic-sky-blue-ish superficial character, but in fact it does represent such a content. So, the tracking theory is false. Again, (C1) expresses the tracking theory's prediction and follows from the specification of the tracking theory together with facts about what SKY-BLUE tracks, while (O2) is supported by our theory-independent considerations.

As we've seen, our theory-independent considerations can form the basis of two different arguments against the tracking theory, the argument from commission and the argument from omission. I think both arguments are effective, though, as we will soon see, the argument from omission is stronger.

I have focused on tracking theories that take perceptual color representations to track surface reflectance profiles on the relevant tracking relations, but it should be clear that similar arguments apply to tracking theories taking perceptual color representations to track the categorical bases of these surface reflectance profiles or dispositions to cause certain physical or functional states. Theory-independent considerations suggest against such content attributions and in favor of content attributions the tracking theory cannot accommodate.

3.5 Other Mismatch Cases

The above arguments invite many sophisticated replies, but before considering some of them, let us consider the scope of the alleged problem.

I want to suggest that there are additional mismatch cases for the tracking theory, both in perception and in thought. Another perceptual case is that of the hot and cold representations involved in our tactile perceptual states representing ourselves or other items as being hot, cold, warm, etc. Perceptual hot and cold representations might be said to track mind-independent physical features, like temperature or heat, or dispositions to cause certain states or reactions in us.[15] But theory-independent considerations suggest that hot and cold representations do not represent such contents. We don't notice such contents upon introspection, and hot and cold representations simply don't behave as if they represented them (we are not disposed to form beliefs with related contents, we do not form higher-order states about our representation of such contents, etc.). Instead, theory-independent considerations suggest that perceptual hot and cold representations represent something like simple, primitive, non-relational, sui generis edenic hotness and coldness. If this is right, then perceptual representations of hotness and coldness are mismatch cases for the tracking theory.

Perceptual representations of smells might be another mismatch case for the tracking theory. Such olfactory representations arguably track something like molecular properties of volatile molecules but represent edenic olfactory properties.[16] Gustatory representations of sweetness similarly might track the presence of glucose

---

[15] Akins (1996) argues that the best-candidate physical properties for what perceptual hot and cold representations track are not temperature and heat but rather gerrymandered properties, such as the relations that hold between a stimulus' temperature, the body part to which the stimulus is applied, the body part's initial temperature, and the body part's rate of temperature change.

[16] See Mendelovici forthcoming-a and MS.

and other sugars but represent edenic sweetness, while gustatory representations of bitterness might track a variety of toxins but represent edenic bitterness. Perceptual representations of heaviness might also be a mismatch case, tracking relational properties of objects but representing intrinsic properties.[17,18]

For every perceptual mismatch case, we might also find a corresponding mismatch case involving **concepts**, the subpropositional representations involved primarily in thoughts. For some of us, the contents of our color concepts might be determined by the contents of our perceptual color representations in a way that makes them mismatch cases. For instance, someone's concept BLUE might represent a range of perceptually representable shades of blue. Such color concepts track something other than what they represent: They track something like ranges of surface reflectance profiles, but they represent something like ranges of edenic colors. If color concepts originally represent these contents, then this is a mismatch case.

There might also be conceptual mismatch cases that do not have perceptual analogues. Moral concepts are good candidates. If J. L. Mackie (1977) is right, our moral concepts represent properties that are prescriptive, in that they offer subjects reasons to act in certain ways, and objective, in that, when instantiated, they exist out there, in the world, independently of subjects and their preferences. But our moral concepts arguably don't track any such properties. Rather, they track harm, disrespect, unfairness, societal norms, disgust, personal aversions, and the like. If moral concepts originally represent these contents, then they are another mismatch case.

Our concept of a self is another potential mismatch case. One intuitive view is that selves are simple enduring substances (see, e.g., Lowe 1996). Perhaps, then, we represent ourselves and others as simple self substances. If there are in fact no simple self substances, then it is quite likely that all we track are human animals, Parfitian relations of psychological connectedness and continuity (Parfit 1984), or simply people's gaits and faces. In such cases, our concept of the self tracks something

---

[17] See Mendelovici 2013b. See also Mendelovici 2013a and 2014 for a representationalist view of moods and emotions on which moods and emotions turn out to be mismatch cases for the tracking theory.

[18] An extreme view is that all perceptual representations represent something other than what they track. (A somewhat less extreme view is that in the case of all "secondary" qualities, we represent something other than what we track.) Although I am sympathetic to the extreme view, my arguments needn't commit us to it. For instance, one might reasonably hold that perceptual representations of spatial, structural, or functional properties, such as representations of shapes and tables, manage to do a good job of tracking what they represent.

See also Chalmers (2006), who suggests that many representations represent edenic properties analogous to edenic redness, and Byrne and Hilbert (2006), who suggest that the arguments for eliminativism about colors should also apply to other cases, such as those of sounds and tastes (though they take this to be a reason to reject the arguments).

other than what it represents. If it originally represents its content, we have another mismatch case.[19,20]

Of course, different people might have different concepts corresponding roughly to the same thing. For instance, some people might be dispositionalists about color or have Parfitian concepts of personal identity. Some of us might have reconstructed our concepts of hotness and coldness to represent temperature or heat. This means that, while some people's concepts of colors, personal identity, or hotness and coldness might be mismatch cases, other people's might not be. But the existence of a single mismatch case is enough to make trouble for the tracking theory. If Mackie's concept of moral goodness is one of objective prescriptivity, Lowe's concept of the self is one of a simple substance, or some child's concept of hotness represents edenic hotness, then, assuming these concepts are supposed to originally represent their contents, the tracking theory faces the mismatch problem.

3.6 Objections

The arguments from omission and commission are fairly simple, but they invite various sophisticated replies. This section considers a few of the most interesting replies, while Appendix A considers a few more replies.

3.6.1 DEFENSE BY IDENTITY

One might attempt to defend the tracking theory by claiming that <SRP>, the content predicted by the tracking theory, *just is* <edenic sky-blue>, the content SKY-BLUE in fact represents. The tracking theory predicts that SKY-BLUE represents <SRP>, and theory-independent considerations suggest it represents <edenic sky-blue>, but this is not a problem because <SRP> *just is* <edenic sky-blue>. This strategy, in effect, denies (C2), the claim that SKY-BLUE does not have the content <SRP>, and (O1), the claim that if the tracking theory is true, then SKY-BLUE does not have the content <edenic sky-blue>. Call this the **defense by identity strategy**.

---

[19] A useful heuristic for finding mismatch cases for the tracking theory is to look for representations of items that resist reduction. The reason they resist reduction might just be that their contents' superficial characters are entirely unlike the (presumably physical) items that they track and that are assumed to form suitable candidates for their reduction base. Other possible cases include representations of responsibility, justice, agency, and numbers.

[20] In Chapter 7, I will argue that practically all concepts have original contents that cannot be accommodated by the tracking theory. Establishing this, however, requires too much argument to be dialectically useful at this point.

A defender of this strategy might concede that it is prima facie implausible that <SRP> is <edenic sky-blue> but maintain that it is already part of her position that the tracking theory's predictions can be surprising, that the contents we observe from a theory-independent perspective can seem distinct from the contents predicted by the theory. We should not be too worried about that, she might add, since there are ready explanations for why we might fail to recognize true identities. These explanations center on the idea that we can represent one thing in two different ways, e.g., under two different modes of presentation, conceptually in one case but nonconceptually in the other, or by using recognitional, demonstrative, or other special concepts in one case but not in the other. So, she might maintain, we, as theorists, might represent <SRP> and <edenic sky-blue> in two different ways, which makes their identity non-obvious to us. Such moves are familiar from the debates on the mind-body problem, where a common strategy is to assert that mental states are identical to physical states and then to attempt to explain away appearances to the contrary. Indeed, one might claim that there is an "epistemic gap" between our concepts of the contents <SRP> and <edenic sky-blue> preventing us from seeing that they are identical, similar to the alleged epistemic gap between mental states and physical states, but that this epistemic gap needn't correspond to a metaphysical gap.[21]

Let us grant that true identities might not always be obvious to us, that this might be explained by appeal to different ways of representing the same thing, and that all this might apply to the case of <SRP> and <edenic sky-blue>.[22] However, all this is irrelevant, since my arguments already allow us to conclude that <SRP> is not identical to <edenic sky-blue>. To see this, note that we can rearrange my premises to argue directly for the non-identity of <SRP> and <edenic sky-blue>:

---

[21] Thanks to Rob Stainton for insisting on objections of this flavor.

[22] There are two notable ways in which <SRP> might end up being identical to <edenic sky-blue>, despite appearing not to be. The first is that there is a single content with both a SRP-ish and an edenic-sky-blue-ish superficial character. This is possible just as it is possible for there to be a single object that is both red and round. (Recall that a C-ish superficial character is a superficial character that includes C-ish-ness; see n. 3 of Chapter 2.)

There is another, far more radical, proposal for how <SRP> might end up being identical to <edenic sky-blue>, one that aims to truly harness the (supposed) power of identity. This proposal maintains not only that <SRP> is identical to <edenic sky-blue> but, further, that having a SRP-ish superficial character is the same thing as having an edenic-sky-blue-ish superficial character. Recall that superficial characters are features or properties of contents, ways that contents are. So, this option would be analogous to claiming that redness is *identical* to roundness. I don't think this proposal is epistemically possible, but nothing hangs on this right now. We will consider a view like this in §3.6.4.

(Returning to the mind-body problem, the first proposal is analogous to substance monism, which is compatible with property dualism, while the second proposal is analogous to property monism.)

(C2) SKY-BLUE does not have the content <SRP>.

(O2) SKY-BLUE has the content <edenic sky-blue>.

(NI1) Therefore, <SRP> is not identical to <edenic sky-blue>.

This argument does not beg any questions against the <SRP>/<edenic sky-blue> identity theorist, since the arguments for (C2) and (O2) do not presuppose that <SRP> is not identical to <edenic sky-blue>: (C2) and (O2) are supported by introspection and considerations of psychological role, which suggest that SKY-BLUE does not represent <SRP> and that it does represent <edenic sky-blue>.

My arguments also give us the resources to argue that if the tracking theory is true, then <SRP> is not identical to <edenic sky-blue>:

(C1) If the tracking theory is true, then SKY-BLUE has the content <SRP>.

(O1) If the tracking theory is true, then SKY-BLUE does not have the content <edenic sky-blue>.

(NI2) Therefore, if the tracking theory is true, then <SRP> is not identical to <edenic sky-blue>.

Again, (C1) and (O1) are justified without assuming that <SRP> is not identical to <edenic sky-blue>, so the argument does not beg any questions against the tracking theorist who wants to identify them.

What these two arguments show is that even though, pre-theoretically, it is a live possibility that <SRP> is identical to <edenic sky-blue>, once we either accept the tracking theory or consult our theory-independent methods for finding out about contents, this possibility gets ruled out.

What of ways of representing and epistemic gaps? Can't they be used to show that somehow I am mistaken here? Ways of representing and the alleged possibility of epistemic gaps without metaphysical gaps can be used to show that a claim that two things are not identical *might* be mistaken, but not that it *is* mistaken. (After all, there is an epistemic gap between lots of things that are in fact not identical, like the Moon and the pile of ungraded papers on my desk.) Appealing to epistemic gaps and ways of representing to defend the claim that <SRP> is identical to <edenic sky-blue> is dialectically ineffective, since I don't merely assert that the two are not identical, but offer a non-question-begging argument for the claim. A dialectically effective response would have to take issue with my premises and the arguments I use to support them.[23]

---

[23] The tracking theorist might also improve her dialectical situation by showing that the view that <SRP> is identical to <edenic sky-blue> can be independently motivated. This would improve her situation not

The upshot of this discussion is that the tracking theorist who wants to insist that <SRP> is simply identical to <edenic sky-blue> cannot defuse my arguments with this claim alone. She must directly engage with the arguments for my premises. For example, she might take issue with (C2) by arguing that my theory-independent considerations do not in fact support it, or she might take issue with (O1) by arguing that the tracking theory does in fact predict that perceptual color representations represent edenic colors. In what follows, I consider some such replies, including ones that make further use of ways of representing (see Appendix A for a few more). I then return to the defense by identity strategy.

3.6.2 WAYS OF REPRESENTING

One might argue that perceptual color representations represent contents in special ways that occlude them from my theory-independent methods, so my methods cannot be used to find out about these contents. For example, perceptual color representations might represent their contents under special modes of presentation, nonconceptually, or in some other special way, which occludes them from our theory-independent methods. If so, this would undercut my arguments for (C2) and (O2), which rely on such methods.

We previously saw that ways of representing might play a role in the defense by identity strategy by explaining why we, as theorists, are not always able to recognize true identities between the contents we theorize about. In other words, according to the defense by identity strategy, we, as theorists, represent the same content in two different ways (e.g., under two different modes of presentation), and the difference in ways of representing prevents us from noticing true identity claims. On the present strategy, ways of representing play a different role: Representing subjects represent perceptual color contents in a special way that blocks our access to them through theory-independent methods. Our theory-independent methods might instead tell us about the relevant ways of representing or about nothing at all.

There are several problems with this strategy. First, there is a general methodological worry: Any strategy that claims that neither introspection nor psychological

---

by dispelling my arguments, but by bringing us to a standoff, with arguments on both sides. However, it is hard to see how one could possibly motivate such an identity claim independently of assuming the tracking theory or a nearby view. See also §3.6.4.

(Notice that an analogous strategy in the case of the mind-body problem is arguably a bit more attractive, since at least there are independent arguments against dualism, such as the argument from mental causation.)

roles can tell us about the contents of intentional states risks denying that we have any theory-independent access to the contents of particular intentional states. If we do not have theory-independent access to the contents of particular intentional states, then there is no way to test competing theories' predictions about *which* contents we represent. This leaves us to decide between theories largely on a priori or metaphysical grounds, even when the theories under consideration make specific predictions.[24] This is quite an unfortunate consequence for a defender of the tracking theory, particularly given that the tracking theory is supposed to stem from a naturalistic mindset, a mindset that is supposed to in some way align with science and empirical ways of finding things out.[25]

A second, and related, problem with this strategy is that if the intentional states predicted by the tracking theory are introspectively inaccessible and play no psychological roles that we can discern, if they leave no detectable trace in our minds or behaviors, then they risk becoming idly spinning wheels. It is not clear why we should posit, or even care about, such contents. If the tracking theory's contents are in fact explanatorily inert idly spinning wheels, this too is an unfortunate consequence for a theory that is supposed to stem from a naturalistic mindset.[26]

A third problem with this strategy is that it is not clear that it can work in the first place because it is not clear why representing contents in certain ways should make them inaccessible to our theory-independent methods. For example, suppose we say that SKY-BLUE's content is represented **nonconceptually**, that is, in a way that does not involve or otherwise require having the concepts that we, as theorists, would use to describe it. The problem is that it is not clear why representing a content nonconceptually should prevent it from playing a psychological role characteristic of the content that it is. Even if nonconceptual contents are represented in a special way, they are still *represented*, and they should still in some way or other behave as if they're

---

[24] I do think that there are relevant metaphysical considerations that can help us decide between competing theories (see §4.4 and §5.2.2), but I do not think they are the only considerations.

[25] One might suggest that intuition can be used to test competing theories' predictions in a theory-independent way, but it is not clear why intuition would be a reliable method here unless it was responsive to the evidence from introspection or psychological role.

[26] One might suggest that the tracking theory's contents can still play a role in determining truth conditions. The problem with this suggestion is that these would not be the truth conditions we care about or have any reason to think exist. This is because the relevant truth conditions would be utterly divorced from our intentional experience. It would be cold comfort to someone who is worried about whether the world is as she takes it to be to tell her that she has no access to how she takes the world to be but it really is that way. The truth conditions we care about and have any intuitive reason to believe exist are those connected to our intentional experience. So, positing the tracking theory's predicted contents cannot be justified by a need to explain truth conditions.

there.[27,28] More generally, one might worry that it is not clear why the relevant ways of representing should result in the kind of occlusion required in order to deny (C2).

The fourth, and I think biggest, problem for this strategy is that even if perceptual color representations have some contents that are occluded from our theory-independent methods, the claim that no perceptual color contents remain unoccluded is implausible. We can at least sometimes introspectively notice our perceptual color states, and when we do, we notice them presenting represented objects as having various colors. Since we notice them introspectively and we are tempted to describe them representationally, they qualify as instances of intentionality (§1.2). Moreover, these states that we introspectively notice play various psychological roles: They are related to the beliefs we form about the objects they represent (e.g., that they are blue, brown, or green), our higher-order thoughts about our perceptual states (e.g., that we visually represent blue cups, brown chairs, or green trees), and our overall phenomenology of representing (e.g., the phenomenology of things "striking" us a certain way, namely, as involving a blue cup, a brown chair, a green tree, etc.). All this suggests that even if perceptual color representations represent contents that are occluded from us, they (also) represent contents that are not occluded. Further, theory-independent considerations concerning these contents suggest that they are edenic color contents, which the tracking theory cannot account for. (O2) is still true and the argument from omission still stands.

One might suggest that our theory-independent methods latch onto modes of presentation, qualia, or something else other than contents. Perhaps, for example, it is modes of presentation that we notice introspectively and that play psychological roles such as those described in the previous paragraph. That's all well and good, but then modes of presentation would turn out to be what we introspectively observe and are tempted to describe representationally, so they would turn out to be contents.

---

[27] Jackson (2004) argues along such lines that the issue of nonconceptual content is a red herring in the debates on representationalism. Jackson's worry, roughly, is that nonconceptual content is still *content*, and so it should behave as such.

[28] Another worry of this sort with the nonconceptual content strategy is that it is not clear why nonconceptual contents should be hidden from introspection in the relevant way. Presumably, the explanation is supposed to go something like this: In order to introspectively notice that we represent <SRP>, we need a concept representing <SRP>, and it needs to be appropriately connected to our perceptual representation of <SRP>. Since SKY-BLUE represents its content nonconceptually, we can represent it without having a concept representing <SRP>, so its content needn't be introspectively accessible. The problem with this story is that it does not explain why even *if* we have the required concepts and the required connections, we *still* cannot recognize anything to do with particular surface reflectance profiles in our perceptual states representing colors. One way to put the import of this problem is that the relevant occlusion mechanism cannot in fact render perceptual color contents sufficiently inaccessible to theory-independent methods to allow us to reject (C2).

But if modes of presentation are contents, then they are within the scope of the tracking theory, and it needs to offer an account of them. The same goes for anything else we might say our theory-independent considerations latch onto in lieu of content.[29]

In short, the problem is that it is quite implausible to flat-out deny that our theory-independent considerations are evidence for something answering to the notion of content. And, whatever this thing is, our theory-independent considerations suggest that it includes edenic color contents, like <edenic sky-blue>. So, (O2) is still true, and the argument from omission still goes through. At best, the ways of representing strategy brings us back to where we started: We are back at having to account for contents of perceptual color representations that don't appear to be identical to anything that they can be said to track. And we gain nothing with this epicycle. It arguably worsens the situation because now we're additionally committed to introspectively inaccessible and psychologically uninvolved, or "hidden," contents that arguably don't do any explanatory work.

3.6.3 THE TRACKING THEORY DOESN'T MAKE PREDICTIONS ABOUT SUPERFICIAL CHARACTER

One might object to my claim that the tracking theory makes predictions about the superficial characters of represented contents, claiming that it only makes predictions about their deep natures. For instance, the tracking theory might predict that SKY-BLUE's content is the property *SRP*, but not that this content has a SRP-ish superficial character. If the tracking theory doesn't make predictions about the superficial character of SKY-BLUE's content, then perhaps we can reject (C1) and (O1).

Like the strategy appealing to ways of representing that we have already considered, this strategy ends up denying that the tracking theory's predictions can be tested using our theory-independent methods. However, in the case of the strategy appealing to ways of representing, the reason for this is that our theory-independent methods are not privy to the facts about our contents' superficial characters, while

---

[29] McGinn (1996) raises a similar objection to the use of a mode of presentation strategy to defend the view that colors are dispositions to cause color experiences:

> Nor is it possible to maintain that colors-as-dispositions are the de re objects of vision, without themselves corresponding to the de dicto content of color perception, since some further properties will need to be introduced in order to capture the de dicto content of perception—and these will present essentially the same problem.... (p. 538)

in the case of the strategy presently under consideration, the reason is that the tracking theory doesn't even make any predictions about such facts in the first place. The idea is that the tracking theory is only concerned with the deep natures, not the superficial characters, of intentional contents, so it is not in conflict with any discoveries our theory-independent methods might lead us to concerning their superficial characters.

If this strategy succeeds in preventing the tracking theory from making any predictions about superficial character, then this would lead to a quite undesirable position for the tracking theorist. The tracking theory would only provide a (presumably partial) theory of the deep nature of contents, and not an answer to the question of *which* contents a particular representation represents, despite providing a mapping from representations to contents when combined with information about what the representations track.[30] In any case, as we will soon see, the strategy does not in fact succeed in preventing the tracking theory from making any predictions about superficial character.

The main problem with this strategy is that, even if it can provide a response to the argument from commission, it does nothing to address the argument from omission. The strategy involves accepting that if the tracking theory is true, then SKY-BLUE's content is identical to the property *SRP*. Now, since superficial characters are features of contents, in order for SKY-BLUE's content to have an edenic-sky-blue-ish superficial character, it would have to have some edenic-sky-blue-ish feature. But *SRP* does not have any edenic-sky-blue-ish feature, and so *SRP* does not have an edenic-sky-blue-ish superficial character. So, if the tracking theory is true, then SKY-BLUE does not have a content with an edenic-sky-blue-ish superficial character, and (O1) is true. It turns out, then, that the tracking theory makes predictions about superficial characters after all, and they are still false.

Put otherwise, the crux of the argument from omission is that the tracking theory cannot accommodate the central feature of SKY-BLUE's content that we can isolate using our theory-independent methods, the edenic-sky-blue-ish-ness. It does not matter whether we call this feature a superficial character or something else, and it does not matter how exactly the tracking theory ends up predicting that SKY-BLUE's content doesn't have it. Indeed, we can drop the talk of superficial character entirely and run the argument from omission in terms of this edenic-sky-blue-ish feature:

---

[30] This is analogous to Bourget's (forthcoming-a) point that physicalism about mental states does not tell us *which* physical state any given mental state is identical to.

(O1′) If the tracking theory is true, then SKY-BLUE does not have a content with
an edenic-sky-blue-ish feature.

(O2′) SKY-BLUE has a content with an edenic-sky-blue-ish feature.

(O3′) Therefore, the tracking theory is false.

SKY-BLUE's content has a certain edenic-sky-blue-ish feature, a certain qualitative,
sui generis, primitive, non-dispositional, and non-relational feature. Even if some
features of SKY-BLUE's contents are not accessible to our theory-independent
methods, this feature *is*, and so it needs to be accommodated by the tracking theory.
The tracking theory predicts that SKY-BLUE's content is *SRP*, which is a property
with various features. If edenic-sky-blue-ish-ness is not among them, then the theory
cannot accommodate the case of SKY-BLUE. It isn't, so it can't.[31]

3.6.4 REITERATED IDENTITIES

The first response strategy we considered was the defense by identity strategy, which
fairly flatfootedly claimed that <SRP> *just is* <edenic sky-blue>. Since <SRP> is
<edenic sky-blue>, SKY-BLUE *does* represent <SRP>, and the tracking theory *does*
predict that SKY-BLUE represents <edenic sky-blue>. This allows us to reject (C2)
and (O1). I argued that this response is dialectically ineffective because it ignores the
argument against the identity claim that I can provide by rearranging the premises
of the arguments from commission and omission.

However, there is a more radical version of the defense by identity strategy, one
that truly aims to harness the (supposed) power of identity by simply reiterating
the defense by identity strategy's basic move. I will argue that this strategy also fails,
and that the reason it fails illuminates the problem with the bare defense by identity
strategy.

Let us focus on how this strategy can be used to argue against (O1), since
the argument from omission is the more powerful of the two arguments. Recall
that I argued for (O1) by arguing that there is nothing edenic-sky-blue-ish about
the property *SRP* (or anything else SKY-BLUE might be said to track). But,
the <SRP>/<edenic sky-blue> identity theorist might suggest, I've neglected
a further identity claim, the claim that edenic-sky-blue-ish-ness is identical to
some feature of *SRP*; perhaps it is identical to, say, SRP-ish-ness. Since *SRP* has
SRP-ish-ness, and edenic-sky-blue-ish-ness is identical to SRP-ish-ness, *SRP* does
have edenic-sky-blue-ish-ness after all, and we can reject (O1). We can call this the

---

[31] Interestingly, this edenic-sky-blue-ish-ness *can* be found in qualia and dispositions to cause qualia, so
this kind of strategy might be used to defend Peacocke's view against some of Boghossian and Velleman's
(1989) objections (see n. 12).

reiterated identities strategy, since it proceeds by reiterating the defense by identity strategy's basic move, that of asserting an identity claim.

Suppose I reply that edenic-sky-blue-ish-ness is not identical to SRP-ish-ness because edenic-sky-blue-ish-ness has some property—say, that of being qualitative—that SRP-ish-ness lacks. The objector might reply that SRP-ish-ness does in fact have that property, because SRP-ish-ness has some further property, P, which is identical to it. The reiterated identities strategy, in effect, reiterates the initial response that, in making a non-identity claim, I am making a mistake. My argument is implicitly committed to multiple non-identity claims, each of which might be called into question. On this response, it's mistaken non-identity claims all the way up.

One hint that something has gone wrong is that the response strategy greatly overgenerates, allowing us to defend any identity claim by simply positing more identities. Consider the following exchange at the customer service desk:

> Customer service representative (Rep): Hello! How can I help you?
> Customer: I have a complaint about my order. I ordered a six-ton African elephant from your website, and what I received is a red brick.
> Rep: Yes! I hope you're enjoying your elephant.
> Customer: I didn't receive an elephant. I received a red brick.
> Rep: Yes! The red brick *is* the elephant.
> Customer: No, it's not. The elephant depicted on your website has a big trunk. The brick has no trunk.
> Rep: Yes, it does! There it is. *(points to surface of brick)*
> Customer: That is the surface of the brick.
> Rep: The surface of the brick *is* a trunk.
> Customer: An elephant trunk is made of flesh. The surface of the brick is made of brick.
> Rep: Yes! Being made of flesh *just is* being made of brick.
> Customer: Let me try again. This brick is six pounds. But the elephant was supposed to be six tons.
> Rep: Yes, of course! The brick is six tons. Six pounds *is* six tons.
> Customer: Look, just refund my three easy payments of $19.99.
> Rep: Of course! I have already issued you a refund.
> Customer: No, I can see right here that you just charged me again.
> Rep: Being charged again *is* getting a refund.
> Customer: Can I speak with your supervisor?
> Rep: Of course! I *am* my supervisor.

In order to defend a prima facie false identity claim, the customer service rep wheels in more prima facie false identity claims, effectively denying any common ground with her interlocutor. If her goal is simply to defend her position, this is a winning strategy; with no common ground to stand on, her interlocutor cannot lodge an argument against her. The customer service rep's strategy is, in effect, a skeptical strategy, a strategy that works because justification has to end somewhere.

Indeed, since it is possible to turn any dispute into a dispute about identities, the reiterated identities strategy can be used to defend *any* claim. For example, suppose that I claim that the Moon is made of cheese. You investigate the Moon, find no cheese, and tell me that I'm wrong. I reply by saying that cheese is identical to rocks, and there are rocks on the Moon, so there is cheese on the moon. I have turned our dispute into a dispute about identities, and now I can employ the reiterated identities strategy. (At any point, I can also assert that you cannot see the truth of my claims because you represent the items I want to identify in different ways, giving rise to an epistemic gap that need not correspond to a metaphysical gap.)

The moral of the story is that positing gratuitous identity claims does nothing to advance one's position. Since the reiterated identities strategy is a winning strategy, it can always be used to defend an identity claim, so the fact that it can be employed in the case of a given identity claim is no reason whatsoever to think that the identity claim is true. In the case of the alleged identity between <SRP> and <edenic sky-blue>, the fact that we can defend this identity by identifying the features of <SRP> with the features of <edenic sky-blue> does nothing to show that the identity holds.

This points to the basic problem with both the defense by identity and the reiterated identities strategies. If the tracking theorist's defense is to be convincing, it is not enough for her to simply take on whatever identity claims suit her theory. Any identity claims she takes on would have to be adequately motivated and defended. So, it is not enough to simply assert that, on her view, <SRP> *just is* <edenic sky-blue> or that, on her view, edenic-sky-blue-ish-ness *just is* some property of *SRP*. These identities would need to be motivated and defended on independent grounds. But it is difficult to see how this can be done. The fundamental problem remains: There is absolutely no reason arising from the examination of the surfaces of objects, the properties of light, or the relations between the two to think that *SRP* involves anything like edenic-sky-blue-ish-ness.[32]

---

[32] What I've described is a "pure" reiterated identities strategy, a strategy that defends the claim that <SRP> is <edenic sky-blue> using the (supposed) power of identity alone. Of course, this strategy might be combined with other strategies, such as that of simply denying that SKY-BLUE's content has a simple, non-dispositional, and non-relational superficial character. This would be analogous to the customer service representative denying that the advertised elephant was six tons, which might be more plausible than identifying being six tons with being six pounds. I have focused on the pure reiterated identities strategy here because, it seems to me, many are taken by the idea that identity claims can be completely opaque to us, giving rise to epistemic gaps that need not correspond to metaphysical

3.7 Reliable Misrepresentation and the Significance of Tracking

I have argued that the tracking theory faces the mismatch problem. This means that intentionality is not a matter of tracking. However, it does not mean that tracking is not important for reasoning and behavior. We can appreciate its importance by considering the usefulness of a certain kind of misrepresentation, reliable misrepresentation.

An intentional state or representation can be said to **reliably misrepresent** when it gets things wrong in the same way all the time. Assuming that objects never have edenic colors, perceptual color states are examples of reliable misrepresentation. They reliably *misrepresent* in that they are always false, and they *reliably* misrepresent in that they occur in similar circumstances on multiple occasions, presumably because they do a fairly good job of tracking various environmental conditions. Many other mismatch cases are also arguably cases of reliable misrepresentation.[33]

The reliability of reliable misrepresentation makes it quite useful to us, despite the misrepresentation. For example, the fact that perceptual color representations track surface reflectance profiles is part of what makes them useful in helping us navigate the world. Despite misrepresenting, they allow us to re-identify objects over time and discriminate between objects of different types. For example, even though an apparently red car doesn't *really* have the property of edenic redness that it appears to have, our perceptually representing it as edenic red allows us to quickly identify it in the parking lot. Likewise, even though ripe tomatoes and unripe tomatoes don't really have the edenic properties of redness and greenness they perceptually appear to have, we can use our perceptual color states to tell them apart. Other reliably misrepresenting states also track items that are significant to us, like temperatures, odors, sugars, and toxins, so they are also likely to be useful in similar ways. We can use them to avoid items that are likely to be harmful to us and seek out items that are likely to be beneficial, even though they misrepresent.

---

gaps, that identities are neither explanatory nor in need of explanation, and that all this grants identity claims a certain immunity from criticism. In contrast, more straightforward ways of simply denying premises do not have the same appeal, so they don't require the same attention. In any case, I consider such revision strategies in §A.2.4 of Appendix A.

[33] Describing intentional states as reliably misrepresenting implies that they have conditions of truth or reference, which I've suggested is not something we can take for granted (§1.3.4). I will eventually suggest that intentional states do have conditions of truth and reference (§9.3.4), and it would not be question-begging to appeal to those arguments here. In any case, not much rests on my claim that many mismatch cases misrepresent. Someone denying that intentional states have conditions of truth and reference might deny this claim, while retaining the claim that many mismatch cases are *reliable* and agreeing with much of what follows.

In some cases, reliable misrepresentation might be more useful than veridical representation of the properties we track. Our perceptual color representations track a complex property but represent something simpler, which might be easier to represent and manipulate than the more complex alternative, and the neglected information might not be particularly useful to us. Knowledge of surface reflectance profiles per se is not important for survival, but being able to re-identify objects over time, discriminate between objects of the same luminance, and pick out the ripe fruit and poisonous frogs *is*. If representing colors can guide our behavior toward the environment just as well as representing surface reflectance profiles, and if representing colors is cheaper or more efficient, then reliably misrepresenting edenic colors might be more advantageous than veridically representing surface reflectance profiles.

Rejecting the tracking theory helps us properly appreciate the role that tracking relations play in producing successful behavior. While cases of reliable misrepresentation most clearly illustrate just how useful mere tracking can be, tracking can play similar roles in cases of veridical representation, and even in cases of internal states that are not intentional at all. In §1.3.3, we considered the possibility that intentionality has something to do with how we generate behavior that helps us get around in the world. While everything I've said is compatible with intentionality playing a special role in our successful interactions with the world, we can now see that tracking is an important but distinct part of the picture. We are able to successfully get around in the world not only because we have representations that represent certain contents that are useful for us to represent but also because we are able to track certain features of our environment that are important for us to keep track of, regardless of whether we also represent them.[34]

---

[34] Some of these points are made in Mendelovici 2013b and forthcoming-a. Hardin (1992) and Wright (2003) make similar claims about the usefulness of non-veridical color vision, and Bermúdez (1999) and Viger (2006) also discuss the usefulness of certain kinds of misrepresentation more generally.

The usefulness of reliable misrepresentation is illustrated nicely by Maturana and Varela's (1992) allegory of the person in the submarine:

> Imagine a person who has always lived in a submarine. He has never left it and has been trained how to handle it. Now, we are standing on the shore and see the submarine gracefully surfacing. We then get on the radio and tell the navigator inside: "Congratulations! You avoided the reefs and surfaced beautifully. You really know how to handle a submarine." The navigator in the submarine, however, is perplexed: "What's this about reefs and surfacing? All I did was push some levers and turn knobs and make certain relationships between indicators as I operated the levers and knobs. It was all done in a prescribed sequence which I'm used to. I didn't do any special maneuver, and on top of that, you talk to me about a submarine. You must be kidding!" (pp. 136–137)

3.8 Conclusion

I have argued that the tracking theory faces the mismatch problem and, so, that we should reject it.

One might suggest that this is not a decisive reason to reject the tracking theory. Every theory has its virtues and vices, and we should consider all the virtues and vices of all competing theories before deciding between them. But this problem with the tracking theory is, I think, unforgivable. We set out observing a phenomenon that we wanted to explain, intentionality. There are at least some cases of this phenomenon to which we have some kind of theory-independent access. The tracking theory fails to accommodate many of them, which makes it empirically inadequate. While the tracking theory may have many other virtues, whatever they are, they cannot make up for empirical inadequacy.[35]

We will return to the tracking theory in the next chapter, which also discusses another theory of intentionality, the functional role theory. We will see that versions of the functional role theory that take tracking relations to be part of the relevant functional roles inherit the tracking theory's mismatch problem. We will also see that there is a deeper problem facing both the functional role theory and the tracking theory: Tracking relations and functional roles are simply not the kinds of things that can give rise to intentionality.

Appendix A: Objections to the Mismatch Problem

I considered some replies to the mismatch problem in §3.6. This (optional) appendix considers a few more.

The replies are divided into two kinds: **Tracking-revising strategies** take issue with my claims about the tracking theory's predictions, i.e., with (C1) and (O1), while **content-revising strategies** take issue with my claims about what SKY-BLUE represents, i.e., with (C2) and (O2).

A.1 Tracking-Revising Strategies

Tracking-revising strategies take issue with my claims about the tracking theory's predictions, denying (C1) or (O1). The reply discussed in §3.6.3 that tracking theories

---

[35] See Mendelovici and Bourget 2014 for the claim that the tracking theory's susceptibility to the mismatch problem and certain other similar failures cannot be made up for by alleged theoretical virtues such as being naturalistic. See also §6.4 for a related discussion of the relative merits of empirical adequacy over theoretical virtues, like that of being naturalistic.

do not make predictions about superficial characters is one such reply. This section considers two more.

A.1.1 REALISM ABOUT EDENIC COLORS

One might suggest that edenic color properties are actually instantiated, i.e., that realism is true of them.[36] If edenic color properties are instantiated, perhaps our perceptual color representations track and represent them, and (C1) and (O1) are false.

In order for this strategy to work, these edenic colors must be causally potent, since tracking theories require that represented properties either cause tokens of our representations or make or have made some causal difference to our well-being or that of our ancestors. The problem is that it is quite implausible that objects have causally potent edenic color properties. These properties would have to be something over and above the ordinary physical properties that perceptual color representations can uncontroversially be said to track. If there are such causally potent properties, it is surprising we have not discovered them yet by other means.[37]

An additional worry is that even if there were causally potent edenic color properties, in order for this strategy to be successful, a tracking theory would have to predict that it is *these* properties, and not surface reflectance profiles or other properties perceptual color representations track, that are singled out by its favored tracking relation. For example, for the optimal functioning theory to successfully employ the strategy, it will have to fall out of the theory that perceptual color representations represent edenic color properties rather than surface reflectance profiles, which would require that it is edenic color properties, and not surface reflectance profiles, that contribute to well-functioning in the relevant way. But this is implausible, since tracking surface reflectance profiles is arguably quite useful, and it is not clear that tracking colors would likewise be useful.

In any case, even if the strategy can be made to work for a given putative mismatch case—that is, even if in a given case what is represented can be found in the actual world and is causally potent, and the tracking theory under consideration successfully singles it out rather than other items the representation in question might be said to track—it is unlikely that this strategy will work in all putative

---

[36] Campbell (1993), Cornman (1971, 1975), and Hacker (1987) propose such primitivist realist views of color. See Hilbert and Byrne 2007, Pautz MS, Hardin 1988, and Gow 2014 for critical discussion.

[37] Hardin (1988) argues against Cornman's (1975) realism along these lines, arguing that if primitive color properties are causally efficacious, then we should be able to test for them by physical means. See also Byrne and Hilbert 2006 for discussion.

mismatch cases. This would require realism about a primitive and causally potent version of a plethora of questionable items, as well as an appropriately selective tracking relation—quite a tall order.[38]

A.1.2 TRACKING UNINSTANTIATED EDENIC COLOR PROPERTIES

Another kind of tracking-revising strategy maintains that perceptual color representations track and represent edenic color properties, which happen to be uninstantiated. If so, we can reject (C1) and (O1). Indeed, perhaps it is possible for the tracking theory to say that perceptual color representations reliably misrepresent, which might seem independently plausible (see §3.7).

This is not immediately out of the question, since some tracking theories can allow for the tracking and representation of uninstantiated properties. For example, the asymmetric dependence theory allows us to track and represent uninstantiated properties when there is a law-like causal connection between a representation and the relevant uninstantiated property, and all other causal connections between the representation and other properties, including instantiated properties, are asymmetrically dependent on it. Fodor (1990, pp. 100–101) suggests this kind of strategy for dealing with the concept UNICORN: There is a causal connection between unicorns and UNICORN, and the causal connection between other items (e.g., pictures of unicorns) and UNICORN is asymmetrically dependent on it.[39]

However, it is implausible that the tracking theory can tell such a story about the representation of edenic colors. Consider again the asymmetric dependence theory. In order to employ such a strategy, it has to say that the SRP-to-SKY-BLUE connection is asymmetrically dependent on the edenic-sky-blue-to-SKY-BLUE connection, which is implausible given the strength of the former connection and the fact that the latter connection is uninstantiated. Indeed, it is doubtful that there even *is* an edenic-sky-blue-to-SKY-BLUE connection. Our perceptual color representations are specifically rigged up to respond to properties like surface reflectance profiles, not uninstantiated edenic properties.

The prospects for this kind of strategy are no more promising for the optimal functioning tracking theory. On this theory, representations represent whatever *would* cause them in optimal conditions, where optimal conditions are conditions

---

[38] Mendelovici 2013b relatedly argues that tracking theories make it too easy to argue for realism about represented properties.

[39] Fodor also suggests that UNICORN might be an internally structured representation and so might not get its content directly from tracking (1990, p. 124). (See also Dretske 1981 for this suggestion.) But this is not an option for perceptual representations of colors, which are unlikely to be internally structured.

that promote survival, flourishing, or other kinds of appropriate functioning. To maintain that our perceptual color representations represent uninstantiated properties, the optimal functioning theorist would have to maintain that our perceptual color representations never occur in optimal conditions. Further, she would have to maintain that were we to be in optimal conditions, edenic color properties, properties that never *actually* cause tokens of our perceptual color representations, *would* at least sometimes cause such tokens. But our perceptual color representations help us survive, reproduce, and fulfill our goals, and so there is no basis on which to maintain that the conditions in which they occur are *never* optimal nor any reason to think that were they to occur in the presence of edenic colors, this would better help us survive, flourish, or function appropriately.

The teleological tracking theory fares no better. On at least some versions of the theory, representations represent whatever properties our ancestors interacted with that aided in the survival and reproduction of the representations' consuming systems in specific ways. In order for such a view to allow for perceptual color representations to represent uninstantiated properties, these properties would have to have been instantiated in our ancestors' environment, corresponding with our ancestors' perceptual states as required, but they must not be instantiated in our current environment. In the case of perceptual representations of color, the claim would be that our ancestors lived in an edenically colored world, while we don't. But the claim that our ancestors lived in an edenically colored world but we don't is ad hoc and implausible. Another problem with this suggestion is that it is quite plausible that just as our perceptual color representations are useful to us, they were similarly useful to our ancestors, which explains why we have them now. So, by the lights of the theory, they should represent whatever it is useful for them to co-occur with in our ancestors, which is the same thing that it is useful for them to co-occur with in us: surface reflectance profiles or the like, not edenic colors. So, *even if* our ancestors lived in an edenically colored world, the theory would likely still predict that our perceptual color representations represent the likes of surface reflectance profiles rather than edenic colors.

The problem can be put more generally: It is a consequence of all tracking theories that there are certain conditions in which a representation cannot misrepresent. Tracking theories only allow for misrepresentation in cases where there is a certain nonsemantic defect, a defect apart from being inaccurate or non-veridical. In the case of optimal functioning theories, misrepresentation can only occur when a representation doesn't help its bearer survive and flourish. This is because what causes or corresponds to the tokening of a representation in conditions in which it helps its bearer survive and flourish *just is* its intentional content. Similarly, teleological tracking theories only allow a representation to misrepresent when it occurs in conditions that are of a different type than design conditions, and asymmetric dependence theories only allow for misrepresentation in cases where a representation is tokened as a result of a comparatively non-robust causal relation.

The fact that the tracking theory only allows for misrepresentation in cases where there is some kind of nonsemantic defect means that it cannot take perceptual color representations to represent uninstantiated properties, since perceptual color representations are as well behaved as any other representations in all the ways that might matter to it: they occur in each version of the tracking theory's favored nonsemantically successful conditions, conditions in which there is no nonsemantic defect. As a result, these occurrences cannot be deemed misrepresentations, and the tracking theorist cannot allow perceptual color representations to represent uninstantiated edenic colors.[40]

A.2 Content-Revising Strategies

Content-revising strategies take issue with my claims about what SKY-BLUE represents, i.e., with premises (C2) and (O2), which are supposed to be supported by our theory-independent methods. The reply appealing to ways of representing discussed in §3.6.2 is an example of such a response strategy, since it appeals to ways of representing to argue against my reasons for claiming that SKY-BLUE represents <edenic sky-blue>. Let us consider some more content-revising strategies.

A.2.1 THE RELIABILITY OF INTROSPECTION

One might object to my use of introspection to argue for (O2) and (C2), my claims about what SKY-BLUE does and does not represent. Introspection, one might claim, is not a reliable guide to represented contents, so it needn't trouble the tracking theorist that it suggests against her predictions.

While some uses of introspection are indeed problematic, my use is fairly innocuous. I only need introspection to have a fairly limited access to intentional states: It need only partially reveal the superficial character of the contents of paradigm cases

---

[40] See also Mendelovici 2013b and 2016, where I argue that tracking theories cannot allow for clean cases of reliable misrepresentation, cases of reliable misrepresentation where nothing nonsemantic has gone wrong, and that this is a problem for them even if there are no *actual* clean cases of reliable misrepresentation. While Mendelovici 2013b and 2016 argue against tracking theories on the basis of the *possibility* of reliable misrepresentation, the present line of argument based on the mismatch problem can be roughly thought of as arguing against tracking theories on the basis of *actual* cases of reliable misrepresentation.

of intentionality, cases that we can notice introspectively and use to fix reference on intentionality (see §2.2.2). This limited introspective access is compatible with our having little or no access to the deep nature of intentional states and contents, our mental processes,[41] nonconscious intentional states, past intentional states,[42] or intentional states we are not attending to.[43] The introspective judgments I make use of are not affected by these limitations because they pertain to the superficial characters of contents that are currently being entertained and attended to.[44]

In any case, my arguments for (C2) and (O2) should be effective for even those who are suspicious of introspective evidence of any kind, since they do not rely on introspection alone. They also make use of considerations of psychological role, which are unaffected by this objection and independently support my conclusions.

A.2.2 DO WE REPRESENT <SRP> IN A PSYCHOLOGICALLY INVOLVED WAY?

One might argue that, contrary to what I've said, SKY-BLUE plays a psychological role that suggests it represents <SRP>. If this is right, then perhaps the tracking theory's content attributions are correct after all.

Let us consider some suggestions as to what the relevant psychological roles suggesting that SKY-BLUE represents <SRP> might be. One suggestion is that perceptual states involving SKY-BLUE cause or otherwise connect with beliefs representing surface reflectance profiles. This might be because the contents of our color-related beliefs are inherited partly from the contents of our perceptual color representations, and so color-related beliefs, as well as perceptual color representations, represent objects as having surface reflectance profiles.

The problem with this suggestion is that it merely allows the psychologically uninvolved contents posited by the tracking theory to permeate throughout the cognitive economy. The fact remains that neither our perceptual representations of color nor our beliefs about colors behave as if they represented surface reflectance profiles. For instance, absent the relevant scientific knowledge, we cannot infer *which*

---

[41] That we have little or no access to our mental processes has been demonstrated in many studies. For example, subjects asked to memorize a list of word pairs including "Ocean-Moon" were more likely to prefer Tide to other brands of detergent, but they did not realize that this preference was at least partly caused by their exposure to "Ocean-Moon" (Nisbett and Wilson 1977).

[42] Cases of change blindness (see Rensink et al. 1997) might be taken to suggest that we have little or no access to past intentional states.

[43] Cases of inattentional blindness (see Mack and Rock 1998) suggest we have little or no access to intentional states we are not attending to.

[44] See also Bayne and Spener (2010) for a congenial discussion of the limits of introspection.

particular surface reflectance profiles an object has from our perceptual experiences of its having a certain color *or* our belief that it has a certain color.

Another suggestion is that intentional states involving SKY-BLUE play a role in discriminating between objects that are SRP and those that are not, so SKY-BLUE does play a psychological role appropriate to representing <SRP>.

The problem with this suggestion is that mere discriminatory abilities, that is, the mere ability to group and tell apart items having certain features, are at best weak evidence that we represent the properties they have in common. This is because mere tracking, tracking that does not give rise to intentionality, is sufficient for discrimination.[45] Note that this is something that even the tracking theorist should accept. A tracking theorist who claims that, on her favored tracking relation, perceptual color representations track and represent surface reflectance profiles should agree that on other tracking relations they also track other properties, such as the categorical bases of surface reflectance profiles. And so, she should agree that perceptual color representations can be used to discriminate between different properties of these types, too. So even the tracking theorist should agree that discrimination is more closely tied to tracking than to intentionality and so that it is at best weak evidence for the claim that a certain content is represented. What we need in order to use discriminatory responses to show that a putative represented content is psychologically involved is some hint that the discriminatory responses are in some sense based on this content, not just that they happen to correspond to the content in some way.

A related suggestion is that our best processing story about color perception takes it to process information about surface reflectance profiles. Cones detect incoming light of various wavelengths, and this information is processed and transformed by other retinal cells and then other parts of the visual system to result in color experiences that also carry information about objects' surface reflectance profiles. All stages of color processing carry information relating to surface reflectance profiles, which suggests that they, and the perceptual color states they sometimes result in, represent surface reflectance profiles in a psychologically involved way. Now, there might be a sense in which it is correct to say that cones, ganglion cells, and other cells and areas involved in color processing, including the perceptual color states we've been concerned with, carry information about wavelengths of light and surface reflectance profiles. After all, we are granting that perceptual color states track surface reflectance profiles, and carrying information about something is one way to track it. But, as we have seen, mere tracking is at best weak evidence for intentionality. We can make

---

[45] See Mendelovici 2013b, 2016, MS, Hardin 1992, and Wright 2003 for similar points.

good sense of the role of surface reflectance profiles in color processing by appeal to tracking and carrying information, without requiring that the resulting perceptual color states *intentionally represent* the properties they carry information about.

In any case, even if it can be argued that considerations of psychological role support taking SKY-BLUE to represent <SRP>, this only provides a response to the argument from commission. It only allows us to say that SKY-BLUE represents a content with a SRP-ish superficial character, and hence that (C2) is false, which provides a response to the argument from commission. But it does nothing to allow us to reject (O2), the claim that SKY-BLUE represents a content with an edenic-sky-blue-ish superficial character, and so the argument from omission is unaffected.

A.2.3 EXTERNALISM AND THE THEORY-INDEPENDENT METHODS

One might argue that perceptual color representations have broad contents, contents the representation of which depends on environmental factors, and that my theory-independent methods for finding out about our intentional states and their contents are ineffective at telling us about broad contents. This would give us grounds to reject (C2) and (O2).

To see why one might think that my theory-independent considerations do not tell us about broad contents, consider the Twin Earth thought experiment: Oscar, who lives on Earth, has a water-related concept that represents $<H_2O>$. Toscar, his intrinsic duplicate, lives on Twin Earth, where the clear watery stuff is XYZ, and as a result, has a water-related concept that represents $<XYZ>$.[46] One might argue that Oscar and Toscar's water-related intentional states play the same psychological roles and are not introspectively discernible. After all, Oscar and Toscar engage in all the same behaviors, and they cannot tell from introspection alone whether their concepts represent $<H_2O>$ or $<XYZ>$.

There are several responses to this worry. One is that it is commonly thought to be an *objection* to externalism, the view that there are broad contents, that broad contents are not introspectively accessible or psychologically involved (e.g., Stich 1983, Boghossian 1997, Sosa 2007). This is why externalists often try to argue that they *are* introspectively accessible (e.g., Burge 1988) and psychologically involved (e.g., Dretske 1995, Williamson 2000). If this attitude is correct, then if there is an incompatibility between the assumptions underlying my methods and externalism, it is externalism that should be rejected.

---

[46] This is, of course, a common variant of Putnam's (1975) well-known thought experiment in support of externalism about linguistic meaning.

Another, potentially more conciliatory, response is to say that in Oscar and Toscar's case, broad contents are in fact at least partially discernible using my theory-independent methods but the contents of perceptual color representations that are predicted by the tracking theory are not discernible at all. While my theory-independent methods do not allow us to fully discern the contents of Oscar and Toscar's concepts, they do narrow down the options by providing partial access to these contents' superficial characters. They do not tell us that Oscar, for example, represents a content with an H_2O-ish superficial character, but they tell us that he represents a content with a water-ish superficial character, where <H_2O> is one such content and <XYZ> is another. For instance, while Oscar and Toscar cannot introspectively tell the difference between <H_2O> and <XYZ>, they can both tell that they represent a content that has a water-ish superficial character, rather than an elephant-ish superficial character. Similarly, Oscar and Toscar's water-related concepts play various psychological roles in relation to their drinking and swimming behavior, the inferences they make about taps, oceans, streams, the requirements for life, etc., and they have an overall "water-ish" phenomenology. All this suggests that Oscar and Toscar's concepts represent contents with water-ish superficial characters. So, one might suggest, theory-independent considerations do tell us something about Oscar and Toscar's concepts: They tell us that they represent contents with water-ish superficial characters, rather than contents with elephant-ish superficial characters or other superficial characters that would be completely unrelated to any introspective appearances or psychological roles.

In contrast, in the case of perceptual color representations, theory-independent considerations provide no hint whatsoever as to the representation of contents with surface-reflectance-profile-ish superficial characters. Theory-independent considerations suggest that SKY-BLUE represents a content with an edenic-sky-blue-ish superficial character, but it is not plausible to maintain that <SRP> has an edenic-sky-blue-ish superficial character in the way that it might be plausible to say that <H_2O> has a water-ish superficial character. Our theory-independent considerations suggest against taking SKY-BLUE to represent <SRP> in the same way that they suggest against taking Oscar's water-related concept to represent <elephant>.

A final response that can be offered to this objection echoes the responses given earlier to some of the other content-revising strategies. Even if perceptual color representations represent broad contents and broad contents are *entirely* shielded from our theory-independent considerations, our theory-independent considerations do reveal *something* very content-like, something involving edenic-sky-blue-ish-ness. This thing, whatever it is, arguably answers to our notion of content and so needs to be accommodated by the tracking theory. So, even if the tracking theory's prediction that SKY-BLUE represents <SRP> cannot be disconfirmed using our theory-independent methods, this does not affect my claims that these methods reveal a content that the tracking theory cannot accommodate. So, even if this strategy can help us reject (C2) and provide a response to the argument from commission, it cannot help us reject (O2), so the argument from omission still stands.[47]

A.2.4 REVISING (O2)

I have suggested that SKY-BLUE represents a content with a qualitative, simple, primitive, sui generis, non-dispositional, non-relational edenic-sky-blue-ish superficial character, i.e., <edenic sky-blue>. But, one might suggest, perhaps our introspective considerations and considerations of psychological involvement do not get us all the way to this claim. Perhaps introspection does not really support the claim that color contents have certain structural features like being primitive or sui generis, and perhaps the psychological role of perceptual color states is also silent on these features. If so, then we might knock those features off of our characterization of SKY-BLUE's content. What we are left with is the claim that SKY-BLUE represents a content with a qualitative sky-blue-ish feature; let us call this content <edenic* sky-blue>. If so, then we might reject (O2) in favor of (O2*):

(O2*) SKY-BLUE represents <edenic* sky-blue>.

By rejecting (O2), this response blocks the argument from omission.[48]

Now, I don't think the reasons for rejecting (O2) in favor of (O2*) are right: Arguably, what we notice upon introspection of perceptual color states are determinately primitive, simple, etc., color features, and, arguably, our perceptual color states behave as if color contents have those features.

In any case, even if we grant that our theory-independent considerations only support (O2*), this is enough to make an argument from omission. The problem

---

[47] Another response to the objection would be to claim that we do not intentionally represent broad contents and, so, that the fact that my theory-independent considerations do not tell us about them is not a problem. In Chapter 7, I argue for a view on which we do not intentionally represent broad contents, though we derivatively represent them, where derived mental representation is not a species of intentionality, but pursuing this line of argument here would take us too far afield.

[48] If we additionally identify <edenic* sky-blue> with <SRP>, then we also have a new way of employing the defense by identity strategy described in §3.6.1 to reject (C2) and avoid the argument from commission. In what follows, I focus on the argument from omission, since this is the part of the response that is new.

is that <edenic* sky blue> involves edenic* blue-ish-ness, which is a qualitative color-like feature, and nothing like that is found in *SRP*. Surface reflectance profiles are dispositions to reflect certain proportions of different wavelengths of light, but neither light, particular wavelengths of light, nor dispositions to reflect, transmit, or emit light are literally *qualitatively blue-ish*. This is simply not part of our best understanding of light or the surfaces of objects. There is no qualitative blue-ish-ness, and hence no edenic* blue-ish-ness, to be found in *SRP*. So, a revised version of the argument from omission still goes through, one that replaces (O2) with (O2*), and (O1) with (O1*):

(O1*)   If the tracking theory is true, then SKY-BLUE does not represent <edenic* sky-blue>.

There are two ways the objector might insist that surface reflectance profiles involve edenic* blue-ish-ness. First, she might simply build a qualitative blue-ish-ness into *SRP*. On the resulting view, we are mistaken as to the true nature of surface reflectance profiles—they *do* involve a qualitative blue-ish-ness, perhaps even as an extra nonphysical component.

This response importantly modifies our understanding of surface reflectance profiles, building in a qualitative blue-ish-ness that cannot be understood in terms of surface reflectance profiles' other features (otherwise, we would not have had to build it in). This strategy results in something very much like primitive color realism, and everything we said about realist strategies in §A.1.1 applies here, too.

The other way to insist that surface reflectance profiles involve edenic* sky-blue-ish-ness is by identifying the problematic qualitative blue-ish-ness with some property of *SRP*: *SRP does* involve a qualitative blue-ish-ness, not because it is tacked onto it, as on the previous suggestion, but rather because some other feature of *SRP*, feature F, *just is* this qualitative blue-ish-ness.

This strategy leads us straight back to the reiterated identities strategy, discussed in §3.6.4, which involves defending a prima facie false identity claim by wheeling in more prima facie false identity claims, effectively denying any relevant common ground with one's opponent. While this strategy makes for a possible defense, it does so because it is effectively a skeptical strategy, taking advantage of the fact that justification has to end somewhere. The fact remains: There is absolutely no reason arising from the physical examination of the surfaces of objects alone to think that they involve anything like edenic* bluishness.

4   Functional Role Theories and Tracking Theories Again

THE PREVIOUS CHAPTER discussed the tracking theory, which states that all actual cases of original intentionality arise from tracking. This chapter considers another theory of intentionality, the functional role theory, which takes original intentionality to arise from representations' functional dispositions with respect to one another and perhaps other items in the world—in short, their functional roles.

I will argue that one version of the functional role theory, the short-arm version, which takes the relevant functional roles to be roles that representations have in relation to other representations or other internal items, faces challenges in securing determinate content and explaining why such functional roles should give rise to intentionality in the first place (§4.2). These problems motivate the alternative long-arm version of the theory, which takes the relevant functional roles to include tracking or other relations to the environment. Unfortunately, as we will see, the long-arm functional role theory inherits the tracking theory's mismatch problem (§4.3). Finally, §4.4 argues that the deep difficulty with both the tracking theory and the functional role theory is that tracking relations and functional roles simply do not have what it takes to give rise to intentionality.

4.1 The Functional Role Theory

According to the functional role theory, original intentionality arises from representations' functional roles. We can put the core view as follows:

> **The functional role theory** All (actual) originally intentional states arise from mental representations' functional roles.

Recall that B arises from A when B is nothing over and above A, perhaps because B is identical to, fully grounded in, constituted by, or realized by A, and that original intentionality is intentionality that does not derive from other instances of intentionality (§2.1). According to the functional role theory, then, the functional roles of mental representations give rise to the most basic kind of intentionality, and any other kinds of intentionality are derived from it.[1]

Harman (1987) distinguishes between two different kinds of functional role theories: **Short-arm** functional role theories restrict the relevant functional roles to internal functional roles, functional roles that representations have in relation to other representations or other internal items, such as roles in inference. In contrast, **long-arm** functional role theories take the relevant roles to include both internal functional roles and long-arm functional roles, functional roles with respect to items in the external environment, such as roles in tracking or directing behavior toward various items.[2]

Short-arm functional role theories generally restrict the relevant kinds of internal roles to roles in inference and reasoning. For example, a short-arm functional role theory might claim that the representation AND represents <conjunction> in virtue of playing the following role in inference, where A and B are representations with propositional contents:

(A1) From judging A AND B, one is likely to judge A.
(A2) From judging A AND B, one is likely to judge B.
(A3) From judging A and judging B, one is likely to judge A AND B.

According to short-arm functional role theories, all it takes for AND to represent <conjunction> is for it to have this sort of functional role. The short-arm functional role theory claims that other representations have their contents fixed in this way,

---

[1] The functional role theory is also sometimes known as "conceptual role semantics" or "inferential role semantics." Defenders of the view include Harman (1982, 1987), Block (1986), Field (1977a, 1977b), and Peacocke (1992).

[2] The tracking theory is a limit case of the long-arm functional role theory, taking the only relevant functional roles to be specific kinds of long-arm functional roles.

too. For example, the concept BACHELOR might have its content fixed by its role in the following inferences:

(B1) From judging O IS A BACHELOR, one is likely to judge O IS A MAN.

(B2) From judging O IS A BACHELOR, one is likely to judge O IS UNMARRIED.

(B3) From judging O IS A MAN and O IS UNMARRIED, one is likely to judge O IS A BACHELOR.

According to short-arm functional role theories, what it takes for BACHELOR to represent <bachelor> is for it to play a functional role like the one specified above. MAN and UNMARRIED likewise get their contents from the functional roles they play, including their roles involving the representation BACHELOR.[3]

According to long-arm functional role theories, the functional roles that give rise to original intentionality include not only internal roles, such as those mentioned above, but also long-arm roles, such as roles in tracking external world properties and generating behavior. For example, on a long-arm functional role theory, the content of BACHELOR might be determined not only by its role in inferences involving UNMARRIED and MAN, but also by tracking relations it bears to the environment (e.g., to the property of being a bachelor) or tracking relations that UNMARRIED, MAN, or other related concepts bear to the environment.

4.2 Worries with Short-Arm Functional Role Theories

The long-arm version of the functional role theory is arguably more promising than the short-arm version (see, e.g., Harman 1987), but it is instructive to consider some of the shortcomings of the short-arm version in order to appreciate some of the possible merits of the long-arm version.

One worry with short-arm functional role theories has to do with how intentionality can arise from functional roles in the first place. Short-arm functional role theories claim that having internal states playing various internal functional roles gives rise to intentionality, presumably in that it either is, constitutes, realizes, or grounds intentionality. But, we might wonder, why should playing an internal functional role give rise to intentionality at all? Once we have a state that plays some internal role, why isn't that the end of the story? Why is there a further bit of the story on which, because of their internal roles, internal states get to have contents? It seems that there shouldn't be, that mere internal roles are not sufficient for intentionality.

---

[3] As before, I assume that many of the vehicles of original intentionality are subpropositional representations, but the discussion can be amended accordingly for those who disagree. See n. 10 of Chapter 1 and §2.1.

BonJour (1998) puts this kind of worry as follows: We can think of the short-arm functional role theory as claiming that there is an isomorphism between the network of inferential relations between representations and the network of entailment and perhaps other relations between contents. Representations then represent the contents that they are associated with by virtue of this isomorphism. But, BonJour claims, it is not clear why the existence of such an isomorphism between the inferential network between representations and the network of relations between contents should make the representations represent the contents.

> Why couldn't there be a set of items standing in [an inferential] structure exactly isomorphic to the [network of relations between contents] while still having no content at all? ... [T]here is no reason at all to take the obtaining of such an isomorphism to be a *sufficient* condition for having a specific content.... (BonJour 1998, p. 177; emphasis in original)

In other words, there is no reason to think that internal functional roles should give rise to intentionality.

It is possible to understand Searle's (1980) Chinese room argument as making a similar point. According to Searle, no amount of syntactic manipulation suffices for having content—mere syntax doesn't get you semantics. Searle argues for this claim using a thought experiment in which a monolingual English-speaking subject is placed in a room with a rule book relating Chinese characters to other Chinese characters. The subject receives strings of Chinese characters through an input slot, looks up those characters in the rule book, and returns the specified characters through an output slot. In doing so, he might be simulating one side of a conversation in Chinese, but neither he nor the room understands Chinese. If this is right, then merely having internal states that play particular internal functional roles does not give rise to intentionality.

This is also a way of thinking of Harnad's (1990) symbol grounding problem. Harnad argues that representations can't get their contents from their functional roles with respect to one another because the representations that any given representation is functionally related to are contentless prior to such content determination. He likens the possibility of representations getting their contents from their functional roles with respect to one another to learning Chinese from a Chinese-Chinese dictionary: To someone who does not know any Chinese, a Chinese-Chinese dictionary merely relates one meaningless symbol to another. Analogously, content can't transfer from one representation to another, because there's no content in the system of representations to begin with. The problem, we might say, is that having internal states playing internal functional roles simply doesn't automatically give rise to intentionality.

It is instructive to consider whether similar worries appear to afflict the tracking theory. Just as one might wonder why functional roles should give rise to intentionality, one might also wonder why tracking relations should give rise to intentionality. Our representations bear various tracking relations to multiple things in their environments, but why, one might ask, should that give rise to the having of *content*? I return to this question at the end of this chapter, but for now, we might agree that such worries do not seem quite as gripping in the case of the tracking theory as in the case of the short-arm functional role theory. A speculative proposal for why this might be the case is that tracking relations seem to relate us to items that are well suited to playing the roles of contents—namely, objects, properties, and states of affairs. These are the kinds of things that we find at the far end of tracking relations, and they look like good candidates for being identified with contents. Internal functional roles, however, do not relate representations to anything that could plausibly play the roles of contents. They only, at best, relate representations to one another. This makes an alleged connection between internal functional roles and intentionality appear problematic in a way that an alleged connection between tracking and intentionality might not.

There is a further question for the short-arm functional role theorist: Supposing that we grant that internal functional roles give rise to intentional states, *which* intentional states do they give rise to? One might worry that the assignment of contents to a system of functionally related representations is underdetermined by the representations' functional roles. To see this, consider again the case of BACHELOR. From (B1), (B2), and (B3), it was clear to us what content BACHELOR is supposed to have: It's supposed to have whatever content is related as described to the concepts MAN and UNMARRIED, namely <bachelor>. However, this only appears clear to us because we assume that MAN and UNMARRIED have already been assigned the contents <man> and <unmarried>. But this is not how content determination works on the short-arm functional role view. Content does not flow from one representation to another (after all, where would it start?). Rather, an entire system of functionally related representations is supposed to have its contents determined all at once. But then the relevant functional roles of BACHELOR are better represented by (B1′), (B2′), and (B3′):

(B1′)   From judging O IS X, one is likely to judge O IS Y.

(B2′)   From judging O IS X, one is likely to judge O IS Z.

(B3′)   From judging O IS Y and O IS Z, one is likely to judge O IS X.

Now it is not so clear how to interpret X, Y, and Z. One possible interpretation is the following:

x represents \<bachelor\>
y represents \<man\>
z represents \<unmarried\>

But an equally good interpretation is this one:

x represents \<mare\>
y represents \<female\>
z represents \<horse\>

And there are plenty of other equally good ways to assign contents.[4]

Of course, the more representations we add, the more constrained the set of admissible interpretations becomes. We might hope to have enough representations to rule out all but one possible interpretation. But this is not so.

The "swapping argument" offered by Bourget (MS) and Mendelovici and Bourget (forthcoming) shows that even if the internal functional roles of a set of representations can determine the logical relationships between their contents (e.g., their entailment relationships), these logical relationships cannot uniquely determine their specific contents. Suppose that there is at least one assignment A of contents to a given set R of representations that is consistent with their internal functional roles and logical relationships. The contents assigned by A can be modeled as intensions, which are functions from possible worlds to certain entities (truth values for thoughts, extensions for concepts[5]). Now picture all the objects at a given possible world W laid on a surface. We can identify each object by its position on the surface, e.g., as "the object at location L." For any concept, we can characterize its extension at W according to A in terms of a specific location (for individual concepts), a set of locations (for monadic concepts), or a structure of locations (for n-ary concepts, where $n > 1$). Now, if we keep these specifications unchanged but swap the locations of some objects on our surface, making sure to swap pairs of objects that are not both inside or outside the extensions of all concepts, our specifications will determine new extensions for some concepts. By construction, the resulting assignment of intensions makes true (or false) all the same thoughts in R as A, but it is a different assignment involving different contents for certain concepts

---

[4] This way of putting the worry assumes that there are subpropositional representations. But the same worry arises if we deny this assumption and take propositional representations to be internally unstructured. Functional relations between full-fledged propositional representations are no more capable of singling out unique content attributions than the functional relations among their parts.

[5] For ease of exposition, I focus on thoughts and concepts, but the same claims apply to propositional and non-propositional representations more generally.

of R. Using this procedure, we can plausibly construct huge numbers of alternative interpretations that are consistent with any set of logical relationships determined by internal functional role.[6]

The upshot is that, while it may be fairly plausible that internal functional roles can get us more content from some content, it is questionable whether they can get us some content from no content, and even if we assume that they can, they arguably cannot assign content determinately.

4.3 Worries with Long-Arm Functional Role Theories

The worries with short-arm functional role theories mentioned above motivate a move to long-arm functional role theories. According to long-arm functional role theories, intentionality is a matter of both a representation's internal functional roles and its functional dispositions with respect to items in the environment. The relevant environmental factors might include tracking relations and dispositions to cause behavior, though most long-arm functional role theorists focus on tracking relations, and I will, too. The intuitive idea is that tracking relations to external items give representations some intentional content, which then gets passed around to the entire system of representations via the representations' internal functional roles.[7]

Long-arm functional role theories might be thought to address both of the above-mentioned worries with short-arm functional role theories. The first worry has to do with why mere internal roles should result in intentionality. To see how long-arm functional role theories might address this worry, recall that the worry is not so pressing for tracking theories. Tracking relations relate us to properties and

---

[6] The core idea of the swapping argument is inspired by Putnam's (1977) model-theoretic argument against correspondence theories of truth. BonJour (1998, pp. 176-177) also raises worries about content indeterminacy for the functional role theory, and Kripke's (1982) quus argument can be understood as posing a content determinacy challenge that applies to functional role theories. Fodor (1978) also raises underdetermination worries with procedural semantics. See also Rey 1980, Baker 1985, and Horowitz 1992.

   Graham et al. (2007) extend such indeterminacy worries to the tracking theory as well, arguing that no non-phenomenal facts can secure content determinacy. Searle (1990) can be interpreted as making a similar argument. See also Strawson (2008), who argues that only phenomenal facts about what we take an intentional state to refer to (our "cognitive intent") can solve the "stopping" problem, the problem of determining what exactly an intentional state refers to.

[7] I set aside two-factor views, which state that there are two kinds of content, one that is a matter of functional role and one that is a matter of tracking (see, e.g., Field 1977a and Block 1998). Two-factor views combine tracking and functional role views in that they take there to be two kinds of original intentionality, one arising from tracking and one arising from functional roles. So, they arguably inherit the problems discussed above for both the tracking theory and the functional role theory.

other items, and these items are good candidates for being identified with contents. To put the point metaphorically, tracking relations seem to "reach out" into the world and "grab" hold of contents. This is why it might be thought that tracking something can suffice for representing it. The long-arm functional role theory can say more or less the same thing. Long-arm relations, the relations that reach into the external world, "grab" contents from the world and inject them into a representational system. They are then transformed and passed around throughout the system, thanks to the functional relations between representations.

Long-arm functional role theories might also be thought to address the content determinacy problem. The problem of content determinacy arises because internal functional roles are arguably not enough to uniquely determine content. The long-arm theory avoids the problem by adding relations between representations and the external world to the mix. These relations impose some constraints on the admissible interpretations of a system of representations. For example, suppose the representation MAN tracks the property of being a man. The long-arm functional role theory might claim that this fixes its content as <man>, which rules out an interpretation of BACHELOR as having the content <mare>. If enough representations have their contents fixed by tracking relations, perhaps there is no longer room for multiple assignments of contents. Again, put metaphorically, tracking relations "grab" content from the world and "inject" it into the representational system. It then gets passed around via internal functional roles. If all goes well, this fixes a unique content for all representations, including the ones that are not directly hooked up to the external world via tracking.[8]

Unfortunately, by invoking elements of the tracking theory, the long-arm functional role theory inherits the tracking theory's mismatch problem (described in the previous chapter). In some cases, the *wrong* content gets "grabbed" from the world and "injected" into the system. For example, the representation SKY-BLUE tracks a particular surface reflectance profile or the like, and, according to the long-arm functional role theory, this at least partly determines its content. SKY-BLUE is functionally related to other representations, which have their contents determined partly by their functional dispositions in relation to SKY-BLUE. In this way, introspectively foreign and psychologically uninvolved content enters the representational system and comes to infect not only representations that get their contents from tracking but also representations that are functionally related to them in the right way.

---

[8] It is not clear, however, that this avoids Graham et al.'s (2007) and Searle's (1990) versions of the content determinacy worry, which apply to tracking theories as well, or Strawson's (2008) "stopping problem."

A possible way out of this worry is to say that representations that bear the relevant kind of tracking relations to the world get their contents not *solely* from tracking but also from their internal functional roles. It might turn out, then, that in the alleged mismatch cases, the internal functional role of a representation is incongruent with what it tracks. For example, SKY-BLUE might track a particular surface reflectance profile but play the internal role appropriate to having the content <edenic sky-blue>. Indeed, I appealed to such discrepancies between what a representation tracks and the content most congruent with its internal role in order to argue that the contents attributed by the tracking theory are psychologically uninvolved (§3.4). The long-arm functional role theorist might suggest that this internal functional role of SKY-BLUE *partly* determines its content and so, we can avoid saying that it represents a particular surface reflectance profile.

Unfortunately, though, what we end up with is a situation in which the two determinants of content pull in different directions, and it is difficult to see how they could inform or qualify each other so as to result in a single univocal content assignment. It looks like the long-arm theorist must choose between having the content of SKY-BLUE determined solely by tracking or having it determined solely by internal functional role, and she would have to make this choice in a principled way (e.g., it won't do to say that content is determined by tracking relations except in mismatch cases). Presumably the same applies to other representations involved in discordant tracking relations and internal functional roles. If we let tracking determine content in such cases, then we face the mismatch problem. If we let internal functional role determine content, then we risk lapsing into indeterminacy worries. It's far from clear that there is a principled way to invoke both ingredients that avoids both problems.[9]

I have focused on long-arm functional role theories where the long-arm relations are tracking relations, but similar points apply to long-arm theories where the long-arm relations are a matter of our behaviors or dispositions to behavior directed at things in the world. Just as there are mismatches between a representation's content and what it tracks, so too are there mismatches between a representation's content and that to which it directs our behaviors. This is because many of the mismatch cases for tracking theories are cases of reliable misrepresentation (see §3.7), and in cases of reliable misrepresentation, represented items do not exist or are not instantiated in the external world, which makes it difficult to see how we can direct

---

[9] One principled way of combining tracking and short-arm functional determinants of content takes perceptual representations to get their contents from tracking and all other representations to get their contents from internal functional role. But this approach doesn't allow us to avoid the mismatch problem, since many mismatch cases are perceptual.

our behaviors toward them. For example, perceptual color representations, which I've argued represent edenic colors (§3.4), do not direct our behaviors toward edenic colors (they do not allow us to discriminate between different edenic colors, identify instances of particular edenic colors, etc.) but instead direct our behaviors toward what they track, e.g., surface reflectance profiles.

In short, the short-arm functional role theory leads to the long-arm functional role theory, and the long-arm functional role theory inherits the tracking theory's mismatch problem, making it empirically inadequate.

4.4 The Real Problem with Both Tracking Theories and Functional Role Theories

The mismatch problem shows that the tracking theory and the long-arm functional role theory have counterexamples and thus *that* they are false. But it doesn't tell us *why* they are false. It doesn't tell us just what is wrong with them.

I want to suggest that the Real Problem with invoking tracking to account for intentionality is that no amount of causal or other tracking relations between mental states and the world suffices to give rise to genuine intentionality. While tracking relations *relate* us to items that might appear to be well suited for being identified with contents, such as objects, properties, and states of affairs, they in no sense make those items available to representational systems, let alone make them available for being passed around from one representation to another. As I suggested above, it can be tempting to think of tracking relations as "grabbing" contents from the world and "injecting" them into our thoughts and experiences, or perhaps as "reaching out" into the world and allowing our minds to make epistemic contact with them. But no mere causal or other tracking relation can make good on these metaphors. Causally or otherwise interacting with objects and their properties doesn't somehow pull them out of the world and place them into our minds. Nor does it allow our minds to somehow reach out into the world to touch them. Bearing a tracking relation to something does not somehow present that thing to us, make us aware of it, allow us to entertain it, or make us have that thing in mind. The Real Problem with the tracking theory and long-arm functional role theory is not that tracking relations sometimes "grab" the wrong contents, but that tracking relations can't "grab" anything at all. All they can do is track.

For this reason, theories relying on tracking relations not only fail to attribute psychologically involved contents in mismatch cases but, worse, preclude the contents they attribute from being psychologically involved in the first place. This is because they cannot make contents available or usable in whatever ways contents are available or usable. They cannot make contents introspectively accessible or available in reasoning or the generation of behavior, and they cannot make contents contribute to how things seem to us or to our representational phenomenology. Items on the far end of a tracking relation are simply not available to us, our reasoning, our introspective abilities, or our understanding of the world. This holds not only in mismatch cases, but also in cases where there happens to be a match between what a representation tracks and what it represents. In such cases, it is not in virtue of tracking relations that a representation's content is psychologically involved. If tracking and long-arm functional role theories sometimes deliver the right answer, they do so by accident.

Recall that one of the problems with the short-arm functional role theory was that it was not clear why playing a certain internal functional role should give rise to intentionality at all. If the claims of this section are correct, then it is also not clear why tracking relations should give rise to intentionality. The Real Problem with tracking and functional role theories, then, is that neither tracking nor internal functional role nor some combination of the two is sufficient for intentionality. These ingredients are simply not enough to give rise to entertaining or otherwise representing a content. In the next chapter, I will argue that phenomenal consciousness *is*.[10]

4.5 Conclusion

In this and the previous chapter, we considered two theories of intentionality, the tracking theory and the functional role theory, which take the source of intentionality to be tracking relations and functional roles, respectively. We saw that these theories face both empirical objections, which tell us *that* they are false, and deep in-principle objections, which tell us *why* they fail. The next chapter considers the phenomenal intentionality theory, which, I will argue, succeeds precisely where tracking and functional role theories fail.

---

[10] Similar thoughts are expressed by BonJour (1998, §6.4), who argues that what he calls the symbolic theory of thought cannot account for our introspective access to our thought contents. Similarly, Johnston (2007) also argues that tracking relations cannot account for the "presence" of experienced contents to our minds. Putnam (1983) also argues that the view that reference is some particular causal relation requires an extra brute fact that *that* causal relation is the reference relation. In conversation, Chris Viger has expressed similar worries that even if tracking relations can connect us to, say, dogs, they cannot account for our understanding or "grasp" of dogs. What these complaints have in common is the idea that mere tracking relations cannot, all by themselves, do anything more than *track*.

III The Phenomenal Intentionality Theory

I NOW TURN to my favored theory of intentionality, the phenomenal intentionality theory (PIT), on which original intentionality arises from phenomenal consciousness. Chapter 5 presents and argues for PIT and overviews the version of PIT that will emerge from the discussion in the rest of this book. Chapter 6 considers PIT's status as a theory of intentionality, arguing that it escapes various theoretical worries.

5   The Phenomenal Intentionality Theory

THE VIEW OF intentionality that I will propose and develop in this and the next few chapters takes its main ingredient to be phenomenal consciousness, the felt, subjective, or "what it's like" aspect of mental life. The overall view can be described very simply: Original intentionality is identical to phenomenal consciousness, and there is no derived intentionality, though there are non-intentional representational states that derive from intentional states.

My specific view is a version of a more general theory, which I will call "the phenomenal intentionality theory," on which all original intentionality arises from phenomenal consciousness. Unlike tracking theories and functional role theories, which locate the "source" (Kriegel 2011, 2013b) of intentionality in the relations between representations and other representations and/or the external environment, the phenomenal intentionality theory takes the "source" of intentionality to be our own subjective inner lives. For this reason, the phenomenal intentionality theory might be described as taking a "consciousness first" (Pautz 2013a) approach to intentionality, taking all intentionality to ultimately derive from phenomenal consciousness.

In this chapter, I first argue for the phenomenal intentionality theory and then begin to home in on my specific version. Along the way, I note various nearby fallback positions that are available to those who accept some, but not all, of my claims.

5.1 The Phenomenal Intentionality Theory

The phenomenal intentionality theory (PIT) takes its main ingredient to be **(phenomenal) consciousness**, the subjective, experiential, felt, or "what it's like" (Nagel 1974) feature of mental life that is introspectively obvious in cases such as those of pain, experiences of redness, and experiences of déjà vu. Like intentionality, phenomenal consciousness is something we can notice introspectively. It is the introspectively noticeable feature that is subjective, experienced, or felt.

We can define **phenomenal properties** as ways things are or might be with respect to phenomenal consciousness, or phenomenal ways things are or might be, and **phenomenal states** as instantiations of phenomenal properties. A **(phenomenally) conscious mental state**, or, simply, a **(phenomenal) experience**, is a mental state that includes, but may not be exhausted by, the instantiation of phenomenal properties. The specific "what it's like," or felt, quality of a phenomenal state or experience is its **phenomenal character**. For example, the experience of pain, the experience of red, and the feeling of déjà vu have what we might call "pain-ish," "red-ish," and "déjà vu-ish" phenomenal characters, respectively.[1]

According to PIT, phenomenal consciousness is implicated in all instances of intentionality. It gives rise to original intentionality, from which all other kinds of intentionality are derived. Recall that B arises from A when B is nothing over and above A, perhaps because B is identical to, fully grounded in, constituted by, or realized by A, and that original intentionality is intentionality that does not derive from other instances of intentionality (§2.1). We can then formulate PIT as follows:

> **PIT** All (actual) originally intentional states arise from phenomenal consciousness.

The underlying idea is that at least some phenomenal states are inherently intentional. They are not "raw feels," mere feelings or qualia. Instead, by their very nature, they automatically represent a content or "say something." As Loar (2003, §12) puts it, phenomenal character is not mere mental paint; it is, by its nature, "paint that points." According to PIT, for example, a phenomenal state with a red-ish phenomenal character might automatically represent the content <red> and

---

[1] On some views of phenomenal consciousness, phenomenal states and phenomenal characters come to the same thing—all there is to a phenomenal state is its specific felt quality. But on other views, the two are distinct. For example, relational views of phenomenal consciousness take phenomenal properties to be relations to distinctly existing phenomenal characters, which might be abstract properties, sense data, or something else (Pautz 2010a, Bourget 2010b, forthcoming-b, Dretske 1996, Lycan 2001, Tye 2015). It is also possible to take phenomenal characters to be aspects of phenomenal states or properties without being phenomenal states or properties in their entirety (see Appendix G of Chapter 9).

a phenomenal state with a red-square-ish phenomenal character might automatically represent the content <red square>.[2]

Intentionality that arises from phenomenal consciousness is sometimes called **phenomenal intentionality**. **Phenomenal intentional properties** are ways things are or might be with respect to their phenomenal intentionality, or phenomenal intentional ways things are or might be. A **phenomenal intentional state** is an instantiation of a phenomenal intentional property, and its content is its **phenomenal content**.[3] In the above example, the state of representing <red square> is a phenomenal intentional state and the content <red square> is its phenomenal content. We can call the view that at least some originally intentional states are phenomenal intentional states **weak PIT**. When combined with the claim that there are intentional states, PIT entails weak PIT.[4,5]

PIT is compatible with the existence of **non-phenomenal intentional states**, intentional states that are not phenomenal intentional states, so long as they are not originally intentional states, that is, so long as they are derived from phenomenal intentionality in some way. Advocates of PIT have offered various views of how exactly non-phenomenal intentional states might derive from phenomenal intentionality. Bourget (2010a) describes four derivation mechanisms: derived intentional states can get their contents from the states they are composed of, the functional relations they bear to phenomenal intentional states, descriptive reference, and deference. Kriegel (2011) claims that non-phenomenal intentional states, such as standing

---

[2] Versions of PIT have been defended by Searle (1990, 1992), Strawson (1994, 2008), Pitt (1999, 2004), Horgan and Tienson (2002), Loar (2003), Kriegel (2003, 2007, 2011), Farkas (2008a, 2008b), Horgan and Graham (2009), Chalmers (2010), Pautz (2010a), Montague (2010), Bourget (2010a, 2017c, forthcoming-c), Mendelovici (2010), Mendelovici and Bourget (2014, forthcoming), and Young (2015). Husserl (1900) and Brentano (1874) are notable historical precedents.

[3] Note that whether a state's contents are phenomenal contents is not a matter of which contents they are (e.g., <grass is green> or <the cat is on the mat>) but rather a matter of in virtue of what the state gets to have this content; we might say a state's phenomenal contents are those that it **phenomenally represents**. So, it is compatible with PIT that two states represent the same content but only one of them phenomenally represents it and hence has it as its phenomenal content.

[4] Weak PIT is not a version of PIT but rather a weakening of PIT, in that it does not require that all originally intentional states are phenomenal intentional states. Similarly, weak representationalism is not a version of representationalism but rather a weakening of representationalism (see, e.g., Chalmers 2004).

[5] Siewert (1998, 2011) and Smithies (2012, MS) are two notable proponents of weak PIT but not PIT. Siewert accepts weak PIT but is neutral on PIT, maintaining that phenomenal consciousness gives rise to original intentionality but allowing that there might also be other sources of intentionality. It is similarly possible to be committed to the view that tracking or functional roles give rise to original intentionality without being committed to the tracking theory or the functional role theory.

Smithies accepts weak PIT while explicitly denying PIT, maintaining that some intentionality derives from consciousness, though not all of it. For Smithies, the distinguishing mark of intentionality that derives from consciousness is that of playing a normative role in the rational justification of belief and action.

beliefs and other nonconscious states, derive from the phenomenal intentional states of an ideal interpreter. Pautz (2013a) suggests that some states derive their contents from sensory phenomenal states and Lewisian principles of interpretation. Horgan and Tienson (2002) defend a view on which some thoughts have broad contents that derive from phenomenal intentional states together with phenomenal intentional "grounding presuppositions." And Searle (1990, 1991, 1992) can be interpreted as holding that some non-phenomenal intentional states derive from potential phenomenal intentional states.[6]

Although I am sympathetic to the derivativist idea (see Chapter 7 and §8.3.2), the version of PIT I will propose maintains that, strictly speaking, there is no derived intentionality. On this view, all intentionality is original intentionality, which arises from phenomenal consciousness. We can call this view "strong PIT":

Strong PIT All (actual) intentional states arise from phenomenal consciousness.

According to strong PIT, all intentional states are phenomenal intentional states. Strong PIT entails PIT (it is, after all, a version of PIT), and, when combined with the claim that there is intentionality, it entails weak PIT.[7]

Although my aim is to argue for a version of strong PIT, I begin by arguing for PIT as a general approach. In Part IV, I arrive at my version of strong PIT by arguing that derivativism fails and the best way to make sense of putative non-phenomenal intentional mental states involves either ascribing to them phenomenal intentionality or denying that they have any intentionality at all.[8]

5.2 Arguments for PIT

I think the most convincing argument for PIT involves showing how it can be fruitfully developed so as to handle a wide variety of cases and shed light on diverse issues, which is part of what the remainder of this book attempts to do. But for now, I will present two preliminary arguments for thinking that this is an approach worth pursuing. In the previous two chapters, we saw that the tracking theory and

---

[6] While many phenomenal intentionality theorists can be interpreted as accepting derived mental intentionality, the idea is most explicitly articulated in Bourget 2010a, Mendelovici 2010, Kriegel 2011, Bourget and Mendelovici 2016, and Mendelovici and Bourget 2014, forthcoming.

[7] Strong PIT has been defended by Pitt (2004), Mendelovici (2010), Farkas (2008a), and Young (2015). Kriegel (2013a) argues that this is also the view of Brentano (1874). Strawson (1994, 2008), at times, is sympathetic to strong PIT, though he allows for derived intentionality in nonconscious states (Strawson 2008).

[8] For an overview and discussion of PIT, see Kriegel 2013b, Mendelovici and Bourget 2014, forthcoming, and Bourget and Mendelovici 2016.

the functional role theory face both empirical and in-principle objections. The two arguments for PIT show that PIT succeeds precisely where these other theories fail.

5.2.1 THE ARGUMENT FROM MATCHING

A **mismatch case** for a theory of intentionality is a case in which a representation's content does not match the content it is predicted to have by the theory, where a representation's content **matches** the content it is predicted to have by a theory when the represented content and the predicted content have the same superficial characters (see §3.3). In other words, mismatch cases are cases in which a theory makes the wrong predictions as to *which* content a representation represents.

In Chapter 3, I argued that there are mismatch cases for tracking and long-arm functional role theories. I focused on the case of perceptual color representations, arguing that tracking and long-arm functional role theories predict that perceptual color representations represent something like surface reflectance profiles, but theory-independent considerations instead suggest that they represent edenic colors. For instance, tracking and long-arm functional role theories might predict that the perceptual color representation SKY-BLUE represents <SRP>, which is identical to a particular surface reflectance profile, *SRP*, but theory-independent considerations from introspection and psychological roles suggest that it represents <edenic sky-blue>. Roughly, the tracking and long-arm functional role theories' content attribution makes an error of commission in that it includes material that is not represented (namely, something to do with surface reflectance profiles), and it makes an error of omission in that it fails to include material that is represented (namely something to do with edenic sky-blueness). In short, the tracking and long-arm functional role theories predict that SKY-BLUE's content has features it doesn't have and that it doesn't have features it does have.

This and other mismatch cases are tough cases for the tracking theory and the long-arm functional role theory, but, I want to suggest, they are easy for PIT (though we might worry that PIT has its own mismatch cases—see below). Let us see how PIT handles the case of perceptual color representations.

In order for PIT to yield predictions that we can confirm using our theory-independent methods, it should tell us what particular intentional states represent. In particular, it should specify the superficial characters (§2.2.1) of particular intentional states. So far, we do not have a specific enough version of PIT to yield such predictions. However, there are general considerations that suggest that PIT has the resources to say that the representation SKY-BLUE represents a content with the right superficial character.

A theory that predicts that the content of SKY-BLUE is <SRP> makes an error of omission because the content of SKY-BLUE has a superficial character with a qualitative, primitive, simple, sui generis, non-dispositional, and non-relational sky-blue-ish-ness that cannot be found in what the theory has to offer, i.e., surface reflectance profiles. PIT, though, does have a qualitative, primitive, simple, sui generis, non-dispositional, and non-relational sky-blue-ish-ness on offer—SKY-BLUE has an associated phenomenal character, which we might call *sky-blue-ish*, and which arguably has the relevant qualitative, primitive, etc., sky-blue-ish-ness. PIT might identify this phenomenal character with the content <edenic sky-blue> or take the phenomenal character to constitute, realize, or ground the intentional content. On all these options, PIT can say that SKY-BLUE has a content that involves a qualitative, primitive, simple, sui generis, non-dispositional, and non-relational sky-blue-ish-ness. In short, <edenic sky-blue> matches[9] *sky-blue-ish*, so a theory that says that the representation of <sky-blue> arises from states with the phenomenal character *sky-blue-ish* has the resources to avoid an error of omission.

We can also see how PIT has the resources to avoid an error of commission. A theory that predicts that the content of SKY-BLUE is <SRP> makes an error of commission because the superficial character of the content of SKY-BLUE doesn't have anything to do with surface reflectance profiles. PIT has room to say that the phenomenal character *sky-blue-ish* yields a content that has superficial features that do not contain such unwanted material—all they contain is a qualitative, primitive, etc., sky-blue-ish-ness.[10] Notice that this does not preclude such a content from having a deep nature that is not revealed by our theory-independent methods, since an error of commission only arises when the *superficial character* of a theory's predicted content contains unwanted material.[11]

In the same way, PIT can accommodate many other mismatch cases for the tracking theory and the long-arm functional role theory. Perceptual states representing hotness and coldness represent edenic hotness and coldness (see §3.5), which

---

[9] I am using the notion of matching in an extended sense compared to the use in Part II. On this extended sense, content A matches item B (which may or may not be a content) when all the features of A's superficial character are had by B (whether or not B has a superficial character and whether or not these features are features of B's superficial character). I use the same term in these two different ways because the two uses are closely related and context clearly disambiguates.

[10] Indeed, it is not implausible that the distinguishing features of phenomenal characters, the features that identify and characterize them as the phenomenal characters that they are, include no unwanted material. If so, then we might be able to simply identify a content's superficial character with these distinguishing features.

[11] This is why it would not automatically be a problem if SKY-BLUE's predicted content had a mental deep nature, as on versions of PIT that simply identify intentional contents with phenomenal characters.

match their associated phenomenal characters, and the concepts of goodness and badness might represent primitive goodness and badness (see §3.5), which also seem to match their associated phenomenal characters. In short, PIT can accommodate the contents of many of the mismatch cases for tracking and long-arm functional role theories.

PIT also fares well in many cases that are not problematic for the tracking theory and the long-arm functional role theory. Shape representations represent shape contents, like <square>, which correspond to their associated "shape-ish" phenomenal characters. Indeed, there seems to be the relevant kind of match in most paradigm cases (§1.2) of intentionality in perception. Perception presents us with a multimodal structured represented scene consisting of the representation of visual, auditory, tactile, and other contents, accompanied by a rich and complex assortment of matching phenomenal characters. For instance, a visual experience of a ripe tomato involves a rich representation of the shape and size of the tomato, its color, texture, and illumination, its location relative to the perceiver, etc. This content matches the experience's phenomenal character, which involves phenomenal characters relating to shape, size, color, texture, illumination, and location. More generally, we might expect that the contents of paradigm cases of intentionality in perception will match their phenomenal characters, making it possible for PIT to accommodate them.

If all this is right, then PIT has the resources to get the right answer in many paradigm cases of intentionality, especially paradigm perceptual cases. Since many of these cases are ones that PIT's main competitors cannot handle, this provides strong support for PIT. Indeed, it is hard to see what other view can handle the cases, since it is not clear that there are any items other than phenomenal characters that match our perceptual color contents and that our intentional states can plausibly be said to single out.[12]

---

[12] One might suggest that a primitivist theory of intentionality, one that takes intentionality not to arise from anything (other than itself), can also accommodate the case of perceptual color states—and, indeed, any case. This is true, but not impressive. Unless it is combined with a further story about how intentionality relates to other phenomena (see, e.g., Chalmers' (1996) naturalistic dualism for such a primitivist theory of consciousness), empirical adequacy is not an accomplishment for primitivism, since it can accommodate any claims about which contents any particular state represents simply by fiat. This does not mean that primitivism is false but only that the fact that it is empirically adequate does not do much to support it.

  My reason for not being a primitivist is that, as we've seen, and as I will further argue, phenomenal consciousness and intentionality are impressively related, so any theory, primitivist or not, will have to accommodate this fact by either identifying them, taking one to be a species of the other, or taking them to be related in some other way. I will argue that the two are in fact identical (§5.3). If this is right, then primitivism collapses into a version of PIT, since it ends up accepting that phenomenal consciousness gives rise to intentionality (by being identical to it). The views might be different in spirit, in that

I have argued that PIT can handle cases that its main competitors cannot handle. This does not, however, show that PIT yields the right predictions in *all* cases of intentionality. In other words, it does not show that PIT does not face its own mismatch problem. Most of the "good" cases for PIT that we have encountered so far are cases of introspectively accessible perceptual states, so one might worry that other kinds of intentional mental states pose a mismatch problem for PIT. These states might include thoughts, nonconscious states, and any states representing rich descriptive contents, object-involving contents, and broad contents.

In Part IV, I argue that PIT can adequately handle these challenging cases (see also §5.4 of this chapter for an overview of the general approach). For now, it is worth noting that most of the challenging cases are not paradigm cases of intentionality. That we represent rich descriptive thought contents, object-involving contents, broad contents, and nonconscious contents is not introspectively obvious, like that we represent. So, what these challenging states intentionally represent—and perhaps even *that* they intentionally represent—is less certain and theoretically up for grabs. The only nonnegotiable challenging case for PIT is that of thought, since thoughts are paradigm cases. But even in this case, it is less obvious just *what* is intentionally represented in any given thought, e.g., whether thoughts or the concepts they involve represent definitions, prototypes, sensory contents, objects and kinds, or something else. So, before even considering PIT's prospects for accommodating the above-mentioned challenging cases, we can make the following argument for PIT: PIT is the only view we've encountered so far that can accommodate all the clear paradigm cases, so there is good reason to think it's true.

5.2.2 THE REAL REASON TO ACCEPT PIT

In the previous chapter, I argued that neither tracking nor internal functional roles nor some combination of the two suffices for intentionality. Internal functional roles don't spontaneously give rise to intentionality, and tracking relations can't "grab" contents from the world and insert them into our minds. In short, tracking relations and functional roles are simply not the right kinds of ingredients to give rise to intentionality. This is the Real Problem with tracking and functional role theories.

In contrast, phenomenal consciousness arguably *is* the right kind of ingredient to give rise to intentionality. That phenomenal consciousness can give rise to intentionality might even seem obvious from the mere consideration of phenomenal

---

primitivism "fits" consciousness to intentionality, whereas PIT does the reverse, but further arguments pull in favor of the spirit of PIT (§6.1).

states. Suppose you are in a phenomenal state with a blue-ish phenomenal character. It might seem that simply by being in this state, you automatically have blueness before your mind; you're automatically representing <blue>. Nothing else need be added to your state in order for you to represent <blue>. In the same way, if you have a phenomenal state with a blue-square-ish phenomenal character, you automatically represent <blue square>.

Of course, we never enjoy a blue-ish or a blue-square-ish phenomenal character in isolation. Our overall phenomenal states are much richer, involving phenomenal characters corresponding to the three-dimensional shapes of represented objects, their distances from us and other objects, the sounds they make, their textures, their temperatures, and many of their other features. But the above claims are arguably true for more complex phenomenal states. Consider your entire visual phenomenal state, which involves a plethora of phenomenal characters. When you are in this phenomenal state, you automatically represent a plethora of visual perceptual contents, e.g., that there are hand-shaped objects and white pages with black marks in front of you, etc. Just as having a blue-square-ish phenomenal character automatically results in the representation of <blue square>, so too does your total visual phenomenal state automatically result in the representation of the visual content you're presently enjoying. The same goes for other kinds of perceptual states. It seems, then, that having phenomenal states suffices for having intentional states and so that phenomenal consciousness is the right kind of ingredient for giving rise to intentionality. In the first instance, this motivates weak PIT, the claim that at least some original intentionality arises from phenomenal consciousness, but I will soon show how these claims can be extended to also motivate PIT.

Horgan and Tienson (2002) argue along similar lines for something like weak PIT:[13] **Phenomenal duplicates**, subjects that instantiate all the same phenomenal properties throughout their existences, share a wide variety of intentional properties. This is supported largely by introspective considerations: Roughly, the idea is that we can introspectively tell that certain types of phenomenal states are inherently intentional and that certain types of intentional states are inherently phenomenal. This allows us to conclude that certain types of intentional and phenomenal states go together and so that phenomenal duplicates share a wide variety of intentional properties. From this, Horgan and Tienson conclude that there is phenomenal intentionality, i.e., that weak PIT is true.

---

[13] More precisely, Horgan and Tienson's conclusion is that there is original intentionality that is *constitutively determined* by phenomenal consciousness.

Siewert (1998) can also be interpreted as arguing for weak PIT using similar considerations: Roughly, the idea is that in virtue of having phenomenal states, one is automatically assessable for accuracy. For example, suppose you have a phenomenal state with a blue-square-in-front-of-you-ish phenomenal character. In virtue of having this phenomenal state, you are accurate or inaccurate depending on whether there is a blue square in front of you. Since being assessable for accuracy is sufficient for having intentional states, at least some phenomenal states give rise to intentional states.[14]

That phenomenal consciousness is the right kind of ingredient to give rise to intentionality is significant: Suppose all of PIT's testable predictions about superficial characters turned out to be true. That would be great. It would mean that PIT was empirically adequate, that it delivered the right answer in all cases. And if the main competing theories were not empirically adequate, then this would provide very strong support for PIT indeed. However, if phenomenal consciousness were not up to the task of giving rise to intentionality, then PIT would be a nonstarter. This is why it is significant that it *is* up to the task.

As I mentioned above, in the first instance, the fact that phenomenal consciousness is the right sort of thing to give rise to intentionality only supports weak PIT, since it does not yet support the claim that phenomenal consciousness gives rise to *all* original intentionality. But when we factor in the Real Problem with tracking theories and functional role theories, we obtain an argument for PIT. Tracking relations and functional roles are two of the main contenders for giving rise to original intentionality, but we have seen that tracking relations and functional roles

---

[14] While I agree that being assessable for accuracy is sufficient for intentionality, and even that having phenomenal states *appears* to make one assessable for accuracy, I don't find it entirely uncontroversial that intentional states give rise to accuracy conditions all by themselves. So, I'm not sure if PIT should ultimately accept that phenomenal states can automatically make one assessable for accuracy. (See §1.3.4 and §9.3.4.) If having conditions of truth and reference requires more than intentionality, then perhaps appearances are deceiving, and having phenomenal states is *not* sufficient for assessability for accuracy, even if it is sufficient for intentionality.

  However, I think there is something importantly right and persuasive about Siewert's argument. In having a phenomenal experience, it certainly *seems* to you that you are assessable for accuracy. It seems to you that the world might either correspond to the phenomenal characters of your phenomenal states or it might not. For example, when you are in a phenomenal state with a blue-square-in-front-of-you-ish phenomenal character, it seems to you that the world might either correspond to this phenomenal character, in that it might involve something blue and square in a certain location in front of you, or it might not. This suggests a revised version of Siewert's argument, one that does not rely on premises concerning the relationship between intentionality and assessability for accuracy that we might ultimately want to reject. The revised argument runs as follows: When you are in certain phenomenal states, it seems to you that you are assessable for accuracy. The best explanation for this *apparent* assessability for accuracy is that because of being in your phenomenal state, you are representing. If that's right, then at least some phenomenal states give rise to intentional states, and there is phenomenal intentionality.

are not up to the task. This gives us reason to take seriously the possibility that *all* original intentionality arises from phenomenal consciousness. Indeed, it is not clear what else could do the trick.[15]

As in the case of the argument from matching, complications arise in the case of thoughts, nonconscious states, and any states with rich descriptive contents, object-involving contents, or broad contents. It is not clear that the relevant contents are phenomenal contents, and so it is not clear whether consciousness has what it takes to give rise to *all* instances of original intentionality. As suggested in the previous subsection, the problematic intentional states are not paradigm cases of intentionality, so what to say about them is somewhat up for grabs. In Part IV, I argue that phenomenal consciousness gives rise to whatever intentionality these states have and, hence, that PIT can accommodate them (see §5.4 for an overview). But, again, even before considering these cases, we can make a fairly strong case for PIT: PIT is the only theory we've encountered so far that can account for original intentionality in terms of ingredients that it can plausibly be said to arise from.[16]

5.3 Identity PIT

So far, I have structured my discussion in terms of the relatively modest goal of determining what gives rise to actual instances of original intentionality (see §2.1). I have argued that it is phenomenal consciousness, not tracking relations or functional

---

[15] One might suggest that a primitivist view of intentionality can avoid the Real Problem. This is true, since primitivism simply posits intentional states but, as in the case of primitivism's response to the mismatch problem, this is not impressive. See n. 12 for my reasons for rejecting primitivism.

[16] One might also object that even if there is an intimate relationship between some intentional and phenomenal states, this does little to support weak PIT and PIT because it is compatible with an alternative view of the relationship between consciousness and intentionality: **representationalism**, the view that all actual cases of phenomenal consciousness arise from intentionality, perhaps together with some further ingredients. Indeed, Gertler (2001b) objects to Siewert's (1998) argument along these lines (see Siewert 2004 for a response), and Bailey and Richards (2014) object to Horgan and Tienson's (2002) argument on similar grounds.

Though not all versions of PIT qualify as versions of representationalism, the version of PIT that I will eventually argue for does. This means that in order to fully argue for my view, I do not have to (and should not) reject representationalism but only the versions of it that are not versions of PIT. In §5.3 and Appendix B, I argue that intentionality arises from consciousness by being identical to it and that all phenomenal states give rise to intentional states. These claims together rule out all versions of representationalism except those that take every phenomenal state to be identical to some intentional state, a claim that is consistent with my version of PIT. When combined with my arguments in Part IV for the claim that every intentional state is a phenomenal state, these claims rule out versions of representationalism that are not versions of PIT. (In §6.1, I argue that the compatibility between representationalism and PIT does not threaten PIT's status as a theory of intentionality in terms of consciousness rather than a theory of consciousness in terms of intentionality.)

roles, that are responsible for actual instances of original intentionality. This fixes on a general approach to intentionality, one that takes its source to be phenomenal consciousness.

This section turns to the further question of precisely *how* original intentionality arises from phenomenal consciousness. My suggestion, roughly, is that original intentionality arises from phenomenal consciousness by being identical to it. Original intentionality is a species of phenomenal consciousness (perhaps the only species of phenomenal consciousness—see Appendix B of this chapter).

We can call the view that every actual originally intentional state is identical to a phenomenal state the **state identity view**. A natural extension of the state identity view identifies all originally intentional *properties* with phenomenal *properties*. On the resulting **property identity view**, originally representing a content is one and the same thing as instantiating a phenomenal property.[17] Another natural extension of the state identity view also identifies the *contents* of originally intentional states with their phenomenal *characters*. I will call this view the **content-character identity view.**[18]

We can call the version of PIT that combines the state identity view, the property identity view, and the content-character identity view **identity PIT**. According to identity PIT, every originally intentional state is identical to some phenomenal state, every originally intentional property is identical to some phenomenal property, and every originally represented content is identical to some phenomenal character. Roughly, identity PIT is the view that original intentionality is a species of phenomenal consciousness.

Alternative views of the relationship between original intentionality and phenomenal consciousness introduce some distance between the two, taking the relationship to be one of constitution, realization, or grounding rather than one of identity. For example, a realization view might take originally intentional states to be realized by phenomenal states without being identical to them. Since this view denies that instantiations of originally intentional properties are identical to instantiations of

---

[17] Since originally intentional states are instantiations of originally intentional properties and phenomenal states are instantiations of phenomenal properties, an identity between originally intentional properties and phenomenal properties entails an identity between originally intentional states and phenomenal states. But it is less clear if the reverse entailment holds: If a single property instantiation can be an instantiation of two distinct properties, then every originally intentional state might be a phenomenal state without every originally intentional property being a phenomenal property.

[18] The content-character identity view does not automatically follow from the state identity view: The state identity view might be true while phenomenal characters are identical to intentional *states*, not their contents. On such a view, what is "felt" when we are in one of these states is not the same thing as what is represented. However, I take it that this view is somewhat unnatural.

phenomenal properties, it also denies that originally intentional properties are identical to phenomenal properties.

My favored view is identity PIT. A prima facie reason to favor it is that it offers a clear story of what originally intentional states, properties, and contents really *are*—they are phenomenal states, properties, and characters—while other views of the relationship between original intentionality and phenomenal consciousness often require a further story to tell us what intentional states, properties, and contents are. For example, the realization view tells us that originally intentional states are realized by phenomenal states, but it does not tell us what kinds of things they are such that they can be thus realized—for instance, are they functional states? The constitution view tells us that originally intentional states are in some sense "made up of" phenomenal states, but it too does not tell us what exactly they are such that they can be made up of phenomenal states without being identical to them. A version of PIT that endorses the state and property identity view but not the content-character identity view tells us what intentional states and properties are but does not tell us what their contents are. In short, identity PIT, which identifies intentional states, properties, and contents with phenomenal states, properties, and characters, respectively, is the only version of PIT we've got that tells us what original intentionality really is. For this reason, I take identity PIT to be the default view and ask whether we have reason to deviate from it.

Introspective considerations provide some positive support for the identity view. Both phenomenal states and originally intentional states are at least sometimes introspectable. When we introspect upon them, we notice various "mental qualities," which may be phenomenal characters, intentional contents, or something else. But when we introspect upon mental states involving both an introspectable intentional content and an introspectable phenomenal character, we do not notice two *distinct* mental qualities. Rather, introspection reveals only *one* mental quality. For example, when you notice the whiteness of this page, it seems introspectively inaccurate to say that your experience involves two distinct whiteness-related mental qualities, a white-ish phenomenal character *and* the represented content <white>. But since the experience clearly does involve the representation of whiteness and a white-ish phenomenal character, we should conclude that the intentional content <white> is identical to the white-ish phenomenal character. In other words, there is only one whiteness-related mental quality, and it may be correctly described as both a represented feature of the represented page and a phenomenal character. Similar points apply to other mental qualities that we introspectively notice in experience.[19]

---

[19] The introspective observations appealed to here are similar to the transparency observations that are often taken to support representationalism. One way of putting the transparency observations is this:

This suggests an identity between intentional contents and phenomenal characters. It also supports the state and property identity views: Since intentional states and properties are characterized and individuated by their contents and phenomenal states and properties are characterized and individuated by their phenomenal characters, it is a small further step to conclude that the observed intentional states and properties are identical to the observed phenomenal states and properties, respectively.

Let us now briefly consider some objections to identity PIT, which might motivate us to reject it in favor of a view that introduces some distance between original intentionality and phenomenal consciousness. The first is that intentionality and phenomenal consciousness have very different natures, with intentionality being a relation to distinctly existing items that play the role of contents and phenomenal consciousness being a mere modification of subjects. If intentionality and phenomenal consciousness do indeed have different natures, then they cannot be identical, but original intentionality might still arise from phenomenal consciousness in some other way, e.g., by being grounded in it.

I address this worry with identity PIT in Part V, where I argue that intentionality is not in fact relational in the relevant sense. But those who do not accept the arguments of that part might prefer a fallback position that rejects identity PIT in favor of an alternative version of PIT, such as one that takes the relationship between original intentionality and phenomenal consciousness to be that of constitution, realization, or grounding.

A second reason to reject the state identity view in favor of one of the alternatives is in order to allow for the multiple realization—or, we might say, the "multiple arisability"—of originally intentional properties: We might want to allow that instantiations of the same originally intentional properties arise in different ways. Since identity PIT identifies every originally intentional property with some phenomenal property, identity PIT precludes this kind of multiple arisability. But multiple arisability is compatible with other views of the relationship between original intentionality and phenomenal consciousness.

It is far from clear that the relevant kind of multiple arisability is possible, but those who think it is might opt for one of the weaker views of the relationship between phenomenal intentionality and phenomenal consciousness. Consideration of possible motivations for allowing for multiple arisability takes us too far afield, so I relegate their discussion to Appendix C of this chapter.

When we pay attention to our experience, what we notice are contents, not mere phenomenal characters or "raw feels" (see Harman 1990 and Tye 2000, pp. 46–51).

5.4 Challenging Cases

While there are reasons to take PIT seriously, the view faces some challenging cases. In Part IV, I argue for PIT-friendly treatments of these cases. In this section, I briefly overview these treatments. As we will see, the view that will emerge is a version of strong PIT, on which all intentional states are phenomenal intentional states.

There are three general approaches that PIT might take toward alleged cases of mental states with non-phenomenal contents: **Inflationism** maintains that the mental states do in fact have phenomenal contents. **Eliminativism** maintains that the mental states do not exist or that they do not intentionally represent the relevant contents.[20] Finally, **derivativism** maintains that the relevant contents are derivatively intentionally represented.[21] My overall strategy for dealing with challenging cases is a combination of eliminativism and inflationism, though in some cases it is derivativist in spirit.

Thoughts

Thoughts are occurrent mental states that we are in when we do what we commonly call "thinking." The problem with thoughts is that the contents we often want to ascribe to them, which might include complex descriptive contents, broad contents, and object-involving contents (see also below), do not seem to match their phenomenal characters, so it is implausible that these contents are phenomenally represented. If they are not phenomenally represented, then it is not clear how PIT can accommodate them.

Chapter 7 responds to this challenge. I argue that thoughts have "immediate contents," which are, roughly, the contents that are "running through our minds" at any given moment. Thoughts' immediate contents arguably match their phenomenal characters, making them good candidates for being phenomenally represented. These immediate contents do not, however, include many of the contents we might intuitively want to ascribe to thoughts. But, I will suggest, even though we do not immediately represent these alleged contents, we do the next best thing: we *derivatively* represent them. I defend a "self-ascriptivist" view of this derived mental representation, on which we derivatively represent various contents by ascribing them to ourselves or our mental states. On this view, thoughts' alleged

---

[20] What eliminativism eliminates need not be the mental state in its entirety but might only be the alleged intentional states it includes. For example, an eliminativist strategy about beliefs might accept that there are beliefs but deny that they intentionally represent, i.e., that they include intentional states. (See also the definition of "intentional mental state" on p. 7.)

[21] These three strategies are described in Bourget and Mendelovici 2016.

contents derive from our dispositions to have a certain kind of thought with a self-ascriptive phenomenal content, a phenomenal content that specifies that a thought or concept's immediate content cashes out into a further content. The resulting derived contents might be thought of as capturing our best understanding of what we mean when we think a thought, or what we really intend to be getting at. As I will argue, derived mental representation is not a type of intentionality, and so, strictly speaking, the derived contents of thoughts are not derived *intentional* contents.

This approach to thought is inflationist in that it takes at least some thought contents to be phenomenal contents, but it is also eliminativist in that it denies that other alleged thought contents are intentionally represented. It is, however, derivativist in spirit in that it maintains that thoughts *derivatively* represent some of the contents they do not phenomenally represent, though it is not a genuine form of derivativism since it denies that the relevant sort of derived representation is a kind of intentionality. It is worth noting, however, that there is a nearby fallback position that accepts my view of thought and takes derived mental representation to be a kind of intentionality. This approach would be both inflationist and derivativist rather than both inflationist and eliminativist.

Broad and Object-Involving Intentional Contents

Broad contents, contents the representation of which is at least partly determined by environmental factors, are arguably not phenomenally represented. For example, in the familiar Twin Earth thought experiment (Putnam 1975), Oscar and his intrinsic duplicate, Toscar, live in different environments, and, as a result, when they think the thoughts they would express with "Water is wet," they think thoughts with different contents. However, assuming intrinsic duplicates are phenomenally alike, Oscar and Toscar enjoy phenomenal states with the same phenomenal characters. So, broad contents are not phenomenal contents.

Object-involving contents are contents that constitutively involve a particular object, property, kind, or other worldly item. For example, suppose Lina perceptually experiences a particular cat, Mitten. We might say that Lina's thought content constitutively involves Mitten. But Mitten is not a constitutive part of the phenomenal character of Lina's experience, nor, arguably, would Lina have had a different phenomenal experience if Mitten were replaced by an indistinguishable duplicate. So, it seems, object-involving contents are not phenomenal contents.

Chapter 7 argues that thoughts and other mental states, including perceptual states, can derivatively represent broad contents and object-involving contents in much the same way that they derivatively represent other non-phenomenal thought contents. This self-ascriptivist strategy is eliminativist in that it denies that broad contents and object-involving contents are intentionally represented, but it is derivativist in spirit in that it claims that such contents are *derivatively* represented, though, again, derived mental representation is not a kind of intentionality. Again, there is a nearby derivativist fallback position that takes derived mental representation to be a kind of intentionality.

Standing States

Standing states are mental states that need not be used, entertained, or otherwise active at the time at which they are had, such as beliefs and desires that one is not currently entertaining or "assumptions" of the visual system. The worry with standing states is that they appear to be intentional, but they are not phenomenal; there is nothing it is like to have a standing state. So, they do not have phenomenal intentionality.

Chapter 8 argues that there are no genuinely intentional standing states. We might have various dispositions to have occurrent states, and we might even have distinct structures in our heads corresponding to these dispositions, but neither of these count as genuinely intentional. However, I also argue that the self-ascriptivist treatment of the alleged contents of thought developed in Chapter 7 can be extended to accommodate the contents of at least some of the standing states we intuitively ascribe to ourselves, and perhaps even some standing states in their entirety.

Like my strategy with states with broad and object-involving contents, this strategy is eliminativist in that it denies that there are intentional standing states, but it is derivativist in spirit in that it claims that standing state contents or standing states themselves can be ultimately derived from phenomenal intentional states. Again, there is a derivativist fallback position that takes this derived mental representation to be a kind of intentionality.

Nonconscious Occurrent States

Nonconscious occurrent states are occurrent states (states that are used, undergone, or activated at the time that they are had) that are not phenomenally conscious. Examples include states in early visual processing, nonconscious states involved in language processing, and nonconscious thoughts. Like standing states, the problem with these states is that many of them seem to be intentional but not phenomenal, so it looks like their contents are not phenomenal contents.

Chapter 8 argues that most allegedly nonconscious occurrent states neither originally nor derivatively represent the contents we might want to ascribe to them. I argue that this eliminativist position is not as drastic as it might at first appear and that it is arguably more in line with what might be considered the standard view on the topic than inflationist and derivativist alternatives.

In contrast with the case of thoughts, standing states, and states with broad or object-involving contents, I do not attempt to capture the contents we might want to attribute to nonconscious occurrent states with a kind of derived representation. The reason for this is that, as I will argue, unlike in the case of the above-mentioned kinds of states, we do not in some sense target or intend the relevant contents. We do not in some sense take ownership over them or intuitively take them to be part of our overall representational perspective on the world. So, there is both no need to capture the contents we might take them to have and no basis on which to take us to derivatively represent them.

While the strategy for most allegedly nonconscious occurrent states is eliminativist, I leave open the possibility that there are phenomenal states we are not aware of that give rise to intentional states we are not aware of. If there are such states, then the strategy for them would be inflationist.

The overall view that I have sketched in this section is a version of strong PIT, since it takes all intentionality to be phenomenal intentionality. This might seem like an unattractive view, since it denies intentionality to non-phenomenal states. However, as we will see in Chapters 7 and 8, it does justice to much of the content and many of the intentional states we might want to recognize on intuitive or theoretical grounds by showing that they are derived from phenomenal intentionality or track various items and play various functional roles.

When strong PIT is combined with identity PIT (the version of PIT that, roughly, identifies original intentionality with phenomenal consciousness—see §5.3), we arrive at **strong identity PIT**, the view that every intentional state, property, and content is identical to some phenomenal state, property, and content, respectively. This, in broad outline, is my overall view.

5.5 Conclusion

According to PIT, intentionality is a matter of phenomenal consciousness, the "what it's like" of being in certain mental states.

I have suggested a fairly strong and simple version of PIT, strong identity PIT, on which every intentional state is identical to some phenomenal state, every intentional property is identical to some phenomenal property, and every intentional state's content is identical to its phenomenal character. In short, according to strong identity PIT, intentionality is a species, perhaps the only species (see Appendix B), of phenomenal consciousness. While this is the view I believe to be correct, I have pointed out various nearby fallback positions.

My aim in this chapter was to provide some initial motivations for PIT, outline my favored version of the view, and preview how I defend and develop it in what follows. As we have seen, PIT is most plausible and best motivated in the case of introspectively accessible perceptual states. Part IV argues that PIT can also make good sense of other kinds of states, such as thoughts, standing states, and occurrent nonconscious states.

Appendix B: The Extent of Phenomenal Intentionality

This chapter argued for PIT, on which original intentionality is phenomenal intentionality. We largely left open, however, the question of *which* states have phenomenal intentionality. Let us turn to this question now.

The discussion so far shows that phenomenal intentionality is pervasive in the case of perceptual states. Many perceptual states are rich in phenomenal character, and this phenomenal character matches their intentional contents. This makes them prime candidates for having phenomenal intentionality.

It is slightly less clear whether thoughts have phenomenal intentionality. Many proponents and sympathizers of PIT have argued that thoughts have rich phenomenal characters corresponding to many of their rich contents (e.g., Siewert 1998, 2011, Horgan and Tienson 2002, Pitt 2004, Kriegel 2011, Montague 2016, and Chudnoff 2013, 2015a, 2015b). In Chapter 7, I present a more moderate view of the phenomenology of thought, on which thoughts have fairly impoverished phenomenal characters, which are responsible for the contents we are immediately aware of in having thoughts but not for many of the contents we intuitively want to ascribe to them.

So far, I've suggested that perceptual states and thoughts have phenomenal intentionality. Let us now turn to the related question of whether all phenomenal states give rise to phenomenal intentionality. If they do, then phenomenal intentionality is as extensive as phenomenal consciousness itself.

If PIT is true, then there is some reason to expect all phenomenal states to give rise to intentionality: If not all phenomenal states gave rise to intentionality, then there would be two very different types of phenomenal states, those that do and those that do not give rise to intentionality. This would be quite strange. Why should some phenomenal states automatically give rise to the representation of a content, while others do not? Absent specific reasons to think that there is such a significant division between phenomenal states, the view that all phenomenal states give rise to intentionality seems more likely.

Let us consider two possible reasons to think that not all phenomenal states give rise to intentional states. One reason is that, strange or not, it must be so, since we know there are mental states that have phenomenal characters but no corresponding intentional contents. Putative examples of such cases are discussed at length in the literature on **representationalism**, the view that all actual cases of phenomenal consciousness arise from intentionality, perhaps together with some further ingredients. Identity PIT combined with the view that all phenomenal states give rise to intentionality qualifies as a version of representationalism, since it maintains that all phenomenal states are identical to intentional states (see §6.1 for why this does not threaten PIT's status as a theory of intentionality). So, this version of PIT faces many of the same alleged counterexamples as representationalism, such as those of pains, moods, emotions, itches, perspectival experiences, and perceptual disturbances like phosphene experiences and blurry vision.[22]

I do believe that all phenomenal states give rise to intentionality. But, since none of what follows depends on this claim, this is not the place to enter these debates.[23] I do, however, want to briefly suggest that PIT is in a better position to deal with many of the alleged counterexamples to representationalism than many prominent versions of representationalism.

The prominent versions of representationalism in question combine representationalism with a tracking theory of intentionality.[24] The resulting **tracking representationalism** must capture the phenomenal characters of our experiences by appeal to what we track, which is severely limiting when we consider the extent of the mismatch problem for tracking theories (see Chapter 3). For example, this makes it difficult for tracking representationalism to account for the phenomenal characters of color experiences, pains, and moods. But versions of representationalism that are not committed to the tracking theory do not face such limitations, and so they do not face the same counterexamples as tracking representationalism; they can appeal to edenic color contents and other contents corresponding to uninstantiated properties

---

[22] A potentially problematic case not discussed much in the debates on representationalism is that of the attitude components of thoughts, e.g., the "belief" bit of a belief that P. If attitudes have corresponding phenomenal characters, then this poses another challenge for the view that all phenomenal states give rise to intentional states. See Appendix E of Chapter 7, which suggests that attitudes have characteristic contents corresponding to their phenomenal characters.

[23] See, e.g., Block 1996 and Kind 2003, 2013 for arguments against representationalism based on pains, moods, bodily sensations, and other kinds of states. For representationalist accounts of such cases, see, e.g., Harman 1990, Tye 1995a, 2000, 2008, Dretske 1995, Byrne 2001, Crane 2003, Bain 2003, Mendelovici 2013a, 2014, Bourget 2015, 2017b, and Smithies MS.

[24] See Tye 2000, Dretske 1995, and Lycan 1996 for such views and Bourget and Mendelovici 2014 and Seager and Bourget 2007 for overviews.

to capture experiences' phenomenal characters (see Bourget and Mendelovici 2014 and Pautz 2006, 2010a).[25]

If all this is right, then consideration of particular cases arguably does not compel us to accept phenomenal states that are not intentional states. Let us now turn to another reason to accept such states.

This reason stems from a PIT-like picture of intentionality that takes intentionality to arise from phenomenal states, but only when they are organized in the right way (see Farkas 2013 and Masrour 2013). On Farkas' view, roughly, phenomenal states give rise to intentionality when they bear the right relations to other past and present phenomenal states. For example, a certain type of perceptual phenomenal state might change in various ways when we have the experience of moving our heads, approaching objects, etc. When all the right relations are in place, we "externalize" phenomenal states of that type, thereby taking them to qualify external objects. This is what makes them intentional states. On Farkas' view, the phenomenal states involved in color vision bear the right relations to other phenomenal states, so they are externalized and hence intentional. In contrast, the phenomenal states involved in pain experiences do not bear the right relations to other phenomenal states, and so they are not externalized and hence are not intentional.

While this picture is attractive in many ways, it is not clear to me why being externalized is a necessary condition for being an intentional state. Perhaps the idea is that phenomenal states that are not externalized do not "say" anything about the mind-independent world and so are not intentional. But why couldn't an intentional state say something about the mind-*dependent* world or simply present us with a content, perhaps a non-propositional content? For example, suppose phenomenal states with a blue-ish phenomenal character didn't bear the relevant relations to other phenomenal states. Suppose, for instance, that vision is normally black and white, but we occasionally experience blue phosphenes. In this scenario, Farkas might be right that we would not externalize blueness—phenomenal states with a blue-ish phenomenal character would not qualify putative mind-independent objects as being blue. But they would still represent <blue>. The scenario would be similar to a related scenario in which the content <cat> sporadically occurred to someone who otherwise never perceived or thought about cats. In this latter case, we should say that our subject has intentional states representing <cat> that are not externalized. Likewise, we should say the same thing about the former case of <blue>. So, even if

---

[25] Elsewhere, I have argued for a non-tracking representationalist picture of moods and emotions on which they reliably misrepresent uninstantiated affective properties (Mendelovici 2013a and 2014) and similar non-tracking representationalist pictures of pains (Mendelovici 2010) and olfactory experiences (Mendelovici forthcoming-a).

we agree with Farkas' story about when phenomenal states are externalized, we might nonetheless maintain that all phenomenal states give rise to intentionality, regardless of whether they are externalized.[26]

The question of whether all phenomenal states give rise to intentionality clearly deserves further consideration, but I take the present discussion to suggest in favor of an affirmative answer. However, for those not convinced by my claims, identity PIT combined with an acceptance of phenomenal states that do not give rise to intentional states makes an attractive fallback position that is compatible with most everything that follows.

I have argued that every phenomenal state gives rise to an intentional state. When combined with strong identity PIT, this means that every phenomenal state is identical to some intentional state and every intentional state is identical to some phenomenal state, a view that qualifies as a version of representationalism as well as a version of PIT. A plausible extension of this view takes every phenomenal property to be identical to some intentional property and every phenomenal character to be identical to some intentional content. On the resulting view, intentionality is not just *a* species of phenomenal consciousness, but *the only* species of phenomenal consciousness.

Appendix C: The Multiple Arisability of Intentional States

Section 5.3 argued for identity PIT, on which every originally intentional state is identical to some phenomenal state, every originally intentional property is identical to some phenomenal property, and every originally represented content is identical to some phenomenal character. I suggested that one reason we might want to reject the identity view in favor of a view that takes the relationship between phenomenal intentionality and phenomenal consciousness to be one of constitution,

---

[26] As Farkas defines the term, intentionality is "the apparent directedness of a mental state at something *beyond itself*, moreover, at something which *could exist independently of being experienced*" (p. 99; emphasis in original). This definition of "intentionality" ties intentionality very closely to externalization, while my definition of "intentionality" does not, which might lead to the suspicion that our disagreement is merely terminological. If the disagreement were merely terminological, that would not be a problem for me, since I only want to argue that externalization is not required for intentionality *in my sense* of "intentionality." However, I do think that even on Farkas' sense, there are reasons for thinking that a phenomenal state failing to bear the right relations to other phenomenal states could nonetheless be an intentional state, since it could nonetheless represent something existing independently of experience. The example of non-externalized blue-ish phenomenal states is arguably such a case: Such experiences represent something, <blue>, that could exist independent of being experienced (at least as far as our subject's experience is concerned).

realization, or grounding is to allow for the multiple arisability of originally intentional properties, where an originally intentional property is **multiply arisable** just in case instantiations of this property can arise in different ways. According to the identity view, any given originally intentional property is identical to some phenomenal property, so it cannot have instantiations that arise independently of that phenomenal property. Alternative views, such as the realization, constitution, and grounding views, allow that instantiations of the same originally intentional property can arise in different ways.

In order to assess this motivation for moving away from identity PIT, let us consider the two central kinds of multiple arisability that we might want to allow for: First, we might want to allow for the metaphysical possibility of originally intentional states arising from non-phenomenal states. Just as the tracking theory and the functional role theory might want to allow that intentionality might arise independently of their favored ingredients in other possible worlds, PIT might want to allow for *possible* cases of original intentionality that are not cases of phenomenal intentionality. For example, it might want to allow that an originally intentional property whose instantiations arise from phenomenal states in the actual world has instantiations that do not arise from phenomenal consciousness in other possible worlds. Perhaps, for instance, originally intentional states with the content <blue triangle> in the actual world arise from phenomenal states, but there are other possible worlds containing intentional states representing the same content that arise from tracking relations to blueness and triangularity.[27]

Identity PIT does not allow for this possibility. This is because it identifies originally intentional properties with phenomenal properties. As a result, any actual or possible originally intentional states have to be instantiations of the corresponding phenomenal properties. In contrast, the realization, constitution, and grounding views can allow that an originally intentional property might have actual-world instantiations that are realized by, constituted by, grounded in, or perhaps even identical to phenomenal states but other-world instantiations that are realized by, constituted by, grounded in, or identical to something else.

It is not clear to me that we need to allow for cases of original intentionality in other possible worlds that are not cases of phenomenal intentionality. I have argued that tracking relations and functional roles do not give rise to intentionality in the actual world. If they do not give rise to intentionality in the actual world, then they are not metaphysically sufficient for intentionality, so they do not give rise

---

[27] Similarly, physicalists about the mind might want to allow that there are possible worlds in which there are nonphysical minds.

to intentionality in any world. So, we do not need to allow for tracking relations or functional roles to give rise to originally intentional states in other possible worlds. For similar reasons, PIT need not allow anything else in the actual world to give rise to intentionality in other possible worlds. We might further argue that it would be surprising if there was some other ingredient that could give rise to original intentionality. It's hard enough to find one that can do the trick! So, absent good reason to think that there are alternative ways of getting original intentionality, we need not accommodate the kind of multiple arisability described above.

The only option that we might want to leave open is that of other possible worlds containing sui generis or primitive instances of original intentionality, instances of original intentionality that do not arise from phenomenal consciousness or anything else. While this suggestion strikes me as more plausible than the suggestion that tracking or functional roles give rise to original intentionality in other possible worlds, it is somewhat difficult to get a grip on. If PIT is right, then intentionality is intimately related to phenomenal consciousness in our world. For the imagined sui generis phenomenon to really count as original intentionality, it would have to be the same type of thing as our original intentionality. But then original intentionality would have to have a nature that allows it to arise from phenomenal consciousness or to be a sui generis phenomenon that exists distinctly from phenomenal consciousness, and it's difficult to see what kind of nature that would be. The case would be very much unlike cases of multiple realizability of functional states by distinct physical states. In these cases, functional states have a functional nature, and it is completely intelligible how diverse physical states can realize something with this nature. But in the alleged case of the multiple arisability of original intentionality under discussion, it is unclear what the relevant nature of original intentionality could be such that it can arise both from phenomenal consciousness and all on its own.

A second kind of multiple arisability we might want to allow for involves instantiations of a single originally intentional property arising from instantiations of independent phenomenal properties. For example, compare a perceptual state representing something as unique red and a thought representing something as unique red. These states might both be instantiations of the same originally intentional property, the intentional property of originally representing <unique red>. But, one might say, they arise from distinct phenomenal states.

Identity PIT cannot allow for such cases. Since it identifies originally intentional properties with phenomenal properties, instantiations of any given originally intentional property cannot arise from instantiations of independent phenomenal properties. In contrast, the realization, constitution, and grounding views can allow for such cases, since they allow that multiple distinct and independent phenomenal states can give rise to instantiations of the same intentional property.

Again, though, it is not entirely clear that we need to allow for such cases, since it is not entirely clear that instantiations of distinct and independent phenomenal properties can represent the same contents. The proposed picture of the two cases described above is dissatisfying because in the case of the perceptual representation of redness, representing redness consists in having a phenomenal state with a rich and vivid red-ish visual phenomenal character, while in the case of the thought about redness, representing redness consists in having a much more attenuated, much less rich, phenomenal character. This phenomenal character might not even be properly described as "red-ish"; it might merely consist of auditory imagery of the word "red" or an amodal representation of redness. One might wonder if such an impoverished phenomenal character really is sufficient for representing redness, given that, in the perceptual case, representing redness involves having a much richer or more vivid phenomenal character. In Chapter 7, I argue that the impoverished phenomenal character of thoughts only yields a correspondingly impoverished content. On this view, the thought and the perceptual state allegedly representing <unique red> turn out to have different phenomenal contents. If the arguments of Chapter 7 are sound, then the above-mentioned example is not one of instantiations of the same originally intentional property arising from instantiations of distinct phenomenal properties, and so we do not need to retreat from identity PIT in order to accommodate it. More generally, if impoverished phenomenal characters cannot yield rich intentional contents, the kind of multiple arisability involved in the above example cannot in fact occur.

There is another reason to want to allow for this second kind of multiple arisability. One might suggest that it is possible to have two intentional states with the same intentional contents but that differ in how "intense" they are. Suppose that in one case, you imagine a red circle while relaxed and focused, while in another case, you imagine a red circle while preoccupied. One might suggest that, on one way of fleshing out the example, in both cases you represent the same intentional content but at different intensities. Metaphorically, we might say that the two states are alike, except that one has the volume turned up higher than the other. Just as turning up the volume on the radio doesn't change which song is playing, so too does increasing an intentional state's intensity not change its content.

The two cases in the preceeding example are both instances of imagination, but we might be able to concoct similar examples of two perceptual states that are alike with respect to content but different with respect to intensity. It might also be that perception and imagination can represent the same contents but with different intensities.[28] Perhaps differences in attention also make for differences in intensity without differences in content.[29]

However, it is not clear to me that there are cases of intentional states with the same contents that differ in intensity. It could be that any apparent difference in intensity is really a difference in content. For example, the imaginative state of a red circle that one enjoys while relaxed and focused might be more detailed or precise than the imaginative state of a red circle that one enjoys while preoccupied. Likewise, perceptual states might be more detailed than imaginative states, even when they represent what we might intuitively classify as being the same contents.[30] And in the same way, differences in attention might make for differences in the details represented, and hence for differences in content.[31] So, it is not clear that there is good reason to accept that we can represent the very same contents more or less intensely.

Since it is not clear that differences in the detail, precision, or determinacy of content cannot account for apparent differences in intensity, I take the case for this kind of multiple arisability to be at best inconclusive. Absent further considerations in favor of the possibility of this kind of multiple arisability, I conclude, somewhat tentatively, that we should stick with identity PIT.

In summary, if we think that instantiations of the same originally intentional property can arise in distinct ways, then there is reason to prefer a realization, constitution, or grounding version of PIT over identity PIT. I am skeptical that there are such reasons, so my bets are on identity PIT. Still, the alternative views are attractive fallback positions for those who want to allow for the multiple arisability of originally intentional properties. Everything that follows can be adapted to be made compatible with these alternative views.

---

[28] Such a view might be inspired by Hume's claims that imaginative states are faint copies of perceptual impressions, though Hume also took imaginative states to differ from perceptual states in being less precise or degraded in various ways (Hume 1739, I.i.1 and I.i.3). See also Byrne (2010) and Kriegel (2015a) for relevant discussion of this view.

[29] More generally, if differences in what one is attending to can make a difference to one's phenomenal states but not to the originally intentional states they give rise to, then instantiations of distinct phenomenal properties can give rise to instantiations of the same originally intentional property (see Nickel 2007, Speaks 2010a, 2015, and Block 2010).

[30] Bourget (2017d) argues that differences in intensity across all experiences are fully explained by differences in content determinacy.

[31] Items that are attended to might be represented more determinately or as more detailed, salient, or foregrounded than items that are not attended to (Chalmers 2004, Nanay 2010, Koralus 2014, and Bourget 2017d).

6   PIT's Status as a Theory of Intentionality

IN THE PREVIOUS chapter, we saw that the phenomenal intentionality theory (PIT) can succeed where alternative theories fail. We ended with a discussion of some challenging cases for PIT, which I promised to address in Part IV. But first, this chapter briefly considers some theoretical worries with PIT that challenge its status as an admissible candidate for a theory of intentionality. For those eager to move on to the problem cases, however, this chapter may be skipped or read out of sequence.

Here, I consider the objections that PIT, or at least my version of PIT, cannot properly be considered a theory of intentionality in terms of consciousness rather than a theory of consciousness in terms of intentionality (§6.1) and that PIT is trivial (§6.2), uninteresting (§6.3), or problematically incompatible with naturalism (§6.4). As we will see, PIT escapes all these worries.

6.1 Is PIT a Theory of Intentionality in Terms of Phenomenal Consciousness?

My favored version of PIT, strong identity PIT, claims that every intentional state, property, and content is identical to some phenomenal state, property, and character, respectively. Additionally, I accept that every phenomenal state, property, and character is identical to some intentional state, property, and content, respectively (see Appendix B of Chapter 5). For our purposes here, let us call strong identity PIT together with this extra claim **strong identity PIT***. On this view, intentionality and phenomenal consciousness are one and the same thing.

One might worry that since strong identity PIT* takes the relation between the intentional and the phenomenal to be that of identity, it doesn't make sense to say that it provides an account of the intentional in terms of the phenomenal. After all, identity is symmetric, so it might seem arbitrary to say that strong identity PIT* accounts for the intentional in terms of the phenomenal rather than the phenomenal in terms of the intentional.

This worry does not apply to all versions of PIT. Versions of PIT that allow for phenomenal states that are not intentional states have a non-arbitrary way of saying that phenomenal states are in some sense prior to or more fundamental than intentional states. The same holds for versions of PIT that take the relation between originally intentional states and phenomenal states to be that of constitution, grounding, or realization. However, the worry does apply to PIT *in general* since not all versions of it can clearly be seen to be theories of intentionality in terms of phenomenal consciousness rather than theories of phenomenal consciousness in terms of intentionality.

One way to bring out the worry is to note that strong identity PIT* (and hence PIT) is compatible with representationalism, the view that phenomenal consciousness arises from intentionality, perhaps together with additional ingredients. Indeed, strong identity PIT* is *the same view as* a version of representationalism that states that every phenomenal state, property, and character is identical to some intentional state, property, and content, respectively, and every intentional state, property, and content is identical to some phenomenal state, property, and character, respectively.[1] But representationalism is often thought of as a theory of consciousness in terms of intentionality (see Dretske 1995 and Tye 2000, but see Chalmers 2004, Bourget 2010b, and Smithies MS, for a different characterization), while PIT is supposed to be a theory of intentionality in terms of consciousness. How can this be if versions of PIT are identical to versions of representationalism?

I want to suggest that, *strictly speaking*, strong identity PIT* (and strong identity PIT and PIT more generally) is not properly considered a theory of intentionality in

---

[1]   Note that this version of representationalism is a far cry from what might be considered the most paradigmatic versions of the view, which take phenomenal consciousness to arise from a combination of functional roles and intentionality, which is taken to be a species of tracking relation. (See Dretske 1995, Tye 1995b, 2000, 2009, and Lycan 1996 for examples of this view and Bourget and Mendelovici 2014 and Seager and Bourget 2007 for overviews.)

terms of consciousness rather than a theory of consciousness in terms of intentionality. However, when strong identity PIT* (or any version of PIT) is combined with some assumptions about the nature of the items to be identified that the advocate of PIT is likely to hold, the resulting combination is properly considered a theory of intentionality in terms of consciousness rather than a theory of consciousness in terms of intentionality. Strong identity PIT* together with these extra assumptions is not compatible with representationalism together with corresponding assumptions.

Before unpacking these points, let us consider the analogous case of the mind-brain identity theory, which is supposed to be a theory of mental states in terms of brain states. The **mind-brain identity theory**, which states that every mental state is identical to some brain state, is compatible with the claim that every brain state happens to be identical to some mental state. Call a version of the mind-brain identity theory that accepts this further claim the **mind-brain identity theory***. But then, one might ask, what makes the mind-brain identity theory* a theory of *mental states* in terms of brain states rather than a theory of *brain states* in terms of mental states, a kind of mentalism about brain states?

Strictly speaking, the mind-brain identity theory* is the same view as the mentalist alternative. So, if a theorist who maintains that mental states are brain states is taken to be offering a theory of mental states in terms of brain states, it must be in virtue of further claims she accepts. The relevant claims might be claims to the effect that mental/brain states are, at bottom, more like what we previously thought brain states are like than the other way around. For example, she might take mental/brain states to be spatially located and physically constituted, and to have the level of internal complexity we might have previously attributed to brain states rather than the level of internal complexity we might have previously attributed to mental states. We can call the mind-brain identity theory* combined with these further commitments the **mind-brain identity theory*+**. While the mind-brain identity theory* is the same view as the mentalist alternative, the "+" version of the view is not equivalent to an analogous "+" version of mentalism. We might say that the mind-brain identity theory*+ "fits" mental states to brain states, while mentalism+ "fits" brain states to mental states.

Similarly, although strong identity PIT* is the same view as a version of representationalism, advocates of PIT and representationalism accept certain further claims about the nature of the items to be identified, yielding incompatible "+" versions of their views. Advocates of PIT hold that intentionality/phenomenal consciousness has more of the characteristics we might have previously attributed to phenomenal consciousness than the characteristics we might have previously attributed to intentionality, while, presumably, advocates of representationalism hold that intentionality/phenomenal consciousness has more of the characteristics we might have previously attributed to intentionality than the characteristics we might have previously attributed to phenomenal consciousness. In short, strong identity PIT*+ (and strong identity PIT+ and PIT+) "fits" the intentional to the phenomenal, while representationalism+ "fits" the phenomenal to the intentional.

Many of the characteristics that we arguably commonly attribute to intentionality differ from those we commonly attribute to phenomenal consciousness. First, intentionality might be taken to be relatively abundant, in that perceptual states, thoughts, standing states, nonconscious occurrent states, and perhaps even non-mental items like stop signs, words, tree rings, and compasses are taken to have it. In contrast, phenomenal consciousness is typically thought to be somewhat scarcer. On some views, only sensory states, like perceptual states, emotional states, and experiences of inner speech, have it, while on other views, occurrent thoughts have it, too. However, normally, standing states and nonconscious occurrent states are not taken to have it, and neither are stop signs, words, tree rings, and compasses.

Second, externalism is often thought to be true of intentionality, in that which intentional states a subject has are supposed to be at least partly determined by features of her external environment (see Putnam 1975 and Burge 1979). In contrast, internalism is usually thought to be true of phenomenal consciousness, in that a subject's phenomenal states are taken to be determined solely by internal factors.

Third, intentionality is often thought to be relational, in that intentional states are taken to be relations to distinctly existing entities that one entertains, is aware of, or otherwise represents, such as propositions (see Chapter 9). In contrast, phenomenal consciousness is usually taken not to be relational in the same way. Having a blue-ish phenomenal state is not generally thought to involve a relation to a distinctly existing entity, a blue-ish-ness; rather, phenomenal states are thought of as non-relational properties of experiencing subjects.

Fourth, intentionality is often taken to be naturalizable, in that it is supposed to arise from broadly physical phenomena, such as tracking relations or functional roles. In contrast, whether or not phenomenal consciousness is taken to be naturalizable, it is often taken to resist naturalization: If it can be naturalized, it is not easy to see how.

These four characteristics we commonly attribute to intentionality and phenomenal consciousness are summarized in Table 6.1.

A view that qualifies as both a version of PIT and a version of representationalism and that takes intentionality/phenomenal consciousness to be scarce, internalist, non-relational, and resistant to naturalization "fits" intentionality to phenomenal consciousness. Such a theory claims that, at bottom, phenomenal consciousness/intentionality is more like what we generally take phenomenal consciousness to be like than what we generally take intentionality to be like. Such a theory is

TABLE 6.1
Some Characteristics that Might be Commonly Attributed to
Intentionality and Phenomenal Consciousness.

Intentionality	Phenomenal consciousness
relatively abundant	relatively scarce
externalistic	internalistic
relational	non-relational
naturalizable	resists naturalization

best thought of as a theory of intentionality in terms of phenomenal consciousness rather than a theory of phenomenal consciousness in terms of intentionality. In contrast, a theory that takes intentionality/phenomenal consciousness to be relatively abundant, externalist, relational, and clearly naturalizable "fits" phenomenal consciousness to intentionality. Such a theory is best considered a theory of phenomenal consciousness in terms of intentionality rather than a theory of intentionality in terms of phenomenal consciousness.[2]

According to the version of PIT I develop throughout the rest of this book, intentionality/phenomenal consciousness is relatively scarce (Chapters 7 and 8), internalistic (Chapters 7 and 9), non-relational (Chapter 9), and resistant to naturalization (§6.4). Strictly speaking, then, this makes my overall view strong identity PIT*+. However, for ease of exposition, I will continue to write as if PIT is implicitly committed to the additional commitments the proponents of PIT are likely to accept, and so I will write as if it is the "+" version of the view.[3]

---

[2] Theories that take phenomenal/intentional states to have some of the features that are generally ascribed to phenomenal states and some of the features that are generally ascribed to intentional states occupy a gray zone. For example, Bourget (2010b, forthcoming-b) and Pautz (2010a) take intentional states to be scarce, internalistic, and not or not clearly naturalizable, but relational. Though they endorse PIT, they also sometimes describe their views as versions of "representationalism."

[3] One might suggest that commitments regarding the features of the items to be identified are already packed into the relevant identity claims, and so when the advocate of strong identity PIT* says "the intentional is identical to the phenomenal," she means something different than a representationalist who utters the same thing. For example, perhaps the advocate of representationalism takes intentionality to be by definition relatively abundant, externalistic, relational, and naturalizable, while the advocate of PIT takes phenomenal consciousness to be by definition relatively scarce, internalistic, non-relational, and not clearly naturalizable. Put otherwise, on this suggestion, strong identity PIT* just is strong identity PIT*+.

Whether this is the case depends on the meanings of the terms "phenomenal consciousness" and "intentionality" for these theorists. While a usage of these terms that packs in the relevant commitments

6.2 Is PIT Trivial?

One might worry that PIT is trivial, following immediately from the definitions of "intentionality" and "phenomenal consciousness." If PIT was trivial in this way, it would be true but unimpressive.

But it is not trivial. Both "intentionality" and "phenomenal consciousness" are defined by pointing to a feature we recognize in a set of examples. In the case of "intentionality," our target feature is the one that we are tempted to characterize using representational terms like "represent," "present," "about," or "directed," whereas in the case of "phenomenal consciousness," our target feature is the felt, subjective, experiential, or "what it's like" aspect of mental life. It does not follow immediately from our definitions that the thing we are tempted to characterize in representational terms is such that it is felt, subjective, or experiential or that it gives rise to these features in some other way. So, PIT does not follow trivially from my definitions.

Indeed, the above considerations show not only that PIT does not follow trivially from our definitions but also, further, that it cannot be established conclusively through reasoning alone, i.e., that it is a posteriori rather than a priori.

One might object that the claim that PIT is a posteriori is in tension with my second argument for PIT, the argument from the Real Reason, which seems to be a priori. Indeed, some versions of this argument seem to involve a priori thought experiments. There is no tension, however, because the argument from the Real Reason is not a priori. The Real Reason to accept PIT is that consciousness is the right kind of ingredient to give rise to intentionality and it is not clear that anything else is. That consciousness can give rise to intentionality is supposed to be evident from introspective consideration of phenomenal and intentional states and a priori reasoning about those states. The relevant kind of introspective consideration depends on more than simply the definitions of phenomenal consciousness and intentionality. It relies on our introspective grasp of what those definitions pick out or refer to, i.e., phenomenal consciousness and intentionality itself. This grasp allows us to learn from the armchair a posteriori truths about what our definitions pick out, which allows us to see that tracking relations and functional roles cannot give rise to intentionality and that phenomenal consciousness can.

Now, of course, we might take what is grasped when we introspect— intentionality and phenomenal consciousness itself—to be packed into our a priori

---

is possible, it would be inadvisable to define either term in such a committal way, since the terms would fail to refer if the phenomena in question failed to have the listed features. In any case, I am not using the terms in this way, so, given my definitions, strictly speaking, strong identity PIT* is not just strong identity PIT*+.

known meanings of our terms "intentionality" and "phenomenal consciousness." Then PIT, and, perhaps, the argument from the Real Reason, would be a priori. But notice that the same is true in the case of any a posteriori identity claim. A prime example of an a posteriori identity claim is "Water is H_2O." But this identity claim too would be rendered a priori if we simply stipulated "water" and "H_2O" to have their shared referent, H_2O, as the a priori known meaning of the terms.[4]

6.3 Is PIT Interesting?

A related worry is that identity PIT is simply uninteresting or unsurprising. If it is true, then it merely points to the fact that something is self-identical, which is a boring kind of fact. Before considering more nuanced versions of this worry, note that the fact that some claim is an identity claim is not in itself an objection to its being interesting, since many identity claims are interesting, such as claims identifying mental states with brain states, colors with surface reflectance profiles, moral facts with naturalistic facts, phenomenal characters with tracked properties, and elephants with bricks (§3.6.4). In any case, even if a particular identity claim is uninteresting, this is not an objection to its appeal as a theory. It is far outside the scope of my project to argue against all the exciting identity theories on offer in philosophy, but I will hazard that the most bold and provocative of such claims, the ones that are most interesting, are most likely to be false and that this is part of what makes them so interesting. We have trouble seeing how these unlikely identity claims might be true, and this makes them surprising, provocative, and exciting. When we come to appreciate a true identity claim, though, it loses some of its mystique. Identity theories, then, are in a bit of a bind: They are likely either interesting but false or true but less interesting. The upshot is that it is no objection to an identity claim that it is uninteresting simply because we can see that it might actually be *true*.

A more nuanced objection is that, while some identity theories shed light on the nature of their targets, identity PIT does not, and this makes it uninteresting. For example, a mind-brain identity theory (the "+" version, at least) purports to tell us new facts about the nature of mental states, such as that they are spatially located.

But this is also true of identity versions of PIT (again, at least the "+" versions). Such views "fit" intentionality to phenomenal consciousness, and in so doing, they uncover new facts about intentionality, e.g., that it is scarce, non-relational, internalistic, and resistant to naturalization—and even simply that it is experiential.

---

[4] Thanks to Tim Bayne and David Bourget for pressing me on the kinds of worries discussed in this section.

Another worry along similar lines is that, while some identity theories account for their targets in terms of their constituent parts, identity PIT does not seem to do so, and this makes it unappealing as a theory of intentionality. For example, the mind-brain identity theory might explain mental states in terms of the constituent parts of the brain states they are purportedly identical to. But if identity PIT is true, an intentional state need not be made up of multiple constituent phenomenal states. It could even be that every intentional/phenomenal state is simple, in that it has no constituent parts.

I agree that identity PIT does not automatically provide a theory of intentionality in terms of constituent parts and that this is a difference between the view and many other identity theories.[5] But I do not think much follows from this. This does not threaten the truth of the theory, since not all things have constituents and even things that do have constituents can be largely understood without a complete account of their constituents.[6] This feature of identity PIT also does not threaten its status as a theory of intentionality, since a theory of intentionality is a theory that tells us intentionality's nature, not necessarily a theory that tells us intentionality's nature *in terms of its constituent parts*. This also doesn't threaten how interesting the theory is, since, although it may be interesting to have a theory of something in terms of its constituent parts, it is not automatically uninteresting to have a different kind of theory that nonetheless tells us about the nature of its target.

6.4 Is PIT Naturalistic?

As we saw in Part II, much theorizing on intentionality assumes that we want a naturalistic theory, a theory appealing only to naturalistic items, which are either fundamental physical items lacking mentality or items constituted by, realized by, or grounded in such items.[7]

---

[5] See, however, Chapter 9.

[6] Compare: A causal tracking theory of intentionality might account for intentionality in terms of causal relations without accounting for causal relations in more basic terms.

[7] We might distinguish between **ontological naturalism**, which is a commitment to a certain ontology purportedly delivered by science, which is usually taken to consist in fundamental physical entities lacking mentality and entities composed of or realized by such entities, and **methodological naturalism**, which is a methodological commitment to a broadly scientific methodology (see Shapiro 1997, Chomsky 2000, Maddy 2001, Horst 2009, Papineau 2010, Mendelovici 2010, ch. 8, and Mendelovici and Bourget 2014 for such distinctions). Mendelovici and Bourget 2014 and Mendelovici 2010, ch. 8 argue that methodological naturalism is the kind of naturalism that matters to theories of intentionality and that PIT is more methodologically naturalistic than tracking theories. But the kind of naturalism at issue in this section is ontological naturalism, the kind of naturalism that is often taken to motivate the tracking theory (see Millikan 1984, p. 87, Fodor 1987, p. 97, and Dretske 1988, p. x).

One might object to PIT on the basis of naturalistic commitments. One objection is that since PIT's ontological commitments include a commitment to phenomenal consciousness, which is not obviously naturalistic, PIT might not end up being naturalistic, and so we should reject it. Mendelovici and Bourget (2014) respond to this objection by arguing that either PIT is naturalistic or naturalism is not an appropriate commitment for a theory of intentionality. In a nutshell, the idea is that either consciousness is a naturalistic item or it is not. If it is, then PIT is naturalistic. If it is not, then we should nonetheless accept consciousness as part of our ontology, since eliminativism about consciousness is not an option. But then naturalism does not reflect the admissible ontological commitments for a theory of intentionality, and so it is not an appropriate constraint on such a theory. Put otherwise, the only appropriate ontological constraint on a theory (at least a theory of things that exist) is a commitment to entities that exist. Phenomenal consciousness exists, so, as far as ontological commitments are concerned, it is acceptable for a theory to invoke it. This is true whether or not phenomenal consciousness can be naturalized.⁸

A second worry pertaining to naturalism is that PIT combined with my claim that only phenomenal consciousness can give rise to intentionality (§5.2) cannot be combined with a naturalistic view of phenomenal consciousness. Along these lines, Pautz (2013a) argues that advocates of PIT that take the failure of naturalism about intentionality to motivate PIT are committed to denying naturalism about phenomenal consciousness. This is because any arguments against naturalistic accounts of intentionality would also provide arguments against PIT combined with a naturalistic view of phenomenal consciousness, for such a combined view would ultimately account for intentionality in terms of naturalistic ingredients. This objection does not directly apply to my view, since I do not claim to have argued against all possible naturalistic views of intentionality. But a restricted version of the objection does apply: PIT together with my conclusions of Part II that tracking and functional role theories fail rule out a tracking or functional role theory of phenomenal consciousness.

Now, clearly, if we cannot account for A in terms of C, then we cannot account for A in terms of B and B in terms of C. So, the general claim that underlies Pautz's objection is clearly correct. But this does not pose a problem for PIT unless we have independent reasons to think that a tracking or functional role theory of phenomenal consciousness is true. And even if we had such reasons and they were

---

⁸ Along similar lines, Strawson (2011) argues that a realistic version of naturalism should accept the existence of phenomenal consciousness. On Strawson's version of naturalism, PIT is unproblematically naturalistic.

compelling, this would only succeed in generating an impasse, with arguments for such a theory of consciousness pitted against arguments against it based on the arguments from Part II and Chapter 5.

In any case, even if it turns out that a tracking or functional role theory of phenomenal consciousness is true, all is not lost for PIT. This would mean that some of the arguments of Part II are mistaken. The problems with those arguments, such a view might say, is that they fail to take into account that tracking relations or functional roles give rise to phenomenal consciousness. Once we take this into account, we can see how tracking and functional roles can indeed give rise to intentionality.

The final objection concerning naturalism that I will consider suggests that even though the above two objections do not warrant the outright rejection of PIT, the fact that tracking and functional role theories are naturalistic is surely a virtue that they have and that PIT lacks. When deciding between theories, we need to weigh all their virtues and vices, including their stance with respect to naturalism.[9]

Before responding to this objection, it is important to clarify what we might mean by a "virtue." A virtue of a theory might be taken to be a feature of the theory that provides evidence of its truth, which we might call a **truth-indicating virtue**, or it might be taken to be a feature of the theory that makes it more desirable that it be true, which we might call a **desire-satisfying virtue**. For example, a particular epistemological theory that defeats skepticism has a desire-satisfying virtue; we would like to defeat skepticism, so we have reason to desire that the theory be true. But, absent independent reason to think that skepticism can be defeated, that an epistemological theory can defeat skepticism is not evidence of its truth, and so it is not a truth-indicating virtue.

Now, the fact that tracking and functional role theories are naturalistic is clearly a virtue in the desire-satisfying sense. This is true for a deeper reason than that we might simply *want* naturalism to be true. It is true because it is more desirable for a theory to invoke items that we already have a fairly good understanding of, like tracking relations, than to invoke items that are not well understood, like (let us grant) phenomenal consciousness. One reason for this is that a theory invoking better understood items is likely to say more about the nature of our target than a theory invoking less well understood items. Tracking and functional role theories, then, might provide a more satisfying account of intentionality, offering a fairly precise picture of how intentionality relates to the rest of the world, especially the physical world. PIT, in contrast, might be thought to say less about intentionality, since intentionality's relation to much of the rest of the world depends on that of

---

[9] Kriegel (2011, p. 172) endorses something like this outlook, arguing that considerations of empirical adequacy need to be weighed against theoretical virtues, like that of being naturalistic.

phenomenal consciousness, which, we are granting here, is not very well understood. But unless we have reason to think that what tracking or functional role theories tell us about the nature of intentionality is *true*, the mere fact that they say more is merely a desire-satisfying virtue.

So, naturalism is a desire-satisfying virtue, but this does not support the truth of naturalistic theories. Since we are interested in finding out which theory is true, rather than which theory we should *hope to be true*, the kind of virtues we are concerned with are truth-indicating virtues. The question, then, is whether naturalism is a truth-indicating virtue. The answer, again, is "yes," but this does not support naturalistic theories over PIT. Naturalism is a truth-indicating virtue because it is a special case of a more general truth-indicating virtue, that of appealing only to things that exist, a point that brings us back to the points of Mendelovici and Bourget 2014 discussed above. Since (let us grant) the naturalistic items invoked by naturalistic theories of intentionality exist, naturalistic theories appeal only to things that exist. But, given that phenomenal consciousness exists, PIT also appeals only to things that exist, so it also has the more general truth-indicating virtue of appealing only to things that exist. While commitment to an ontology consisting only of naturalistic items is a truth-indicating virtue, so too, and for the same reasons, is commitment to an ontology consisting only of naturalistic items *and* consciousness. So, naturalism provides no support of the truth of naturalistic theories over PIT.

We might add that the idea that we need to weigh all the virtues and vices of competing theories before deciding between them is attractive but incorrect—and, in the case of the dispute between the theories under consideration, particularly misleading. It suggests that the tracking and functional role theories can accept the mismatch problem and the Real Problem as vices but "make up" for them with other virtues. But, as suggested in §3.8, some vices are simply unforgivable. The mismatch problem shows that tracking theories and the best versions of functional role theories are empirically inadequate. They make the wrong predictions in certain paradigm cases of intentionality. But empirical inadequacy is not a vice you can make up for with other virtues. If a theory is empirically inadequate, it is false. Even if naturalism were a truth-indicating virtue that favored tracking and functional role theories over PIT, this would not make up for their being *false*.[10]

6.5 Conclusion

Making sense of how an identity theory like strong identity PIT can be nontrivial and interesting and how it can shed light on a phenomenon, particularly when it

---

[10] See also Mendelovici 2010, ch. 8 and Mendelovici and Bourget 2014 for similar points.

does not reveal an underlying structure of constituent parts, is tricky, but I have argued that there is good sense to be made of strong identity PIT's status as a theory of intentionality. For those who are still taken by the idea that PIT is in some sense uninformative as a theory, note that many contemporary philosophers have assumed or argued that it is false, which alone suggests that it is nontrivial and interesting.

In short, PIT is a legitimate contender for a theory of intentionality, one that is worth taking seriously. Let us now turn to how it can be made to work.

IV Challenging Cases

IN THE PREVIOUS part, we saw that PIT is a well-motivated theory of intentionality, succeeding precisely where alternative theories fail. However, we also saw that PIT faces challenges in accommodating various kinds of mental states. This part turns to these challenging cases: Chapter 7 considers the case of thoughts, including thoughts with broad contents and object-involving contents, and Chapter 8 considers nonconscious states, including standing states and nonconscious occurrent states. I will argue that there are natural PIT-friendly ways of treating these challenging cases that can be motivated largely on independent grounds.

This part has two aims: First, in showing how PIT can deal with apparently problematic cases in natural and uncontorted ways, I hope to show that the theory is viable and interesting. Second, by seeing how PIT might be developed in a wide range of cases, I hope to further flesh out and motivate my favored version of PIT. On my view, which is a version of strong PIT, the intentional mind is restricted to the phenomenal mind, which is itself fairly limited, but derived mental representation and other representation-like phenomena play many of the roles that intentionality might have previously been thought to play.

7 Thought

IN PREVIOUS CHAPTERS, I argued for the phenomenal intentionality theory (PIT), the view that all original intentionality arises from phenomenal consciousness. Thoughts are a challenging case for PIT, since we at least sometimes take them to represent a variety of contents that do not seem to match their corresponding phenomenal characters, such as rich, complex, and sophisticated descriptive contents, object-involving contents, and broad contents.

This chapter argues that thoughts have both phenomenal contents and derived contents, which are derived from phenomenal contents, and that the above-mentioned problematic contents are merely derivatively represented.

I proceed as follows: §7.1 clarifies the challenge, §7.2 argues that thoughts have phenomenal contents, §7.3 argues that many of thoughts' alleged contents are derivatively represented, and §7.4 argues that derived mental representation is not a kind of intentionality, which makes the proposed view of thought content compatible with strong PIT.

7.1 The Challenge for PIT from Thought

Thoughts are occurrent intentional mental states that we are in when we do what we commonly call "thinking." Judgments, entertainings, occurrent beliefs, and occurrent desires count as thoughts, but perceptual experiences, emotional experiences, and standing states do not. My focus in this chapter is on thoughts that we are in some sense aware of having. Thoughts that we are not in any sense aware of having, if there are any, are instances of allegedly nonconscious occurrent states and are covered by what I say about such states in Chapter 8.[1]

I will assume that the vehicles of intentionality underlying thoughts are made up of **concepts**, which are subpropositional representations involved primarily in thoughts. For example, the thought that Mitten is a cat might involve the concepts MITTEN and CAT, which represent the contents <Mitten> and <cat>, respectively. For convenience, I will structure much of the discussion around the contents of concepts.[2]

The problem with thoughts and the concepts they involve is that their **alleged contents**—the contents they are often thought to have, either on the basis of intuition or on the basis of philosophical or psychological theory—do not seem to be phenomenal contents, so it is not clear how exactly PIT can account for them. To see the problem, let us consider in some detail the case of the concept WATER, which might be taken to represent a reference-fixing descriptive content like <the clear, potable liquid that flows from taps, is essential for human life, and fills rivers, lakes, seas, and oceans around here>, a descriptive content that doesn't serve to fix on a referent, like <clear, potable liquid>, or an object-involving content, like <H_2O>, which involves the externally existing kind H_2O. Some of these contents, like <H_2O>, might be broad contents, contents the representation of which is at least partly determined by environmental factors.

It is implausible that WATER phenomenally represents the above-mentioned contents. To see why, consider the phenomenal character corresponding to the use of the concept WATER, or, in short, WATER's phenomenal character. There are different views of what this phenomenal character might be, which we can organize in terms of a distinction that is sometimes made between conservative and liberal views of cognitive phenomenology. According to **conservatism**, there

---

[1] In this chapter, I am mainly concerned with providing a PIT-friendly account of the *contents* of thoughts, not of their *attitudes*, e.g., the attitudes of judgment or desire. I discuss the prospects of combining my account with various views of the attitudes in Appendix E of this chapter, which is best read after the rest of the chapter.

[2] See also n. 10 of Chapter 1.

are no phenomenal characters beyond **sensory phenomenal characters**, which might include perceptual, imagistic, verbal, and emotional phenomenal characters. A conservative view of WATER's phenomenal character might take it to consist in verbal imagery of the word "water" or visual imagery of water.

According to **liberalism**, there are **cognitive phenomenal characters**, which are non-sensory phenomenal characters that are special to thoughts in that they do not generally occur in other types of mental states, such as perceptual states, bodily sensations, or emotional states. A possible liberal view of WATER's phenomenal character is that it is or includes a simple or sui generis water-ish phenomenal character, a phenomenal character that is not normally found outside of thought. Other possible liberal views take it to be a complex cognitive phenomenal character corresponding to various aspects of WATER's alleged content.[3]

The problem is that WATER's alleged contents do not seem to match[4] its phenomenal character, whether it is a sensory phenomenal character consisting of verbal and perceptual imagery, a complex cognitive phenomenal character, or a simple sui generis cognitive water-ish phenomenal character. For instance, WATER's alleged descriptive contents, like <the clear, potable liquid that flows from taps, is essential for human life, and fills rivers, lakes, seas, and oceans around here>, are quite complex and nuanced, specifying many of water's features, such as its being clear, potable, and essential for human life. These contents fail to match the sensory or cognitive phenomenal characters that WATER might be said to have. WATER's alleged object-involving content, $<H_2O>$, also does not match its phenomenal character: there doesn't seem to be anything particularly H_2O-ish about our phenomenal state when we use the concept WATER, especially if we don't know that water is H_2O. Since WATER's alleged contents don't match its phenomenal character, it is implausible that these contents are phenomenally represented. Similar claims hold for other concepts and thoughts.[5]

We can isolate the following two challenges facing PIT in the case of thought, which will correspond to the two parts of my proposal:

---

[3] See Strawson 1994, Siewert 1998, Horgan and Tienson 2002, Pitt 2004, Chudnoff 2015a, Kriegel 2015b, and Montague 2016 for arguments for liberalism and Tye and Wright 2011 for a defense of conservatism. See also Bayne and Montague 2011 for a representative collection of essays on cognitive phenomenology.

[4] Content A matches item B (which may or may not be a content) when all the features of A's superficial character are had by B. See n. 9 of Chapter 5 for this extended sense of "match."

[5] Further, unless intrinsic duplicates have thoughts with different phenomenal characters, broad contents can't be phenomenal contents. And unless these phenomenal characters literally involve external objects as constituents, which I take to be prima facie implausible (except perhaps in cases of object-involving contents about our own mental states or their contents or phenomenal characters), they cannot capture object-involving contents. (See §5.4.)

Challenge 1: Specify the phenomenal content of thoughts.

Challenge 2: Accommodate the alleged contents of thoughts.

One might reject either challenge. For example, one might maintain that thoughts do not have phenomenal contents at all, though perhaps they derivatively represent something like their alleged contents. Such a view is somewhat against the spirit of most versions of PIT, which take phenomenal intentionality to be pervasive (see, e.g., Horgan and Tienson 2002, Pitt 2004), and, if we think that thoughts do have phenomenal characters, it is incompatible with the claim that all phenomenal states give rise to original intentionality, which I want to accept (see Appendix B of Chapter 5). In any case, in what follows, I argue that thoughts do have phenomenal contents and so that this challenge, whether or not we should accept it, is met.

One might reject the second challenge by questioning our reasons for taking thoughts to represent some of the above-mentioned alleged contents. For example, a descriptivist might question whether thoughts represent object-involving contents, and an internalist might question whether they represent broad contents (see Farkas 2008a and Pitt 1999). While I am sympathetic to these positions, I think that we in some important sense take ourselves to represent such contents, as evidenced by the fact that many of us have strong intuitions in their favor. Object-involving and broad contents figure in our best ways of understanding ourselves and the commitments our thoughts carry. This is reason to want to find a theoretical home for these alleged contents. The same goes for other alleged contents that we might be tempted to reject. In any case, as we will see, a virtue of my account is that it does not force any individual to accept any alleged contents that she does not in some sense antecedently accept.[6]

In what follows, I develop an account that responds to both challenges. My proposal meets the first challenge by specifying a kind of thought content apart from thoughts' alleged contents that *is* plausibly phenomenally represented. It meets the second challenge by specifying a way in which thoughts derivatively mentally represent many of their alleged contents. Appendix D argues that a similar strategy can be used to capture some allegedly non-phenomenal contents in perception.[7]

---

[6] Note that it is our intuitions, not our introspective access to our own intentional states, that motivate taking object-involving contents seriously. Our introspective observations can at best only tell us that we have thoughts with object-involving *superficial characters*, not thoughts that literally involve objects, i.e., thoughts with object-involving *deep natures* (see §2.2.1 for the superficial character/deep nature distinction and §9.3.1 for related discussion). See also Mendelovici 2018 for analogous points about the claim that we represent non-propositional contents.

[7] Much of the discussion of PIT in the case of thought centers on arguing for liberalism (see, e.g., Horgan and Tienson 2002 and Pitt 2004). However, as the discussion in this section shows, both liberal and

7.2 Thoughts' Phenomenal Contents

This section argues that thought has a kind of content that is distinct from its alleged content and that is a good candidate for being thought's phenomenal content. This content, which I call **immediate content**, is the content that "runs through our minds" or that is immediately available to us when we are in an intentional mental state. Subsection 7.2.1 argues that thoughts have immediate contents, §7.2.2 argues that thoughts' immediate contents are distinct from their alleged contents, §7.2.3 discusses some congenial philosophical and scientific views of concepts, and §7.2.4 argues that immediate contents are good candidates for being thoughts' phenomenal contents.

7.2.1 THOUGHTS HAVE IMMEDIATE CONTENTS

Immediate contents are the contents we are immediately aware of when we are in an intentional mental state. Metaphorically, they are the contents that are "before our mind's eye," or that "run through our heads." My claim is that thoughts, at least the ones that we are in any sense aware of, have immediate contents. For example, when it suddenly occurs to you that you have been lecturing past the end of class or that the department meeting was yesterday, not today, there is some content that you entertain and that you are aware of. What you are aware of in these cases are your thoughts' immediate contents.[8,9]

One might agree that in the above examples we are aware of *something* but suggest that what we are aware of is not a content. Perhaps what we are aware of are mere fleeting phenomenal characters, the representations involved in thoughts, or our representing a certain content. Let us consider these alternatives in turn.

---

conservative advocates of PIT face a challenge in accounting for the alleged contents of thoughts, so the truth of liberalism is not enough to avoid the problems with thought. As we will soon see, my general strategy for solving the problems is compatible with both liberalism and conservatism, though my preferred version of this strategy happens to be a liberal one. All this shows that, perhaps surprisingly, the success or failure of a PIT-friendly account of thought content does not stand or fall with the truth of liberalism. (Thanks to Charles Siewert for encouraging me to emphasize these points. See also Siewert 1998 for a congenial way of thinking of the issues.)

[8] By "immediate contents" I do not mean contents that directly acquaint us with their targets, that we know without mediation, or that have some other special epistemological status (though it might turn out that immediate contents have some such features). I simply mean the contents that we have "before our mind's eye" when we have a thought—no more, no less.

[9] Although my focus is on thought, perceptual states also have immediate contents. When you perceive a dog, your perceptual state might represent various immediate contents corresponding to its shape, color, the ways it is moving, its distance away from you, and perhaps even its high-level features, such as that of being a dog (more on this in Appendix D).

The first suggestion is that what we are aware of are mere phenomenal characters, phenomenal characters that are not *also* contents. While what we are aware of might be phenomenal characters (indeed, this is the view that I will recommend), it does not seem they are *mere* phenomenal characters. Some examples of states that might be taken to have mere phenomenal characters are pains, moods, and emotions. These states, it might be claimed, are mere raw feels (but see Appendix B of Chapter 5 for reasons to reject this view). If what we were immediately aware of in having thoughts were mere phenomenal characters, then having a thought would be as these states are claimed to be on a view on which they have mere phenomenal characters, involving an awareness of nothing more than a raw feel. But having thoughts is nothing like this. We are not aware of mere raw feels. Instead, what we seem to be immediately aware of in having a thought is something that the thought "says," i.e., a content. Indeed, the very fact that thoughts are uncontroversial as examples of intentional mental states but controversial as examples of phenomenal mental states suggests that their features that we are aware of are intentional, even if they are also phenomenal.

It is also implausible that what we are immediately aware of are merely the representations involved in thought, i.e., the items having intentional properties but not the intentional properties themselves. Representations might be symbols in a language of thought, brain states, functional states, or states of an immaterial soul. But it does not seem that we are aware of any such things in having a thought. Again, what we are aware of is something that thoughts "say," not the thing that does the saying.

On the most straightforward way of understanding the third suggestion that what we are immediately aware of is our thinking a particular content, it is not in conflict with my claims. According to this suggestion, we are immediately aware of two things: a content and the act of thinking that content (or the fact that we are thinking it). This suggestion agrees with my claim that there are contents that we are immediately aware of. It adds the further claim that we are immediately aware of thinking them, which is something that I am neutral on.

One might object that it is not clear that immediate contents are genuine contents because it is not clear that they have all the features required for something to qualify as a content. For example, one might suggest that contents must have, be, or determine truth conditions, play a specific role in a folk psychological theory of mental states and behavior, or figure in certain cognitive scientific, psychological, or neuroscientific theories. However, given the ostensive way we fixed reference on intentionality in Chapter 1, having any of these features is not automatically a requirement for something to count as a content. This does not mean, of course, that immediate contents do not have some or all of the aforementioned features but just that their status as contents is not dependent on their having them.

We can conclude that thoughts, and presumably the concepts they involve, have immediate contents, contents that we are immediately aware of when we are in an intentional state.

7.2.2 CONCEPTS' IMMEDIATE CONTENTS ARE DISTINCT FROM THEIR ALLEGED CONTENTS

I will now argue that the immediate contents of thoughts and concepts are distinct from their alleged contents and provide some options as to how to characterize these contents. I will start with some examples in which a concept's immediate content is distinct from its alleged contents and then argue that most cases are like my examples. I will focus on concepts, but since concepts make up the vehicles of thought, my claims apply fairly directly to thoughts as well.

Numbers and Numerals

A number concept—say, the concept of 373,987—might have as its alleged content the number 373,987 or a description of the number, perhaps involving our under-standing of succession or our ability to count. However, when we use our concept of 373,987, what we are immediately aware of is arguably not the number itself or a description of it but rather the numeral "373,987," perhaps in addition to the fact that it stands for a number or number-like thing and a rough ballpark sense of the number itself.

Bourget (2017c) argues that when we think about numbers, what we grasp are numerals, not numbers. The considerations he uses to argue for his claim also support my claim that the immediate contents of our number concepts are numerals rather than numbers or descriptions of numbers. One intuitive consideration is that, as far as what is in our immediate awareness is concerned, it seems that numerals like "373,987" could stand for entirely different numbers than they in fact stand for, which suggests that when we use such numerals, we are not immediately aware of the numbers or descriptions of numbers they stand for. Another consideration is that the same arithmetic equations seem more or less obvious depending on the notation we use to symbolize them. For example, seeing that $7 \times 100 = 700$ is easy in decimal notation but difficult in binary notation ($111 \times 1100100 = 1010111100$). This suggests that, at least when dealing with large numbers, we perform number-related tasks by working with numerals, not numbers or descriptions of numbers. This in turn suggests that in many cases when we use our number concepts, the contents we are immediately aware of are not numbers themselves but only numerals (perhaps together with a sense that they stand for numbers or number-like things and a ballpark sense of the magnitudes of the numbers they stand for).

We can think of our number concepts' immediate contents as mental tags or symbols standing for numbers or related contents. In most cases, when we think number-related thoughts, our immediate contents involve these tags, instead of what we in some sense take them to stand for. This might be because it is easier or more efficient for us to be immediately aware of numerals and related contents than of numbers or descriptions of numbers, or because we are simply unable to become immediately aware of numbers or descriptions of numbers themselves.[10]

If all this is right, then number concepts have immediate contents that are distinct from their alleged contents.

Stipulated Concepts

Suppose that while working through some complicated philosophical reasoning, you reach an intermediary conclusion—say, that physicalism is committed to the a priori entailment of the phenomenal facts by the physical facts. You might stipulate <Let Ent = physicalism is committed to the a priori entailment of the phenomenal facts by the physical facts>. You might then use your ad hoc concept ENT in your further deliberations. For instance, you might use it to represent to yourself a premise in an argument against physicalism.

ENT might be said to have as its alleged content the content you defined it as standing for, <physicalism is committed to the a priori entailment of the phenomenal facts by the physical facts>. However, when you use ENT, this content is not running through your head in its entirety; it is not what you are immediately aware of. Instead, what you are immediately aware of is another content, <Ent>, which might consist in the word "Ent," mental imagery, a gisty, partial, or schematic understanding of ENT's stipulated definition, or a "new" simple or sui generis content.

Note that the key observation is not that you have difficulty putting the content of ENT into words or that you can use the concept without doing so. It is that when you use ENT, you do not seem to be immediately aware of its alleged content (its stipulated definition). You can see this from the fact that using ENT does not seem to come with an immediate awareness of the notions of physicalism or a priority. In contrast, when you entertain ENT's stipulated definition, perhaps by spelling it out to yourself, you *are* immediately aware of such notions or something nearby. This difference between what you are immediately aware of when you use ENT and when

---

[10] Bourget (2017c) argues that, at least in the case of large numbers, we think in numerals because we are simply unable to grasp the corresponding numbers.

you entertain its stipulated definition suggests that what you are immediately aware of when you use ENT is not its alleged content.

Just as we can think of numerals as tags for numbers or other related contents, we can think of <Ent> as a mental tag for ENT's stipulated definition. When we reason using ENT, we do not run its entire stipulated definition through our heads. Instead, we are only immediately aware of the simpler content <Ent>, which we in some sense accept as standing for the full definition. As in the case of number concepts, being immediately aware of <Ent> might be easier or more efficient than being immediately aware of ENT's full definition.

If all this is right, then ENT has an immediate content that is distinct from its alleged contents.

I want to suggest that these claims about number concepts and stipulated concepts apply more generally to pretty much all concepts. What we are typically immediately aware of when we use concepts is not their alleged contents but rather some simpler immediate contents that serve as mental tags for their alleged contents.

Earlier, we saw that concepts have various kinds of alleged contents: reference-fixing descriptions, descriptions that do not serve to fix reference, and object-involving contents. In order to argue that concepts' immediate contents are not their alleged contents, I will consider these various types of alleged contents in turn and argue that, in most cases, they are not concepts' immediate contents.

Reference-fixing descriptive contents contain enough information to zero in on a referent, but it is implausible that we are immediately aware of all this information every time we use a concept.[11] For example, the concept SUPERVENIENCE might represent the reference-fixing description <Properties in class A supervene on properties in class B iff all worlds that are alike with respect to the B properties are alike with respect to the A properties>, but, just as we are not immediately aware of the full stipulated definition of ENT every time we use the concept, we are not immediately aware of SUPERVENIENCE's full definition every time we use that concept.

Descriptive contents that serve to merely characterize a concept's referent, rather than to fix reference on it, also contain more information about a concept's target than we seem to be immediately aware of when we use the concept. For example, the concept BIRD might be taken to represent a prototype (Rosch 1975), which might include features such as having wings, having feathers, laying eggs, and having the ability to fly. But when we think <Tweety is a bird>, we are not immediately aware

---

[11] Indeed, largely thanks to Kripke (1972), it is controversial that we in any sense have such information. But see Jackson 1998a, Kroon 1987, and the arguments to come for defenses of the claim.

of all this information pertaining to birds. Perhaps we use this information to classify Tweety as a bird or to make inferences about Tweety's features based on the fact that he is a bird, but this does not require that it is immediately running through our minds when we think <Tweety is a bird>.

It might seem that object-involving contents, like worldly properties, kinds, and objects, are better candidates for being concepts' immediate contents. Perhaps when we use the concepts SUPERVENIENCE, BIRD, and WATER, we are immediately aware of the supervenience relation itself, the kind *bird*, and the kind H_2O, respectively. However, although we can name these contents with simple expressions, like "the supervenience relation," "the kind *bird*," and "the kind H_2O," these kinds of contents are oftentimes quite complex and hidden from us in a way that makes it implausible that they are our immediate contents. The supervenience relation is the relation that obtains between pairs of classes of properties when a world cannot differ with respect to the properties in one, supervening, class without differing with respect to the properties in the other class. If the supervenience relation were SUPERVENIENCE's content, it would be quite complex, just like the concept's corresponding descriptive content. Again, it is implausible that we are immediately aware of such a content every time we think about supervenience.

Similarly, the kind H_2O is the kind composed of molecules containing two hydrogen atoms and one oxygen atom, which is arguably more complex and sophisticated than what we are immediately aware of when we think about water. It is also hidden from us in that we in no sense have immediate access to all this information about H_2O on the basis of our WATER concept alone, which suggests that we are not immediately aware of such a content. The kind *bird* might similarly be a kind that has a particular genetic profile or evolutionary history. Again, this kind would make for quite a complex, sophisticated, and hidden content, and, again, it is implausible that we become immediately aware of it just by using the concept BIRD.

If the foregoing is right, then most concepts do not immediately represent their alleged contents. Now, as in the cases of number concepts and stipulated concepts, we are still aware of *something* when we use concepts like SUPERVENIENCE, BIRD, and WATER, so these concepts have immediate contents of some sort. And again, there are various options as to what these immediate contents might be: A concept's immediate contents might be or partly consist in inner speech (e.g., the word "supervenience"); mental imagery (e.g., a mental image of one thing above another); a gisty, partial, or schematic grasp of the concept's alleged contents (e.g., an idea of some kind of logical dependence); a sui generis, perhaps simple, content, not understandable in terms of other contents (e.g., a notion of supervenience as its own kind of thing); or a combination of these options. It is an open question which of these kinds of contents are any given concept's immediate contents, and the answer might differ for concepts of different items or for concepts of the same item had by different subjects or by the same subject on different occasions. We will discuss these options in more detail in §7.2.4.

For now, though, we can conclude that, like number concepts and stipulated concepts, most concepts have immediate contents, and these immediate contents are distinct from their alleged contents. Like number concepts and stipulated concepts, it might even make sense to describe immediate contents as serving as tags standing for more complex contents that are beyond our immediate awareness. It might be easier or more efficient for us to bring these simpler immediate contents to mind than our concepts' full alleged contents, or we might simply be unable to become immediately aware of these alleged contents.

7.2.3 THIN AND THICK CONCEPTS

The view that thoughts and concepts have immediate contents that are distinct from their alleged contents is congenial to some views in philosophy, psychology, and neuroscience that draw similar distinctions between the concepts used in thought and other mental activities pertaining to an item, on the one hand, and fuller representations we have of that item, on the other.

Barsalou (1993, 1999) distinguishes between what he calls "concepts," which are temporary constructions in working memory that allow one to perform certain tasks relating to an item, such as tasks involving categorization or inference drawing, and one's body of knowledge pertaining to an item, which is stored in long-term memory. Barsalou's concepts are constructed on the fly from one's body of knowledge in long-term memory. Since concepts are constructed based on the demands of the task at hand, we can have multiple concepts relating to any given item. For Barsalou, both concepts and the relevant bodies of knowledge are largely perceptual, in that their contents are derived from perception.

Prinz (2002) defends a similar view that distinguishes between "proxytypes" corresponding to an item, which are temporary constructions in working memory, and long-term memory networks, which contain the full body of knowledge we have concerning the item. Proxytypes are so called because thinking and other concept-involving tasks make use of them *in place* of their corresponding long-term memory network. So, for example, while we have a long-term memory network containing diverse representations of dogs, when we think about dogs, we do not make use of this entire network but only a part of it, which in some sense stands for the whole. Like Barsalou, Prinz takes proxytypes to be constructed on the fly, so which part of our dog network we use on any given occasion depends on the task at hand. And, again like Barsalou, Prinz takes both proxytypes and long-term memory networks to be perceptual.

Views of learning and concepts that are based on **chunking**, the process by which a larger number of individual chunks of information are bundled together to form a smaller number of chunks of information (Miller 1956), are also congenial to my proposal. For example, Wickelgren (1979, 1992) claims that when we learn a new concept or proposition, a new cell assembly representing a new idea (a "chunk idea") is recruited to stand for a group of old cell assemblies representing old ideas (the "constituent ideas"). The new and old cell assemblies are associatively linked in both directions, allowing us to move from the chunk idea to the constituent ideas and vice versa. What is interesting about Wickelgren's picture is that chunking involves not only the association of "constituent ideas" with one another but also the recruitment of new "chunk ideas" to in some sense stand for them. Similar ideas are found in Hebb (1949) and elsewhere.

Along similar lines, Eliasmith (2013) proposes a theory of neural processing that posits what he calls "semantic pointers." Semantic pointers are *pointers* because they "point" to more sophisticated representations, in much the same way that a pointer in a computer program points to information stored at a particular memory location. Semantic pointers are *semantic* because they are themselves representations that contain information—they contain a "lossy" compressed version of the information present in the more sophisticated representations that they point to. On Eliasmith's view, much cognition involves operations over pointers rather than what they point to, but, when needed, semantic pointers can be "dereferenced" to access the information that they point to.

The above views roughly claim that there are two distinct types of concepts and contents corresponding to categories or other represented items: "thin" concepts with correspondingly "thin" contents, which suffice for many tasks relating to the item, and "thick" concepts with correspondingly "thick" contents, which correspond to a fuller understanding of the item. Not only are these thin and thick concepts distinct, but, on most of these views, their contents are also distinct. For Eliasmith, thin concepts represent lossy compressed versions of their corresponding thick contents, while for Prinz and Barsalou, thin concepts represent proper parts of their corresponding thick contents.

These thin contents roughly correspond to my immediate contents, while the thick contents even more roughly correspond to the kinds of derived contents that I will introduce later. Like immediate contents, thin contents are the contents of occurrent thoughts, though thin contents are often taken to play other roles, such as roles in recognitional tasks, which immediate contents might or might not play.

In short, my immediate contents are, more or less, the thin contents that occur in thoughts.[12]

I will say more about derived content shortly, but for now it is worth noting that derived contents need not correspond to the thick contents described by the above views. As we will see, derived contents correspond to what we take ourselves to represent, which might include reference-fixing descriptive contents, object-involving contents, and broad contents. None of these contents need correspond to existing structures in the brain, so they need not have the same kind of psychological reality as thick concepts are supposed to have on the above views.

7.2.4 THOUGHTS' PHENOMENAL CONTENTS

The first challenge facing PIT in the case of thought is that of specifying thoughts' phenomenal contents. In setting out this challenge, we saw that the alleged contents of thoughts and concepts do not match their phenomenal characters, so they are unlikely candidates for being thoughts' phenomenal contents. In the previous subsections, we also saw that thoughts and concepts have immediate contents, which are distinct from their alleged contents. These immediate contents, I want to suggest, are thoughts' phenomenal contents.

We can support the claim that thoughts' immediate contents are phenomenal contents with an argument from matching, similar to the argument for PIT in §5.2.1. If thoughts' immediate contents match their phenomenal characters, it is plausible that they are phenomenally represented. To make this argument, I will consider several broad options regarding which immediate contents any given concept represents and argue that on all these options, it is quite plausible that concepts have matching phenomenal characters.

A concept might have a verbal, affective, perceptual, or other kind of **sensory immediate content**. For example, the concept SUPERVENIENCE's immediate content might be the word "supervenience" and a visual image of one thing above another. This view is congenial to Barsalou and Prinz's neo-empiricist views of concepts, on which thin concepts represent perceptual contents. For example, they might say that a concept of a dog represents the word "dog" or an image of a dog, which is drawn from a thicker concept of a dog that includes these and other contents.

---

[12] Another way in which thin contents might go beyond immediate contents is for there to be nonconscious thoughts that have thin contents but not immediate contents.

It is not implausible that concepts with sensory immediate contents also have matching sensory phenomenal characters. For example, if SUPERVENIENCE's immediate content is simply a quasi-auditory content corresponding to the word "supervenience" and a visual image of one thing above another, then it is not implausible that it has a matching quasi-auditory and visual phenomenal character. This suggestion would only commit us to sensory phenomenal characters, so it is compatible with conservatism about cognitive phenomenology.

A concept might instead, or in addition, have a **schematic immediate content**, an immediate content that is a compressed, gisty, abstract, or otherwise schematic version of its corresponding thick or alleged content. For example, the immediate content of SUPERVENIENCE might be a gisty unarticulated grasp of a definition of supervenience, with aspects corresponding to various parts of the definition. This option is congenial to views of thin contents on which they are "lossy" compressed or schematic versions of thick contents, like Eliasmith's view. Such contents might include a gisty or abstract characterization of thick contents without including all their details.

Again, it is not implausible that concepts with schematic immediate contents have matching schematic phenomenal characters. For example, if SUPERVENIENCE's immediate content is a gisty unarticulated grasp of a definition of supervenience, it is not implausible that it has a matching gisty supervenience-ish feel. The schematic phenomenal characters suggested by this proposal might be abstract or otherwise schematic sensory phenomenal characters, in which case they can be accepted by the conservative about cognitive phenomenology. Alternatively, they might be schematic phenomenal characters unique to thought, which only the liberal can accept.

A concept might instead, or in addition, have a unique, special, or **sui generis immediate content**, an immediate content that is not simply a part of its alleged contents but that is a "new" content, all of its own. Such immediate contents might be internally unstructured, not having parts that are also contents. Perhaps, for example, the content that occurs to us when we think about knowledge is not some partial grasp of our full understanding of knowledge but rather a "new" sui generis simple content, <knowledge!>. Such a view is consistent with Wickelgren's proposal that entirely new chunk ideas get recruited to stand for their corresponding chunk constituents.

Again, it is not implausible that concepts with sui generis immediate contents have matching sui generis phenomenal characters, phenomenal characters that are not just parts of their alleged contents. For example, if KNOWLEDGE's immediate content is a sui generis unstructured content, it is not implausible that it has a matching sui generis unstructured knowledge-ish phenomenal character. This proposal is most clearly compatible with a liberal conception of cognitive phenomenology, since it is unclear on what basis we could plausibly maintain that the required sui generis phenomenal characters are sensory.[13]

The above kinds of contents are not mutually exclusive: An immediate content might qualify as being of more than one kind. For example, an abstract perceptual immediate content might qualify as both sensory and schematic, and, as I will suggest below, an immediate content can be both schematic and sui generis.

The above options can also be combined in that an immediate content might include parts or aspects of different kinds. For example, the concept BIRD might have an immediate content that includes a sensory content involving visual imagery of a bird as well as a schematic content involving a gisty grasp of the fact that birds are a kind of animal. The concept KNOWLEDGE might have an immediate content with a sensory component involving quasi-auditory imagery of the word "knowledge," a schematic component involving a schematic grasp of knowledge's relations to truth, justification, and belief, and a simple sui generis <knowledge!> component. As before, it is not implausible that concepts with such immediate contents that are combinations of sensory, schematic, or simple components have matching combined phenomenal characters.

It could also be that we have multiple concepts corresponding to a given category or other item, each with different immediate contents. Indeed, this seems likely, given the plausible claim that what exactly enters in our immediate awareness corresponding to a given item seems to differ in different circumstances. This is very much in line with Barsalou and Prinz's claim that concepts are created on the fly based on task demands. Again, if what enters our immediate awareness corresponding to an item differs in different circumstances, it is not implausible that our phenomenal characters differ as well.

I have outlined various options as to concepts' immediate contents and phenomenal characters, suggesting that it is quite plausible on all the options that immediate contents and phenomenal characters match. There may be strong phenomenological or other considerations for preferring one set of options to another for any given concept, but for the purposes of defending PIT, it does not really matter which set of options we accept, so I will leave the question open.

However, before continuing, I will digress to mention one view that I find attractive, which is that most concepts' immediate contents are (or at least include a part or aspect that is) sui generis, simple, and schematic, involving a gisty grasp

---

[13] But see Bayne and Spener 2010 and Mendelovici and Bourget 2013 for relevant discussion of the unclarities of the sensory/non-sensory distinction.

of some parts or aspects of their corresponding alleged contents. This might be possible if immediate contents are (or have parts or aspects that are) **internally unstructured**, in that they do not involve proper parts that are also immediate contents, but **externally structured**, in that they have properties of having values on certain dimensions.[14] An example of such internally unstructured but externally structured contents is the contents of perceptual color representations. Any given color content is internally unstructured, not literally having hues, saturations, and brightnesses as distinct parts. At the same time, it is externally structured, since it has values on the dimensions of hue, saturation, and brightness.

Something similar might be true of the immediate contents of many concepts. For example, the immediate content of KNOWLEDGE might be an internally unstructured sui generis content, <knowledge!>, one that is not simply excerpted from its alleged contents, which, we might suppose, include contents like <true>, <justified>, and <belief>. Despite being internally unstructured, <knowledge!> might share properties with the contents <true>, <justified>, and <belief>. This might account for the sense we have that the immediate content of KNOWLEDGE involves some kind of inarticulate gisty grasp of some of its alleged contents. In short, <knowledge!> has properties in common with its alleged contents but does not include them as parts.

The view I find attractive, then, is that concepts' immediate contents are or include parts or aspects that are simple, sui generis, and schematic in the ways described above and that they have matching simple, sui generis, and schematic phenomenal characters. They might also, in some cases, include sensory parts or aspects with matching sensory phenomenal characters. While this is my preferred view, everything that follows is compatible with the alternative views outlined above.

So far, I have argued that concepts' immediate contents can plausibly be said to match their corresponding phenomenal characters. This makes it plausible that the immediate contents of thoughts and concepts are phenomenal contents: Either they are identical to phenomenal characters, or our representing them arises from our phenomenal states in some other way.

Indeed, it is not clear how else we could come to represent immediate contents if not phenomenally. The contents predicted by tracking and functional role theories arguably do not match thoughts' immediate contents. For example, the concept

---

[14] This terminology comes from Chalmers (2016).

    Externally structured contents are naturally represented in a multidimensional state space organized by similarity. See Churchland (1989a, 1995, 2005), Palmer (1999), and Rosenthal (2010) for various ways of developing the idea of a perceptual state space representing mental contents or other mental features based on their similarities along various dimensions.

WATER arguably tracks H_2O, or perhaps clear watery stuff, so the tracking theory can only accommodate the concept's alleged descriptive or object-involving contents. Similarly, WATER plays a functional role characteristic of a concept that represents a complex description that refers to or characterizes H_2O, or watery stuff in general, so again, the functional role theory can at best only capture WATER's alleged contents. So, tracking and functional role theories arguably face a mismatch problem in the case of thoughts' immediate contents.

If all this is right, then we can strengthen the argument from the mismatch problem against tracking theories and functional role theories discussed in Chapters 3 and 4 and the argument from matching for PIT discussed in Chapter 5: Concepts and thoughts have immediate contents that cannot be accommodated by tracking and functional role theories but that can be accommodated by PIT.

More relevant to our present purposes, we can see how we have met the first challenge, that of identifying the phenomenal contents of thoughts. I have argued that concepts have immediate contents that are distinct from their alleged contents. These immediate contents can plausibly be said to match their phenomenal characters. This makes it plausible that the phenomenal contents of concepts—and those of the thoughts they constitute—are none other than these immediate contents.[15]

7.3 Self-Ascriptivism about Thoughts' Alleged Contents

I now turn to the second challenge, that of accounting for thoughts' alleged contents, including rich descriptive contents, object-involving contents, and broad contents. I will suggest that thoughts derivatively represent these contents. On the view I will propose, **self-ascriptivism**, we derivatively represent various alleged contents by ascribing them to ourselves or our mental states.[16]

It is instructive to consider non-mental cases of derived representation. On some views, words, signs, and other non-mental items derive their contents from the contents of mental states. For example, stop signs mean <stop!> and the word "cat"

---

[15] In order to fully account for the immediate content of thought using the immediate contents of concepts, we need an account of how phenomenal contents combine to form more complex phenomenal contents. This is a general challenge for PIT, one that might be thought to arise in a particularly acute form when PIT is combined with a non-relational view of intentionality, so I defer discussion of it to §9.3.3.

[16] An early version of the view proposed here is presented in Mendelovici 2010. The current version is greatly indebted to countless discussions with David Bourget about the view itself and derived mental representation more generally.

means <cat> at least largely because we take, stipulate, or accept stop signs to mean <stop!> and "cat" to mean <cat>, where this might be a matter of our explicit and tacit intentions and agreements. In short, we might say that "cat" means <cat> and stop signs mean <stop!> because in some way or other we ascribe them these contents.

I want to suggest that a similar kind of derived representation also occurs in mental states. Just as we can ascribe contents to external objects, so too can we ascribe contents to ourselves and our mental states. Consider the stipulated concept ENT. We take its immediate content, <Ent>, to mean or stand for a more complex content, <Physicalism is committed to the a priori entailment of the phenomenal facts by the physical facts>, which we might abbreviate <Ent+>. After all, we *stipulated* that <Ent> is to stand for <Ent+>, and if we asked ourselves what we mean by <Ent>, we would answer <Ent+>. I want to suggest that because of all this, the content <Ent> derivatively represents <Ent+>, just as "cat" derivatively represents <cat>. I also want to suggest that, by extension, the *concept* ENT derivatively represents <Ent+>.

The guiding idea is that the way we target contents that we aren't immediately aware of is by in some way ascribing them to ourselves or our mental states. In slogan form, we mean what we take ourselves to mean.[17] There are different ways in which we might self-ascribe contents, some of which are more demanding than others. For example, we might overtly stipulate that one content is to stand for another, as we do in the case of ENT. A less demanding way of self-ascribing a content is by (perhaps implicitly) taking it to be what we really mean or intend by some other content.

In what follows, I elaborate upon this less demanding way of self-ascribing contents and show how it can form the basis of an account on which we derivatively represent many of our thoughts' alleged contents. My proposal is tentative and will inevitably fail to capture many subtleties. My aim is not to provide a definitive account of the minimal sufficient conditions for taking ourselves to mean a content by another content but rather to provide a proof of concept: I want to provide a realistic sketch of a picture of how we can derivatively represent rich and complex contents that are beyond our immediate awareness.

---

[17] This idea is similar in spirit to one of Frank Jackson's (2001, 1998a, 1998b) guiding ideas for his descriptivism about language, the Lockean idea that words are voluntary signs. According to this idea, the reference conditions of a word are not imposed on us by the world, but are in an important way up to us. For example, we might use "Aristotle" to refer to whatever happens to be causally related to our use of the term in such-and-such a way, but we could have just as easily used the term to refer to whoever was the teacher of Alexander.

I begin by offering an account of how we take ourselves to mean one content by another (§7.3.1) and then offer an account of derived mental representation based on it (§7.3.2). Subsection 7.3.3 explains how this meets the second challenge.[18]

7.3.1 TAKING ONE CONTENT TO MEAN ANOTHER

I suggested that a relatively undemanding way of self-ascribing a content involves taking one content to stand for or mean another. But how can we understand this taking?

As a first pass, we might say that taking one content, C, to mean another content, C+, is a matter of being disposed, upon sufficient reflection, to have thoughts stating that C "cashes out" into C+. In the case of ENT, I am disposed to have thoughts like <<Ent> just is <Ent+>> or <what I mean by <Ent> is <Ent+>>. These thoughts say that <Ent+> is an elucidation, unpacking, precisification, expansion, or, more generally, a **cashing out** of <Ent>. They say that <Ent+> is in some sense a better version of <Ent>: <Ent+> gets at what <Ent> was going after, but in a more precise, explicit, detailed, or perspicuous way.

We can call thoughts that state that an immediate content at least partly cashes out into another content **cashing out thoughts**. In some cases, such as the case of ENT, cashing out thoughts provide a complete specification of what we mean by a content. However, it is more often the case that any given cashing out thought only provides a partial specification. For example, if I ask myself what I mean by <bachelor>, I might have multiple cashing out thoughts, such as <Part of what I mean by <bachelor> is <something that's unmarried>>, <Another part of what I mean is <something that's

---

[18] Self-ascriptivism is similar in spirit to the derivativist strategies defended by Bourget (2010a), Kriegel (2011), Pautz (2013a), and other advocates of PIT in that it takes some kind of non-phenomenal representation to be determined by phenomenal intentionality. It is also similar to various proposals made by advocates of the views of thin and thick concepts described in §7.2.3, on which thin concepts (or contents) in some sense "stand for" their corresponding thick concepts (or contents). For example, Prinz's (2002) proxytypes are so called because they are *proxies* for information stored in their corresponding long-term memory networks. (See also Eliasmith 2013 and Wickelgren 1992.)

My proposal differs from these approaches in that it takes its paradigm case of derived representation to be that of conventional representation, where we derivatively represent by specifying, intending, or otherwise taking one thing to mean another. Derived mental representation, of my sort, is not simply derived in the sense of being constructed out of original intentionality or in the sense of simply being a matter of one content or concept being used in lieu of another. The derived contents my account delivers are contents that subjects target or intend, in the same way that we target or intend the contents or meanings of conventional representations. As we will see in §8.2, this makes it more plausible that self-ascriptivism's derivation mechanisms succeed in passing intentionality around from phenomenally intentional states to derived states. However, as I argue there and in §7.4, derived mental representation is not in fact a type of intentionality.

male>>, etc. These cashing out thoughts together, but not severally, specify what I mean by <bachelor>.[19,20,21]

There are a few further points to be made about cashing out thoughts.

First, the cashing out relation figuring in cashing out thoughts is transitive: If you accept that A cashes out into B and that B cashes out into C, then you are committed to A cashing out into C. For example, suppose you have the cashing out thoughts <<bachelor> cashes out into <unmarried man>> and <<unmarried man> cashes out into <unmarried male human>>. Then you are committed to <bachelor> cashing out into <unmarried male human>.

Second, the cashing out relation is such that if A cashes out into B, then for any content C that has A as an element and any content C+ that is identical to C except that in it B plays the role of A, C cashes out into C+. We can call this property that of being **inheritable**, since the cashing out relations between contents are inherited by the structured contents of which they are a part. For example, suppose you have the cashing out thought stating that <man> cashes out into <male human>. Then you are committed to <unmarried man> cashing out into <unmarried male human>.

---

[19] In some cases, due to cognitive limitations, we might not be able to entertain in a single thought what we take ourselves to mean by a content. For example, I might understand the conceivability argument against physicalism as an argument having three particular premises and a particular conclusion but, due to cognitive limitations, not be able to have a thought specifying that the full argument is a cashing out of <the conceivability argument>. Still, for each statement in the argument, I might have a cashing out thought stating that it is a statement in the argument playing a particular role. For example, I might think <By <the conceivability argument> I mean, in part, <an argument that has as a premise that zombies are conceivable>>.

[20] Cashing out thoughts that are stipulatory (e.g., <by <Ent> I hereby mean <Ent+>>) do not have truth values. But cashing out thoughts that are not stipulatory might have truth values (e.g., <<Ent> just is <Ent+>>) and might be true (e.g., <<Ent+> is an expansion of <Ent>>, on some views of the immediate contents of ENT) or false (e.g., <<Ent+>, that is what I was thinking all along by <Ent>>). For our purposes, it doesn't matter whether cashing out thoughts have truth values, and, if they do, what they are. All that matters is that we are disposed to have the relevant cashing out thoughts.

Compare: As far as derived representation in language is concerned, what matters is that we tacitly or otherwise accept that "cat" means <cat>, but it does not matter whether these acceptances have truth values or, if they do, what they are (for example, it doesn't matter if our acceptances entail that "cat" means <cat> independently of us, which presumably would be false).

[21] Chris Viger has suggested to me that the phenomenology of thought also includes a sense that our contents can be cashed out in various ways. This suggestion is plausible: It seems that we do have an awareness that our understanding of a target is not limited to what is directly before our minds at any given moment. The suggestion is also congenial to my view: If there is such a phenomenology, then we might have not only dispositions to have cashing out thoughts specifying that one content is to stand for another but also occurrently represented phenomenal contents in some sense pointing to the fact that we have such dispositions to have cashing out thoughts, which would make our contents' cashings out quite literally intended by us. Although I don't want to make this a requirement for taking a content to mean another content, a nearby view to the one that I am proposing does. See also n. 19 of Chapter 8.

Finally, cashing out thoughts specify our taking one content to mean another, but we need not actually have such thoughts in order to count as meaning one content by another. It is enough to be *disposed* to have such thoughts. For example, I need not constantly think to myself that <Ent> cashes out into <Ent+>; it is enough that I am disposed to have such thoughts.[22]

With these points in mind, we can use the notion of a cashing out thought to characterize that of taking a content to mean another content:

> (Taking) Subject S **takes** a representation's immediate content C **to mean** C+ if S has a set of dispositions to have cashing out thoughts that together specify that C cashes out into C+ (upon sufficient reflection).[23]

There are a few things to note about (Taking).

First, (Taking) makes what an immediate content cashes out into relative to a subject. This is because cashing out thoughts specify what *a subject* means by a content. Making (Taking) relative to a subject allows different subjects to take the same contents to mean different things. For example, I might take <bachelor> to mean <unmarried man>, while you might take it to mean <available man>.

Second, in (Taking), C is always an immediate content of some representation, but C+ may or may not be an immediate content of a representation. This is because, at least in the case of the kind of derived mental representation I will soon use (Taking) to define, it is always immediate contents that we take to mean something, but what we take them to mean might be either the immediate contents of other actual or potential states, or other items that are not immediate contents, such as worldly items. In the cases we have discussed so far, immediate contents cash out into other immediate contents, but §7.3.2 discusses cases in which they cash out into other items.[24]

---

[22] In Chapter 8, I argue that, strictly speaking, dispositions such as these do not count as genuinely intentional, or even derivatively representational, so strictly speaking, on my overall view, the relevant takings need not be intentional or derivatively representational mental states. (We might, though, happen to have derivatively representational states specifying that one content cashes out into another, but this is not required by my account.) See also n. 19 of Chapter 8 for why self-ascriptions need not themselves be self-ascribed in order to do their work. Thanks to Declan Smithies for prompting these clarifications.

[23] (Taking) only provides sufficient conditions for taking a content to mean another content in order to allow that there are other ways of achieving the same result. This is appropriate because the notion of taking aims to capture the somewhat fuzzy pre-theoretic idea of (perhaps tacitly) accepting that one thing stands for another.

[24] One might worry that taking C to be a content makes cashing out thoughts metasemantic, in that they are about contents, and that it is implausible that we have dispositions to have such metasemantic thoughts. However, there are undemanding ways of having metasemantic thoughts. For example, one way of thinking that I mean a content is to think the content itself and then think <*that* is what I meant>,

Third, nothing in (Taking) rules out the possibility that an immediate content C means more than one content. This would happen if the cashing out thoughts that a subject is disposed to have together specified that an immediate content cashes out into more than one content. This allows for the possibility of our taking a single immediate content to mean, for example, both a description *and* an object-involving content.

Fourth, (Taking) generally generates a plethora of contents that we take ourselves to mean. Since the cashing out relation is transitive and inheritable, we count as taking our contents to mean not just whatever content we are disposed to think they cash out into but also whatever content we are disposed to think *that* content cashes out into, whatever content is obtained by replacing any of these contents' parts with whatever we are disposed to think *they* cash out into, and so on. In this way, we can end up taking our immediate contents to mean contents that are fairly distant from what is in our immediate awareness, contents that, due to cognitive or other limitations, we might not even be able to entertain in a single mental act—or at all. This does not contradict my guiding principle that we mean what we take ourselves to mean. In effect, our cashing out thoughts state that we are more than happy to "replace" occurrences of one content in our thoughts with those of another, more precise, detailed, or perspicuous content. When we apply all these "replacements" at once, we arrive at our best understanding of the immediate content we were initially entertaining. This is the content we were in some sense targeting all along.

Finally, since what counts as sufficient reflection is vague, which contents we take our immediate contents to mean can be indeterminate. This is by design. While there are clear cases in which we take a content to mean another content, which contents we in some sense target as our meanings is often indeterminate. For example, while it might be clear that I take <Ent> to mean <Ent+>, it might be indeterminate whether I take <uncle> to cash out into <a parent's brother>, <a parent's brother or a parent's brother-in-law>, or <any older male family member>. When I entertain the content <uncle>, I might not in some sense target one of these particular contents but instead simply aim more or less in their general direction. The vagueness in the definition of (Taking) allows for this kind of indeterminacy, since we might be disposed to have different cashing out thoughts in different circumstances, and which circumstances count as the relevant ones is left a little bit open. However, an

---

where <*that*> refers to the content rather than the referent of the content. So, for example, I might think <bachelor ... unmarried man, *that* is what I meant>. In effect, this allows us to mention a content by using it. (This way of mentioning by using is similar to that described in Davidson's (1968) account of "saying that.")

alternative self-ascriptivist view might aim to specify the conditions of manifestation for the relevant dispositions more precisely so as to avoid such indeterminacy.[25,26]

7.3.2 DERIVED MENTAL REPRESENTATION

Self-ascribing contents is sufficient for derived representation, and taking one mental state to mean another is one way in which we can self-ascribe contents. So, when we take immediate content C to mean C+, C derivatively represents C+ (for us). By extension, we can say that when an intentional mental state or representation has an immediate content with derived contents, it too counts as having those derived contents.[27] So, we can specify a notion of derived mental representation as follows:[28]

(DMR) Immediate content C (and any state or vehicle with immediate content C) **derivatively represents** C+ (for S) if S takes C to mean C+.[29]

My project here is to provide a PIT-friendly account of thoughts' alleged contents, which are the contents we want to ascribe to thoughts, such as descriptive, object-involving, and broad contents. For our purposes, it is useful to distinguish between two types of alleged contents that we might want to capture, those that can be phenomenally represented, at least in principle, and those that cannot. For example, the concept MODAL REALISM might have as its alleged content a description that can, at least in principle, be phenomenally represented. In contrast, we might not be able to phenomenally represent object-involving contents like WATER's

---

[25] In earlier work (Mendelovici 2010), I provided a schema for derived mental representation that could be filled in with different manifestation conditions to yield different notions of derived mental representation, which I suggested could capture different kinds of alleged contents, which might be useful for different purposes. This approach can be combined with the present way of specifying derived mental representation to yield a pluralist view of derived contents. I have dropped this part of the picture here because I think that which contents we take ourselves to mean is indeterminate, and attempts to remove this indeterminacy, while they might indeed be useful for constructing certain notions of content useful for certain purposes, are not helpful for capturing the alleged contents we intuitively target, which is my main goal here.

[26] Buckner (2011, 2014) provides a view similar to self-ascriptivism on which a representation's content is determined by the way its subject is disposed to revise the representation in the future.

[27] This last step allows us to say that concepts and thoughts, and not just their immediate contents, derivatively represent their alleged contents, but it is not mandatory. If we do not take this last step, we can instead say that, strictly speaking, concepts do not derivatively represent their alleged contents, but their immediate contents do, which should be good enough to offer a theoretical home for alleged contents in a way compatible with PIT.

[28] For now, it does not matter whether derived representation is a kind of derived *intentionality*. We turn to this issue in §7.4.

[29] (DMR) provides only sufficient conditions for derived representation in order to allow that there are other ways of derivatively representing. We will encounter another such way in §8.3.2.

alleged content <H$_2$O>, which is the natural kind H_2O itself, and GEORGE's alleged content <George>, which is George himself, perhaps because worldly objects and kinds are simply not the kinds of things that can enter phenomenal consciousness.[30]

Again, it is instructive to consider non-mental cases of derived representation. We can distinguish between the following two ways of ascribing contents: First, we can ascribe a content by directly relating a vehicle of representation to the content itself, e.g., by stipulating that the vehicle of representation is to stand for the content. For example, we might stipulate that the word "bachelor" is to stand for <unmarried man>, a content that our stipulation directly specifies. We can call this kind of derived representation **direct derived representation**, since it involves directly specifying the derivatively represented content.

Second, we can ascribe a content by indirectly specifying it, e.g., by using a definite description or other denoting expression or mental state to pick out the content, without directly representing the content ourselves. For example, we might stipulate that a salt shaker is to stand for whoever is the funniest person alive, which might, unbeknownst to us, be Eleni. We can call this kind of derived representation **indirect derived representation**, since it involves indirectly specifying a vehicle of derived representation's content. While direct derived representation only allows us to derivatively represent contents that we can at least in principle antecedently represent independently of the derivation mechanism in question, indirect derived representation allows us to represent contents we might not even in principle be able to represent without the derivation mechanism.

The self-ascriptivist account I have suggested allows for derived mental representation of both kinds. Direct derived mental representation involves taking an immediate content to mean another immediate content, while indirect derived mental representation involves taking an immediate content to mean the referent of another immediate content. The difference between the two cases lies in the contents of the cashing out thoughts we are disposed to have. Our cashing out thoughts can directly specify that C means an immediate content *or* that C means *the referent* of an immediate content (which usually isn't itself an immediate content, though it may be).

For example, the cashing out thought <by <water>, I mean <water+>>, where <water+> is a reference-fixing description of H$_2$O, specifies that <water> cashes out into <water+>. In contrast, the cashing out thought <by <water>, I mean water+>

---

[30] I am assuming that phenomenal contents cannot include worldly objects and kinds. This seems plausible enough, at least on a view that identifies phenomenal contents with phenomenal characters (§5.3), since, presumably, phenomenal characters do not include worldly objects and kinds.

specifies that <water> cashes out into water+ *itself*, i.e., whatever <water+> refers to, which, let's say, is the kind H_2O. The key difference between the two cashing out thoughts is that in the second, <water+> is used, and so has its usual referent, H_2O, while in the first, it is mentioned. As a result, a subject disposed to have the first cashing out thought means <water+> by <water>, while a subject disposed to have the second cashing out thought means <H_2O>, which is just H_2O itself, by <water>.[31]

The above example illustrates how my account can capture descriptive contents (like the reference-fixing description <water+>) through direct derived representation, and object-involving contents (like the kind-involving content <H_2O>) through indirect derived representation. The example of the object-involving content <H_2O> is also an example of the indirect derived representation of a broad content. Oscar and Toscar have the same dispositions to have cashing out thoughts, but, since their environments are importantly different, <water+> picks out different kinds for them. So, they indirectly derivatively represent different contents, with Oscar derivatively representing <H_2O> and Toscar derivatively representing <XYZ>.

Deferential contents are a special case of indirect derived representation that can yield both descriptive and object-involving broad contents. Suppose I am disposed to have the cashing out thought <by <water>, I mean whatever the experts mean by "water">. Then my concept WATER derivatively represents whatever experts happen to mean by "water." If what experts mean by "water" is a descriptive content like <water+>, then my representation WATER indirectly derivatively represents this descriptive content. If what experts mean by "water" is the object-involving content <H_2O>, then my representation indirectly derivatively represents this object-involving content.[32] This example also illustrates how indirect derived representation yields broad contents, which can be either descriptive or object-involving: in both of these deferential cases, my content is a broad content, since which content

---

[31] In this example, WATER refers to H_2O via a reference-fixing description, <water+>. More generally, the self-ascriptivist proposal is congenial to descriptivism, providing a psychological home for reference-fixing descriptions in our dispositions to have cashing out thoughts. Descriptivism is controversial due to arguments by Kripke (1972), Putnam (1975), and others, but, as we will soon see, self-ascriptivism can supply the building blocks necessary to answer such arguments along the lines suggested by Kroon (1987), Jackson (1998a), and Chalmers (2002, 2012), including deference to our past, future, or ideal selves, our recognitional abilities, and rigidified, causal, and metalinguistic descriptions. In any case, my proposal is compatible with other views of reference. What is required for us to indirectly derivatively represent a content is that we can refer to it.

[32] What the experts mean by "water" is presumably a matter of the derived content of the experts' concept WATER, which is, presumably, not itself deferential in the same way.

it is that I represent depends on environmental factors, namely, what experts mean by "water."

Another kind of deferential content involves deferring to past stages of ourselves or ourselves in certain idealized circumstances. For example, suppose that after a long night at the bar, I am unable to recall what I stipulated <Ent> to mean. I might nonetheless have the cashing out thought <by <Ent>, I mean whatever I meant by <Ent> yesterday> or <by <Ent>, I mean whatever I would mean while sober and well-rested>. Again, this sort of indirect derived representation allows for both descriptive and object-involving broad contents.[33]

Note that all this is compatible with my guiding idea that we mean what we take ourselves to mean. Although in deferential cases, we hand over control of our meanings to someone else or to a different version of ourselves, we do this willingly. Indeed, all cases of indirect mental representation involve willingly handing over control of our meanings.[34]

Another special case worth mentioning is that of recognitional concepts. There are two kinds of recognitional concepts we can use my account to make sense of. The first kind is an instance of direct derived representation. Suppose that the alleged content of TART is a particular range of contents of taste experiences, which we recognize when we encounter but have no other means of characterizing. Here is how my account can capture this content: For each instance of a taste content in the range, we are disposed to have a partial cashing out thought stating that tartness is such that *that* instance is an instance of tartness. These partial cashing out thoughts together specify that the immediate content of TART cashes out into this range of taste contents. By (Taking) and (DMR), TART then derivatively represents this range of taste contents.

Indirect derived representation allows us to make sense of a second kind of recognitional concept, one whose derived content is or is determined by the set of worldly items that a concept in some sense applies to. This kind of recognitional

---

[33] Whether deferring to past or future stages of oneself necessarily yields contents that are broad depends on whether we count historical or future facts concerning the state of a subject from the skin in as environmental facts. If we do, then the kind of content obtained from past and future deference is automatically broad, but if we do not, then it may be narrow. (See Farkas 2008b for relevant discussion of how to construe internalism.)

[34] The guiding idea that we mean what we take ourselves to mean is also why I do not want to say that what we take a content to mean depends on our dispositions to have cashing out thoughts in ideal or otherwise "good" circumstances. If we meant what we would mean in ideal or otherwise "good" circumstances, this would impose contents on us that we might not intend. My inebriated self at the bar who insists that by <supervenience> she means <a relation of metaphysical priority and dependence> has just as much of a right to mean what she takes herself to mean as my sober self in "good" circumstances.

concept involves being disposed to have cashing out thoughts stating that an immediate content partially cashes out into whatever is the referent of certain other immediate contents. For example, suppose that for each instance of a taste content in a particular range, we are disposed to have a partial cashing out thought stating that tartness is such that the referent of *that* instance is an instance of tartness. These cashing out thoughts together specify that the immediate content of TART cashes out into that particular range of worldly properties, and so, by (Taking) and (DMR), TART derivatively represents the object-involving content consisting in that range of properties.

Recognitional concepts of both sorts might be quite common, with apparently sophisticated concepts being recognitional or having a recognitional part. For instance, perhaps we are disposed to have cashing out thoughts stating that <knowledge> partially cashes out into a partial description like <a mental state that involves having a true, justified belief> and, for each case in a certain class of cases, cashing out thoughts stating that knowledge is such that *that* case is an instance of knowledge. By (Taking) and (DMR), KNOWLEDGE derivatively represents the partial description and the class of cases. This might be the best way to capture what we take <knowledge> to mean. The same might be true of many other concepts.[35]

7.3.3 MEETING THE SECOND CHALLENGE

The second challenge for PIT was to show that it can accommodate the alleged contents of thoughts. To meet this challenge in the way I have proposed, alleged contents must be derived contents, and derived mental representation must not presuppose any kinds of intentionality that cannot be accommodated by PIT.

There are various sorts of alleged contents that we might want to capture, including rich descriptive contents and object-dependent contents, either of which might be broad. We've seen that self-ascriptivism has the resources to capture all these types of alleged contents: Descriptive contents can be directly or indirectly derivatively represented, while object-dependent contents can be indirectly derivatively represented. Broad contents are indirectly derivatively represented descriptive or object-dependent contents.

---

[35] Why not just take all concepts to be recognitional concepts of this sort? On such a view, what our concepts represent is a (perhaps infinite) disjunction of the represented items we take them to apply to. The reason not to take this approach to all concepts is that in order to count as derivatively representing such contents, we would have to take our immediate contents to mean them, and it is not clear that we do so in all cases. Additionally, in some cases, we have at least some contents of other types, e.g., descriptions, that we take our immediate contents to mean and that would be neglected by such an account.

Which particular contents of the aforementioned types a given subject represents depends on her particular dispositions to have cashing out thoughts. It might turn out that any given subject does not represent some types of alleged contents. It might even turn out that there are some types of alleged contents that no one represents. So, our account might end up being slightly or even massively revisionary with respect to which alleged contents we represent. However, in cases where our reasons for thinking we represent a particular sort of alleged content stem from our intuitions about particular cases, we are likely to derivatively represent content of that sort. This is because our intuitions about our representation of certain alleged contents and our derived representation of those same contents arguably come from the same source: our taking ourselves to represent them. For this reason, we should expect this account to be fairly successful at capturing the contents we have intuitive reasons to take ourselves to represent.[36]

In any case, there is reason to let the chips fall where they may when it comes to derived mental representation. The guiding idea of this section is that the only way to target a content that we do not immediately represent, that is not "forced" upon us by experience, is to in some sense accept ourselves as representing it. If this guiding idea is correct, then there is simply no way to target contents that are neither forced upon us nor accepted by us. So, for example, in a case in which I am simply not disposed to have cashing out thoughts like <by <water>, I mean <water+>>, it is simply not correct to say that my concept WATER represents <water+>. I neither phenomenally represent this content nor take myself to represent it, so imposing the content on me would be in violation of our guiding idea. If, for whatever reason, I happen not to

---

[36] There are two noteworthy scenarios on which my proposal might end up being quite revisionary. The first is one on which it turns out that the only contents we can immediately represent are sensory contents (a possibility we left open in §7.2.4). On this scenario, the only contents we would be able to derivatively represent would be possible sensory contents and their referents, since directly derivatively representing a content requires that it can be immediately represented, and indirectly derivatively representing a content requires that a content that refers to it can be immediately represented. However, the limitations are not as severe as might be thought. It is not clear that complex and sophisticated derived contents cannot be constructed out of sensory contents, which might include schematic sensory contents (see Prinz 2002 for a defense of such a view). In any case, it is not implausible that we in fact represent non-sensory, as well as sensory, immediate contents, along with corresponding sensory and cognitive phenomenal characters (see §7.2.4), so the potential for such limitations arguably does not arise.

The second scenario in which my view might end up being quite revisionary is that in which there is no reference, which is a possibility that our starting point left open (§1.3.4). If it turns out that there is no such thing as reference, then there is no indirect derived representation, and there are no object-involving contents. In this case, I agree that the view is revisionary, but it arguably gives us the right answer, since if there is no reference, then any intuitions we have that we represent particular contents with an object-involving nature are presumably entirely mistaken. In any case, in §9.3.4, I suggest that there probably is such thing as reference.

take C to mean C+, then the right answer is that I don't derivatively represent C+.[37]

Let us now turn to the second condition for meeting the second challenge. Since PIT takes all original intentionality to be phenomenal intentionality, in order to meet the second challenge, my account of derived content must not require that there be any original intentionality that isn't phenomenal intentionality.

My account meets this requirement. What it is to represent a derived content is to have various dispositions to have cashing out thoughts, thoughts with contents of the form <C cashes out into C+>. These contents have three elements: C, C+, and the cashing out relation. C is always an immediate content of some (actual or possible) representation, so it is a phenomenal content. In the case of direct derived representation, C+ is also an immediate content, so it is also a phenomenal content. In the case of indirect derived representation, C+ is a referent of immediate contents or direct derived contents, which are phenomenal contents, so it is a matter of phenomenal contents and how the world is (and anything else that might be required for reference, so long as it is not a source of non-phenomenal original intentionality).

The third element of cashing out thoughts, the represented cashing out relation, is also a phenomenal content. Unlike the alleged contents we've discussed, this content is simple and unsophisticated enough to plausibly be just a matter of having a certain phenomenal experience. All that is required is that we are able to have phenomenal experiences like that of one thing being an expansion, precisification, unpacking, magnification, or more detailed version of another, that of accepting one thing as a replacement for, substitution for, or better version of another, or simply that of one thing being what we meant or intended by another. It is not implausible that there are phenomenal states with the required kinds of phenomenal characters. Although I think that representing such contents is probably a matter of cognitive phenomenal characters, it is also not wholly implausible that they can be accounted for in terms of purely sensory phenomenal characters.[38]

---

[37] The same holds in cases where self-ascriptivism ascribes a content that we reject for theoretical reasons, as in the case of someone who is an internalist for theoretical reasons but who nonetheless has externalist intuitions about particular cases. Even in this case, the view gives us the right answer: The internalist takes herself to represent broad contents but simply cannot accept that she does on theoretical grounds. She, too, represents what she takes herself to represent. We should not decline her this basic good simply because of her misguided theoretical beliefs.

(In any case, such an internalist should be comforted by the fact that the representation of these broad contents stems entirely from internal factors: her own phenomenal states and dispositions to have further phenomenal states.)

[38] Note that cashing out thoughts are fairly undemanding to have. Presumably children and some animals can have phenomenal states representing that one content is equivalent to or a better version of another. Thanks to Declan Smithies for prompting this clarification.

If all this is right, then the self-ascriptivist picture is compatible with PIT, and we have met the second challenge of accommodating thoughts' alleged contents.

7.4 Is Derived Mental Representation a Type of Intentionality?

I have purposefully avoided calling derived mental representation "derived intentionality" in order to remain neutral on the question of whether it is indeed a type of intentionality. Recall that we fixed reference on intentionality ostensively by pointing to paradigm cases, which are introspectively accessible cases such as those of perceptually representing a red square or thinking that it's raining (§1.2). Whether derived mental representation counts as a kind of intentionality depends on whether it is the same kind of thing as our paradigm cases.

I want to suggest that derived mental representation is sufficiently different in nature from paradigm cases of intentionality so as to not qualify as a kind of intentionality, though it arguably satisfies a broader everyday notion of representation. Since paradigm cases involve introspectively accessible contents and immediate contents are the contents we are immediately aware of, the contents we notice in these cases are quite plausibly immediate contents, which are phenomenal contents. So, the question of whether derived mental representation is a kind of intentionality turns on whether derived mental representation belongs to the same kind as phenomenal intentionality.

I think the answer is clearly "no." There are many dissimilarities between phenomenal intentionality and derived mental representation, but one of the most significant differences is that what a representation derivatively represents, but not what it phenomenally represents, is always relative to a subject. Strictly speaking, when S takes C to mean C+, C doesn't just derivatively represent C+; C derivatively represents C+ *for* S. Compare: When we take stop signs to represent <stop!>, they represent <stop!> for us. They don't represent <stop!> for ants, cats, or tables, and they don't represent <stop!> in and of themselves. In contrast, when we *phenomenally* represent a content, we do so full stop.[39]

There is another important difference between derived mental representation and phenomenal intentionality: There are determinate facts of the matter as to which contents we phenomenally represent. These facts depend on what our

---

[39] This is not to say that phenomenal intentionality does not involve a certain subjectivity in that phenomenal contents are *experienced* and *present to* the representing subject (see Kriegel 2013b for the idea that phenomenal intentionality is subjective). Thanks to Laura Gow for prompting this clarification.

phenomenal experience is like, which is a determinate matter.[40] In contrast, since (Taking) makes reference to a disposition whose conditions of manifestation are only vaguely specified, it can be indeterminate what we derivatively represent. This difference between derived mental representation and paradigm intentional states is another reason to think that derived mental representation is not a kind of intentionality.

Section 5.4 distinguished between inflationist, eliminativist, and derivativist strategies PIT might take toward alleged cases of mental states with non-phenomenal contents. Inflationism claims that the mental states do in fact have phenomenal contents, eliminativism claims that the mental states do not exist or that they do not have the relevant contents, and derivativism claims that the mental states derivatively intentionally represent the relevant contents.

The view of thoughts presented in this chapter is both inflationist and eliminativist. It is inflationist in that it takes thoughts to have phenomenal contents, and it is eliminativist in that it denies that thoughts intentionally represent their alleged contents. It is, however, derivativist in spirit in that it takes alleged contents to be derivatively represented, but, strictly speaking, it does not qualify as a version of derivativism because it does not take derived mental representation to be a kind of intentionality.[41] The overall strategy, then, is consistent with strong PIT, the view that all intentionality is phenomenal intentionality (see §5.1).

Of course, the formulation of the above claims is sensitive to the way we fix reference on intentionality. If we fix reference in a way other than my own, we might end up picking out a disjunctive kind that includes both phenomenal intentionality and derived mental representation. Then the view I propose would qualify as a kind of derivativism and be incompatible with strong PIT. Relatedly, those who think that my ostensive definition picks out a broader kind than phenomenal intentionality, a kind that includes derived mental representation, would take derived mental representation to be a kind of derived intentionality. The derivativist version of self-ascriptivism about thoughts' alleged contents is another fallback position for those who believe that there is something very deep in common between original intentionality and derived mental representation.

---

[40] Of course, there might be vagueness in our *descriptions* of these facts.

[41] See also Strawson (2008), who claims that derived representation is a kind of aboutness but not a kind of intentionality.

7.5 Conclusion: PIT about Thought

I have suggested a PIT-friendly view of thought content on which thoughts have both immediate contents, which are phenomenal contents, and derived contents, which we represent simply because we take ourselves to represent them. In short, we think in phenomenal tags that we take to stand for more complex and sophisticated contents.

There is an optimistic and a pessimistic take on the resulting view. The pessimistic take is that we only ever represent our impoverished immediate contents and any impression to the contrary is a mere illusion, brought on by our disposition to have cashing out thoughts. When we "look for" certain alleged contents, we find them before our mind's eye, at least sometimes and to a certain extent, which leads to the mistaken impression that we were thinking them all along. But this is merely a kind of refrigerator light illusion, since we were not in fact thinking them all along. On this construal of the overall view, the phenomenon of derived mental representation gives us the illusion of rich and contentful thought, when in reality, all we ever think are our impoverished phenomenal contents.[42]

My preference is for a more optimistic take, one on which, although the only contents we *intentionally* represent are our limited and impoverished immediate contents, our dispositions to have cashing out thoughts allow us to effectively bootstrap our way out of the confines of our own consciousness, opening us up to a world of rich, complex, and sophisticated contents, even including actual objects and other items in the external world. These contents are the contents we in some sense target, intend, or take ourselves to represent, so, in some important sense, they are genuinely *ours*.[43]

Appendix D: Derived Mental Representation in Perception

The account of derived mental representation developed in this chapter applies not only to thoughts but also to intentional mental states more generally, including perceptual states. This is useful, since it might be thought that the challenges facing PIT in the case of thought—namely, those of accommodating the representation of rich descriptive contents, object-involving contents, and broad contents—also

---

[42] This is the picture I endorsed in Mendelovici 2010. Bourget (2017c, forthcoming-c) endorses a similar picture on which we represent less than we tend to think we do.

[43] Bourget (2010a) can be interpreted as having such an optimistic spin, claiming that various derivation mechanisms give rise to genuine intentionality.

arise in the case of perception. For example, a perceptual state representing a pine tree *as a pine tree* (Siegel 2005, 2010) might be thought to have a rich descriptive or object-involving content, and a perceptual state of a particular object might be thought to have a content involving that object as a constituent part (Schellenberg 2010). If the phenomenal characters of perceptual states do not match such alleged contents, then they pose a challenge for PIT.

As in the case of thought, we can say that perceptual states *derivatively* represent such contents. Presumably, in having perceptual experiences, there is some content we are immediately aware of, so at least some perceptual states have immediate contents. If a subject is disposed to have cashing out thoughts that together specify that a perceptually represented immediate content, C, cashes out into C+, then she takes C to mean C+. And if she takes C to mean C+, then C derivatively represents C+ (for her), and so does any state or representation immediately representing C, including any *perceptual* state or representation immediately representing C.

For example, suppose that when a subject sees a pine tree *as a pine tree*, she has a visual experience that, in some sense, represents not only particular shapes and colors but also the property of being a pine tree or the kind *pine tree*. Here is how my account accommodates this case: The perceptual state has a particular immediate content, C, which is phenomenally represented. C might consist in a particular configuration of shapes and colors or even a gisty pine-tree-ish content.[44] The subject is also disposed to have various cashing out thoughts to the effect that C cashes out into <an evergreen coniferous tree with needle-shaped leaves>, or simply <kind of tree that experts call "pine">. Such cashing out thoughts together specify a content, C+, that might be thought of as our subject's best characterization or understanding of a pine tree. By (Taking), our subject takes C to mean C+, and by (DMR), her perceptual representation with the immediate content C derivatively represents C+.

Similarly, suppose we want to say that a particular subject perceptually represents an object-involving content, such as the content <Mitten>, which is the flesh-and-blood cat, Mitten. My account accommodates this case as follows: Our subject has a perceptual state with a certain phenomenal content, C, which might consist in various sensory contents (e.g., cat imagery), schematic contents (e.g., a gisty depiction of Mitten), or sui generis contents (e.g., a primitive content <Mitten!>). Our subject is also disposed to have cashing out thoughts specifying that C cashes out into whatever item has such-and-such features, which, if all goes well, is Mitten

---

[44] The view that the immediate contents of perceptual states include non-sensory parts or aspects is congenial to the view that perceptual experience involves cognitive phenomenology (see Montague 2009).

himself. Our subject thereby takes C to mean <Mitten>—i.e., Mitten himself—and so her representation of C derivatively represents <Mitten>.[45]

One attractive consequence of allowing for derived mental representation in perception is that it lessens the disappointment that might come with an error theory about the contents of perceptual color states.[46] In Chapter 3, I argued that perceptual color representations (originally) represent edenic colors, which happen not to be instantiated. As a result, perceptual color representations reliably misrepresent: roughly, they get things wrong in the same way all the time. However, depending on our dispositions to have cashing out thoughts involving our perceptual color contents, our perceptual color representations might *derivatively* represent properties that putatively colored objects actually have. For example, as a result of coming to realize that there are no edenic colors, I might come to reconstruct my color concepts so that they pick out properties I think objects in fact have—say, dispositions to cause color experiences. This reconstruction might be a matter of coming to take the immediate contents of my color concepts to mean such dispositional contents. In line with such changes, I might also come to take the immediate contents of my *perceptual* color representations to mean the same dispositional contents. This might involve, for example, being disposed to have cashing out thoughts that together specify that, say, <sky-blue>, my perceptual color content, cashes out into <the disposition to cause perceptual states representing <sky-blue> in subjects like me in normal viewing conditions>. My perceptual color representations would then derivatively represent dispositions to cause certain perceptual states, which objects do have. They would then have two contents, one immediate and one derived, only the first of which would be in error.[47]

Appendix E: Attitudes

The category of thoughts includes occurrent beliefs, occurrent desires, occurrent hopes, occurrent fears, and other propositional (or non-propositional) attitudes. It is typically thought that such states involve two components: an **attitude**—e.g., belief,

---

[45] Derived mental representation in perception requires that the original contents of perceptual states can figure in cashing out thoughts, which requires that the phenomenal contents of perceptual states can figure in thoughts. This might involve perceptual phenomenal contents embedding in cashing out thoughts (or cashing out thought-perception hybrid states), or cashing out thoughts descriptively or demonstratively referring to them.

[46] Of course, this is only a desire-satisfying virtue, not a truth-indicating virtue (see p. 118).

[47] Thanks to Charles Siewert for encouraging me to elaborate on how derived mental representation applies in the case of perception.

desire, hope, or fear—and a content, which is *what* is believed, desired, etc. So far, I have not said anything about attitudes, since my target is intentionality, the having of contents. But, since attitudes are an integral part of thoughts, PIT should at least be compatible with an account of attitudes. This appendix overviews three views of attitudes and argues that PIT is compatible with all of them, though my version of PIT is particularly congenial to one in particular.[48]

The standard view of attitudes is arguably **attitude functionalism**, the view that an intentional mental state's attitude is a matter of its functional role (Fodor 1987). For example, desires might be intentional mental states that play the functional role characteristic of desire, such as that of causing us to try to bring about their contents given what we believe.

An alternative view is **attitude phenomenalism**, the view that an intentional mental state's attitude is a matter of its having certain characteristic phenomenal characters (Horgan and Tienson 2002, Pitt 2004, Jorba 2016). For example, beliefs might have a phenomenal character of conviction, while desires might have a phenomenal character of yearning or attraction.

A third view is **attitude representationalism**, the view that an intentional mental state's attitude is a matter of its having certain characteristic contents (Pearce 2016).[49] On such a view, each distinct attitude involves a characteristic content, the representation of which makes it the attitude that it is. For instance, to desire something might be to represent it as good, desirable, or rewarding. To believe something might be to represent it as being the case, or true. On this view, a belief that P and a desire that P are alike with respect to some parts or aspects of their contents but differ with respect to others.[50]

---

[48] Recall that on my use of terminology, an intentional state is an instantiation of an intentional property, while an intentional mental state is a mental state that includes, but may not be exhausted by, the instantiation of intentional properties. So, thoughts are intentional mental states but may not be intentional states. (See §1.2.)

[49] See also Kriegel (2015b), who argues that belief-like and desire-like states have characteristic contents.

[50] One question for the attitude representationalist, suggested to me by Adam Pautz, is whether when one thinks a bare that-clause content, e.g., *snow is white*, one automatically bears a particular attitude toward it. One view is that such states count as mere "considerings," the cognitive analogues of imaginings. Another view is that such states count as beliefs. On the former view, we needn't add any characteristic contents to a that-clause content in order to count as considering it, whereas on the latter view, we needn't add any characteristic contents to a that-clause content in order count as believing it. I don't think the question of which particular attitude-related contents a particular thought has can be easily settled, but my sympathies lie with the view that the default attitude is that of belief. Intentional states generally seem to carry a kind of commitment to the truth of what is represented (consider, for example, perceptual states), and avoiding such a commitment requires neutralizing it (for the attitude representationalist, this might involve thinking a content like *things might or might not be such that P*).

The above views are not mutually exclusive. For example, if attitude phenomenalism is true and the relevant phenomenal properties are special functional properties, then attitude functionalism is also true. More interestingly for my purposes, as we will soon see, attitude phenomenalism and attitude representationalism might both be true.

It is not my purpose to decide between these views. Instead, here, I want to show that PIT is compatible with all these options.

On attitude functionalism, what makes a mental state a belief, desire, or other type of attitude is its functional role. Assuming that attitudes are not intentional features of mental states, attitude functionalism places attitudes outside the scope of PIT, since PIT is only a theory of intentionality. Is PIT compatible with such a view of attitudes? It seems so. There is no obvious barrier to PIT accepting the view that intentional mental states can play various functional roles and that a mental state's attitude is a matter of playing such roles.

Similarly, PIT is compatible with the claim that attitudes are a matter of phenomenal states, so PIT is compatible with attitude phenomenalism. However, when combined with my favored version of PIT, which takes every phenomenal property to be identical to some intentional property (see Appendix B of Chapter 5), attitude phenomenalism entails attitude representationalism. So, if one wants to be an attitude phenomenalist but not an attitude representationalist, one should reject the claim that every phenomenal property is identical to some intentional property. While I don't want to reject this claim, rejecting it has no downstream ramifications, so it is a nearby fallback position for those who want to endorse attitude phenomenalism but not attitude representationalism.

On attitude representationalism, whether or not it is combined with attitude phenomenalism, attitudes are squarely within the scope of PIT and, more specifically, within the scope of a phenomenal intentionality theoretic account of thought, since

---

Adam Pautz has suggested to me that neither of the above two options is satisfactory: The view that considering is the default attitude is implausible, since it is unclear whether merely considering a content combined with the alleged further characteristic contents of various attitudes can really amount to having those attitudes, and the view that belief is the default attitude undercuts the motivation for attitude representationalism, since once we allow that one kind of thought has an extra built-in attitude independent of any characteristic contents, we might as well allow that they all do. I don't think that either of these objections is decisive: The attitude representationalist that takes considering to be the default attitude might say that all it is to have a belief, desire, etc. is to consider that a particular content is true, good, etc.; no more work needs to be done by these considerings. Such a view might amount to a deflated understanding of belief, desire, and other attitudes. And the attitude representationalist who takes belief to be the default attitude might maintain that coming with a kind of commitment to truth is not a further feature of a thought (or an intentional state more generally), but rather falls out of the very nature of being a thought (or an intentional state). Thinking that P just is committing to its truth.

thoughts have attitudes. PIT must then maintain that they arise from phenomenal consciousness or that they are merely derived representational states. Neither option is entirely implausible. The first option takes the contents individuating the attitudes to be phenomenal contents. One consideration in support of this view is that, as Horgan and Tienson (2002), Pitt (2004), Goldman (1993), and Jorba (2016) have argued, there is a clear phenomenal difference between thoughts with the same that-clause contents but different attitudes, e.g., between a belief that it's raining and a desire that it's raining. So, it is not entirely implausible that the contents individuating the attitudes are phenomenal contents. However, as in the case of the alleged contents of thoughts, one might worry that these phenomenal contents don't match the contents the attitude representationalist takes to individuate the attitudes.

The other option for combining attitude representationalism with a phenomenal intentionality theoretic account of thought takes the contents individuating the attitudes to be derived. On such a view, intentional states involving different attitudes would involve impoverished, perhaps sensory, schematic, or sui generis, phenomenal contents, which we take to mean fuller or more precise specifications of attitude contents. For example, a desire for ice cream might involve a gisty desire-ish content that we take to mean <good>, <desirable>, <rewarding>, <to be had>, etc. Then the representation representing this gisty desire-ish content would derivatively represent this content. One attraction of this combination of attitude representationalism with self-ascriptivism is that it nicely accommodates a diverse range of attitudes beyond those of belief and desire, such as those of fearing, hypothesizing, aspiring, hoping, wishing, and regretting. First, it can accommodate these attitudes without according them too much psychological reality: We have such attitudes simply because we *take* ourselves to have such attitudes. Second, it makes sense of subtly different attitudes, such as those of hoping and wishing, by taking the difference between them to lie largely in how we construe them.

Attitudes are an integral part of thoughts, so an account of the content of thoughts, and of intentionality more generally, should be compatible with an account of attitudes. I have overviewed three accounts of the attitudes and argued that PIT is compatible with all of them. My sympathies lie with a combination of attitude representationalism and the view that attitudes have fairly thin phenomenal contents and fairly sophisticated and subtle derived contents, but the other options provide fallback positions for those who are not convinced of this view.

8   Nonconscious States

ACCORDING TO THE phenomenal intentionality theory (PIT), the intentional mind, or at least the originally intentional mind, is the conscious mind. This might seem like a hopelessly outdated view, one that flies in the face of cognitive science. Indeed, one might argue that one of the most important contributions of the cognitive revolution was the acceptance of nonconscious mental states and processes.

Searle (1990) notably argued that all intentional states are either conscious or potentially conscious, claiming that his conclusions wreak havoc on cognitive science. The view I defend in this chapter may seem to be even more extreme than Searle's, since it denies intentionality to all nonconscious states, regardless of whether they are potentially conscious. But my approach is in fact quite conciliatory. Rather than wreak havoc on what we might take to be the standard view of nonconscious states, the view implicit in much scientific theorizing about the mind and brain, my view, I argue, is very much in line with it.

This chapter proceeds as follows: §8.1 clarifies the challenge for PIT, distinguishing two different types of nonconscious states that we might want to accommodate: standing states and allegedly nonconscious occurrent states; §8.2 overviews and provides my reasons for rejecting versions of PIT that take nonconscious states to have derived intentional contents; §8.3 argues for my preferred view of standing states; and §8.4 argues for my preferred view of nonconscious occurrent states.

8.1 The Problem with Nonconscious States

Recall that PIT is the view that all originally intentional states arise from phenomenal states (see Chapter 5). PIT faces a challenge when it comes to nonconscious states: It seems that there are nonconscious intentional mental states, states that are intentional but not phenomenally conscious. How, then, do they get their contents?[1]

We can divide the nonconscious states we might want to accommodate into two general types: The first is that of **standing states**, mental states that need not be used, entertained, or otherwise active at the time at which they are had. Standing states can be contrasted with **occurrent states**, mental states that are used, entertained, or otherwise active at the time at which they are had. Examples of standing states include beliefs, desires, and memories that are not continuously being entertained at the time that they are had, as well as "assumptions" of the visual system (Marr 1982) and states of knowing the grammar of our language (Chomsky 1965) that are not continuously in use. For instance, suppose you have a desire to eat ice cream, a desire you intend to satisfy after reading this chapter. Presumably, you are not continuously occurrently desiring that you eat ice cream while reading this chapter. Still, you nonetheless count as having the desire, even if it is not continuously occurring to you, so it is a standing state. In contrast, the intentional states this text is causing in you right now are occurrent states.

The second type of nonconscious state that we might want to accommodate is that of **nonconscious occurrent states**, which are occurrent states that lack phenomenal character. Some examples of nonconscious occurrent states are nonconscious occurrent states in early visual processing, nonconscious occurrent visual states of blindsight patients, and nonconscious thoughts.

Both standing and occurrent nonconscious states admit of a further distinction between personal and subpersonal states: Some standing and occurrent nonconscious states are **personal states**, states that can be said to be had by entire persons. Examples of nonconscious personal states include standing beliefs, standing desires, and nonconscious thoughts. Even though we cannot introspectively observe nonconscious personal states, we sometimes ascribe such states to ourselves and others, perhaps based on intuition or a folk psychological theory of mind (see §1.3.1)

---

[1] See Smithies (2012, MS, ch. 1), who argues that there are such nonconscious states and that they pose a problem for PIT.

or perhaps based on scientific theories of mind and behavior. In contrast, some standing and occurrent nonconscious states are **subpersonal states**, states that are properly attributed to subsystems of persons rather than to persons themselves. For example, standing and occurrent states in early visual processing might be such states. Our reasons for accepting subpersonal states are usually that they are posited by scientific theories (see §1.3.2).[2]

The problem posed by all kinds of nonconscious states is the same: Many of them seem to be intentional mental states, but they also seem to lack phenomenal character—there seems to be nothing it is like to have a belief one isn't occurrently thinking or to nonconsciously process linguistic information. As a result, it seems that their intentionality cannot be phenomenal intentionality. So, it is not clear how PIT can accommodate them.

In §5.4, we saw that there are three general strategies PIT might take toward any alleged intentional but non-phenomenal mental state: According to inflationism, the mental state does in fact have phenomenal contents. According to eliminativism, the mental state does not exist or does not intentionally represent the relevant contents. Finally, according to derivativism, the mental state derivatively intentionally represents the relevant contents.

In what follows, I argue that there are no genuinely intentional standing states. However, I also suggest that the notion of derived mental representation developed in Chapter 7 can be extended to apply to some personal standing states, so that at least some personal standing state contents, and perhaps even some personal standing states in their entirety, qualify as derivatively represented. Since I do not take derived mental representation to be a kind of intentionality (see §7.4), this view is, strictly speaking, eliminativist, but there is a nearby derivativist fallback position for those who take derived mental representation to be a kind of intentionality.

The view of nonconscious occurrent states that I will recommend is a combination of inflationism and eliminativism: Some allegedly nonconscious intentional states *might* have phenomenal characters and phenomenal contents that we are not aware of. However, it is implausible that all of them do. For those that don't, I recommend eliminativism, which, I will argue, is very much in line with the standard view of these states.

In short, my view is a combination of eliminativism and inflationism about allegedly nonconscious states. Before considering the view in detail, let us first consider the derivativist alternative.

---

[2] See Drayson 2014 for discussion of the personal/subpersonal distinction.

8.2 Derivativist Strategies

Several advocates of PIT have proposed a derivativist treatment of nonconscious states. Kriegel (2013b), an advocate of PIT who endorses derivativism about a wide variety of nonconscious states, somewhat metaphorically expresses the derivativist view as follows:

> [I]ntentionality is injected into the world with the appearance of a certain kind of phenomenal character ... [O]nce this phenomenal character appears, and brings in its train "original intentionality," intentionality can be "passed around" to things lacking this (or any) phenomenal character. (p. 3)

On this picture, once we have original intentionality, it can be "passed around" to items lacking phenomenal consciousness. I will later suggest that intentionality cannot transfer from one object to another and that this is the core reason to reject a derivativist picture. But first, let us canvass some derivativist options.

One derivativist view is **potentialist derivativism**, on which potentially conscious states derivatively represent the contents they would originally represent if they were phenomenally conscious (Searle 1990, 1991, 1992, Bourget 2010a; see also Graham et al. 2007, Kriegel 2013b, and Pitt MS-b for discussion). According to potentialist derivativism, nonconscious states derive their intentional properties from the intentional properties of the phenomenally conscious states a subject merely *potentially* has. We can think of this picture using Kriegel's metaphor as follows: The potential original intentionality of phenomenally conscious states is passed around to corresponding nonconscious states.

Another view is **functionalist derivativism**, on which nonconscious states are derivatively intentional because they bear the right kinds of functional relations to actual and potential occurrent states, including phenomenal intentional states (Graham et al. 2007, Horgan and Graham 2009, Loar 2003, Bourget 2010a, Pautz 2008, 2013a, Chalmers 2010, p. xxiv). This view is much like the functional role theory described in §4.1, except that it includes phenomenal intentional states. Recall that one worry with the functional role theory was that it cannot assign contents determinately. Functionalist derivativism addresses this worry by taking phenomenal intentional states to, as Graham et al. (2007, p. 479) put it, "serve as 'anchor points' of determinate intentionality" (see also Pautz 2008, p. 267). The idea is that these anchor points, perhaps together with other factors, constrain the possible interpretations of a system of representations enough so that there is only one admissible interpretation.[3] This picture is particularly well illustrated

---

[3] But see Bourget MS, which argues that these views do not in fact avoid indeterminacy worries.

by Kriegel's metaphor: On this picture, intentionality gets passed around from phenomenal intentional states to non-phenomenal states that are appropriately functionally related.

Pautz's (2008, 2013a) **consciousness-based best systems theory** is a version of functionalist derivativism inspired by Lewis' (1974) a priori functionalism that takes the relevant functional roles to be determined by folk psychology.[4] According to this view, a subject derivatively intentionally represents a non-phenomenal content C just in case the "best interpretation" assigns to her an intentional state with the content C. The best interpretation, roughly, is the one that satisfies the a priori principles of folk psychology, including the "principle of rationality," which states that a subject's behavior is generally rational given her beliefs and desires, and the "principle of humanity," which states that a subject's intentional states are the ones that it is reasonable for her to have given her evidence, which, for Pautz, is a matter of her history of phenomenal intentional perceptual states.[5]

A third derivativist view is **interpretivist derivativism**, according to which nonconscious states derivatively intentionally represent the contents that a possible ideal interpreter would interpret them as having using intentional systems theory (Kriegel 2011). **Intentional systems theory** is a theory that aims to predict a system's behavior by attributing to it beliefs and desires and assuming that it is rational (that is, assuming that its behavior aims to satisfy its desires given its beliefs). On Kriegel's picture, roughly, a nonconscious state x derivatively represents a content C when a (possible) ideal agent employing intentional system's theory is disposed to have a phenomenal intentional state stating that x intentionally represents C. On this picture, intentionality gets passed around from the possible ideal agent's phenomenal intentional states to other subjects' nonconscious states.[6]

Finally, we might add to our list of derivativist options **derivativist self-ascriptivism**, the view that we derivatively intentionally represent various contents by ascribing them to ourselves or our mental states. Derivativist self-ascriptivism is a combination of self-ascriptivism (§7.3) and the view that the resulting derived mental representation is a kind of intentionality. (In §7.4, I argued for *eliminativist* self-ascriptivism but noted that derivativist self-ascriptivism is a

---

[4] Adam Pautz has also called this view "phenomenal functionalism" (see his 2008 and 2013a).

[5] Pautz further claims that similar considerations constrain the interpretation of a subject's language and that the meaning of linguistic expressions in a subject's language can in turn influence the intentional states she counts as having (2013, pp. 225–226).

[6] Pautz's consciousness-based best systems theory, which I've classified as a version of functionalist derivativism, can also be thought of as a version of interpretivist derivativism, but one that does without the interpreter. See also Pautz 2013a, n. 32.

nearby fallback position.) On derivativist self-ascriptivism, intentionality gets passed around from self-ascriptions to other items.

Let us now turn to assessing derivativism. Kriegel (2011) suggests that one reason to prefer derivativism to eliminativist strategies is that it offers a more conciliatory position, since it allows us to say that nonconscious states intentionally represent, albeit derivatively. However, I will soon argue that consideration of the putatively intentional states in question reveals that an eliminativist (and, in some cases, an inflationist) strategy is in fact more conciliatory than the alternative derivativist strategies. If these arguments are sound, then they dispel Kriegel's motivation for derivativism.

Even if derivativism yields predictions that are more in line with our prior expectations, as Kriegel claims, there is a fundamental concern with the view, which is that intentionality is just not the kind of thing that can be passed around as would be required. The worry is that *even if* derivativism appears to give us what appear to be the right answers in all cases, the view fails because the various derivation mechanisms are not in fact sufficient for generating new instances of intentionality. We might call this problem the **Real Problem** with derivativism, since it is analogous to the Real Problem for tracking and functional role theories.[7]

Of course, everyone will agree that not any old relation something bears to an actual or possible intentional state results in derived intentionality. One thing cannot "catch" another thing's intentionality simply by being sufficiently close to it or by bumping into it. So, even if a derivativist theory's predictions are in line with prior expectations, there remains a further question of whether the derivation mechanisms in question can really "pass" content around as required.[8]

I want to suggest that the kinds of relations potentialist, functionalist, and interpretivist derivativism invoke are not sufficient for generating instances of intentionality. Before considering these versions of derivativism, let us first consider derivativist self-ascriptivism. In this case, there is prima facie reason to think that

---

[7] One kind of complaint against particular derivativist strategies is that they cannot accommodate all the putative cases of nonconscious intentionality. Graham et al. (2007) and Kriegel (2011) argue that potentialist derivativism cannot accommodate intentional nonconscious states that are not even potentially phenomenally conscious, such as any allegedly intentional states involved in early visual processing. Kriegel (2011) also argues that functionalist derivativism cannot accommodate nonconscious intentionality in entirely non-phenomenal beings. Smithies (MS, ch. 1) similarly argues that what amount to various forms of derivativism cannot adequately account for all alleged cases of nonconscious intentionality. My worry, in contrast, is that *even if* derivativism appears to give us the "right answers" in all cases, the view fails because the various derivation mechanisms are not sufficient for intentionality.

[8] In conversation, Kati Farkas has expressed similar concerns with derivativist self-ascriptivism, which I completely agree with. Her approach in Farkas 2008a reflects such concerns.

intentionality gets passed around. Consider a case where you simply stipulate to yourself: <By <P>, I mean <grass is green>>. In this case, your mental content <P> comes to stand for <grass is green> (for you). Section 7.4 argued that this sort of derived representation is not a case of derived intentionality, though it may satisfy an everyday notion of representation. The point here, however, is that there is some prima facie plausibility to the idea that self-ascriptions can "pass" intentionality around. Taking something to have a certain content *makes* it have that content (for you).

Things are not so clear on potentialist derivativism. On this view, items that are potentially phenomenally conscious inherit the content that they would have were they to be phenomenally conscious. For example, if a merely potentially phenomenal state is such that, were it to be made phenomenally conscious, it would have the phenomenal intentional content <grass is green>, then it has the derived intentional content <grass is green>. The problem is that it is unclear just why a potentially phenomenal state should qualify as being derivatively intentional, as opposed to merely *potentially* intentional. After all, while the state is potentially phenomenal, it is not *derivatively* phenomenal, so why does it get to count as derivatively intentional rather than merely potentially intentional? Note that whether or not we say that potentially originally intentional states are derivatively intentional is not merely a matter of terminological choice. In Chapter 1, we fixed reference on intentionality ostensively by pointing to paradigm cases of the phenomenon. Saying that potentially originally intentional states are themselves intentional commits us to their belonging to the class of items we picked out using this ostensive definition.[9,10]

Next, let us consider functionalist derivativism. On this view, intentionality flows from actual or potential phenomenal intentional states to other functionally related states. The worry here is that it is not clear why intentionality should transfer from actual or potential phenomenal states to other states. In general, bearing a causal relation to something with intentionality does not result in the intentionality being passed around. Internal states with intentionality might bear lots of causal relations to all sorts of other internal states and external items, but not all these items thereby become intentional. Why, then, would *any* of these items become intentional?

---

[9]   Searle (1991), roughly, argues that the only thing that can be used to decide which contents nonconscious states represent is the contents they would have if conscious. Even if this is right, this at best only supports the claim that there is a determinate way in which we can assign them contents on the basis of the features they would have if conscious. It does not provide a reason for thinking that nonconscious states are intentional in the first place.

[10]   Similarly, Strawson (1994, 2004) argues that mere dispositions do not give rise to intentional states. See §8.3 for more discussion.

Why isn't the full story simply that we have actual and potential phenomenal intentional states that are causally and dispositionally related to actual and potential non-intentional states?

On Pautz's (2008) view, the relevant functional roles are fixed by a priori folk psychological principles. These principles functionally define beliefs, desires, and other states in terms of their connection to one's evidence, which, for Pautz, is the phenomenal content of one's past and present perceptual states. I am doubtful that folk psychology defines beliefs, desires, and other such states in this way, but let us assume that it does. Then it would indeed turn out that we have beliefs, desires, and other folk psychological states and that they are derived from phenomenal states in the way that Pautz describes. But it would still be a further question whether such states have *intentionality*, and it is not clear why we should accept that they do. (If we say that folk psychological states have intentionality by definition, then we are operating with a different definition of "intentionality" than the ostensive one, and their having intentionality in this sense is consistent with their failing to have intentionality in the sense under discussion; see also §1.3.1.)

Compare: Suppose we define a "sofa-thinking-that C" as a sofa seating a person thinking that C. If people ever sit and think on sofas, then there will indeed be sofa-thinking-that Cs for various contents C. But it does not follow that any intentionality has transferred from people to sofas. Similarly, simply defining folk psychological states in terms of their relations to phenomenal intentional states does not suffice for intentionality to transfer from the phenomenal intentional states to the folk psychologically defined states. It wouldn't make the defined states have a derived form of the phenomenon we defined ostensively in Chapter 1.[11]

Finally, let us consider Kriegel's interpretivist derivativism, the view that nonconscious states have as their derived intentional content the content that an ideal interpreter would attribute to them using intentional systems theory. Like

---

[11] In response to this, Adam Pautz has told me that he can accept that his view does not deliver a kind of intentionality, but only a kind of "intentionality*." If so, then we have no disagreement regarding the points made here. However, an immediate problem with this construal of his theory is that now it is not clear what it is supposed to be a theory *of* (except perhaps the a priori known meanings of folk psychological terms). If the target of the theory is not intentionality, more needs to be said about what exactly its target is supposed to be (and why it is a correct theory of it). Compare: Without a stated target, the tracking theory tells us only that there are tracking relations, which is something that everyone can agree with.

   In contrast, eliminativist self-ascriptivism is a theory of how we target contents that we are not immediately aware of. In Chapter 7, I urged that the only way we can do so is through self-ascriptions (see also §10.2). The view has a stated target, and I've argued that there are in-principle reasons to think it successfully captures it and, further, that it is the only view that can.

derivativist self-ascriptivism, interpretivist derivativism takes the passing around of intentionality to require something like ascriptions of intentional states. But whereas derivativist self-ascriptivism claims that we derivatively represent a content when *we* ascribe it to our internal states, interpretivist derivativism claims that we derivatively represent a content when *an ideal agent* would ascribe it to our internal states. In both cases, derived intentionality results from an agent ascribing a content to something else.

Recall that on self-ascriptivism, when a content or representation comes to derivatively represent some content, it only, strictly speaking, derivatively represents the content *for the subject making the ascription*. In the above example, the subject who stipulates <By <P>, I mean <grass is green>> does not thereby make it the case that the content <P>, or even her internal state representing that content, comes to represent <grass is green> in and of itself. Instead, she makes it the case that <P>, and perhaps also her internal state representing <P>, comes to represent <grass is green> *for her*. The same holds in non-mental cases of derived representation. Strictly speaking, stop signs represent <stop!> *for us*. They do not represent <stop!> for ants, Martians, or for stop signs, and they do not unqualifiedly represent <stop!> in and of themselves. Similarly, then, if an ideal interpreter interprets a subject's internal state x as having content C, this should only result in x representing C *for the ideal interpreter*, and not for the subject, for x, or in and of itself. Put otherwise, even if interpretivist derivativism describes a derivation mechanism that succeeds in getting content to pass from phenomenal intentional states to nonconscious states, the contents it ascribes are only relative to the ideal interpreter. These content attributions are irrelevant to the subject, just as a stop sign's meaning for us is irrelevant to the stop sign.[12]

The only way to derivatively represent content that is relevant to the subject of derived representation is for *the subject* to ascribe that content to herself or her states or contents. This brings us back to derivativist self-ascriptivism. While I take derivativist self-ascriptivism to be the most viable derivativist option, I think it too ultimately fails to get intentionality to flow from phenomenal states to non-phenomenal states. The problem is that what self-ascription gives rise to is not a derived version of intentionality but rather something utterly different

---

[12] One might object that the ideal interpreter's content attributions predict the *subject's* behavior, not her own, so the contents are derivatively represented by the subject. While we may grant that the content attributions are predictive of the subject's behavior, it is still not clear why this should make them in any way significant to *her* rather than existing merely in the eye of the beholder, i.e., the ideal interpreter. These contents are not contents that the subject in any way accepts, acknowledges, or uses. They merely provide for a convenient way of predicting her behavior.

from intentionality. What it gives rise to is one thing standing for another thing *for someone*. Our ascriptions make a stop sign stand for <stop!> *for us*, and our self-ascriptions make internal states stand for contents they don't phenomenally represent *for us*. But, as argued in §7.4, intentional states are not relative to subjects in this way. Rather, intentionality is a matter of a state or subject entertaining or otherwise having a content in and of itself. So, taking one thing to stand for another does not result in a derived version of intentionality. Genuine intentionality is an entirely different kind of beast.

We can conclude from the preceding discussion that derivativist self-ascriptivism is the most viable version of derivativism, but even *it* does not deliver derived *intentionality*, rather than mere derived *representation* that happens to be derived from intentionality. However, of the derivativist options, derivativist self-ascriptivism makes the best fallback position for advocates of PIT who want to accept derived intentionality.

If, as I've recommended, the advocate of PIT rejects derivativist strategies, she is left to choose between inflationism and eliminativism about any given alleged case of nonconscious intentionality. Since, in most cases, it is implausible to maintain that allegedly nonconscious intentional states are in fact phenomenally conscious, this leaves us with a largely eliminativist view of these states, which is my preferred view. The remainder of this chapter argues that such a largely eliminativist strategy is quite plausible and can be motivated independently of PIT.

8.3 Standing States

Standing states include both personal states, like standing beliefs, standing desires, and memories, and subpersonal states, like "assumptions" of the visual system. Standing states pose a challenge for PIT because they seem to be intentional but not phenomenal.

This section argues that there are no intentional standing states. Section 8.3.1 considers the claim that there are personal standing states, like beliefs and desires, that are intentional, and argues that there are none. Section 8.3.2, though, suggests that (eliminative) self-ascriptivism can be extended so as to apply to at least some alleged personal standing state contents or even personal standing states in their entirety. Section 8.3.3 suggests that folk psychological notions of standing (and perhaps occurrent) states arguably track a combination of phenomenal intentional states and derived mental representational states. Finally, §8.3.4 considers to what extent these points can be extended to cover subpersonal standing states.

8.3.1 PERSONAL STANDING STATES

One might claim that there are personal standing states, like beliefs and desires, and that they are intentional. We can distinguish two views of personal standing states on which they are intentional: On the **distinct structures view**, personal standing states are or include distinct internal structures that continuously intentionally represent their contents, where **distinct (internal) structures** are distinct, fairly localizable, and persistent structures in our heads. On this view, the contents of personal intentional standing states are in some sense "written" in our brains. The second view, **dispositionalism**, is the view that personal standing states are dispositions to have occurrent states with the same or similar contents or other relevant dispositions, such as dispositions to behave in particular ways. Both views agree that there are personal intentional standing states, but they disagree on whether they are distinct structures or dispositions. Mixed views are also available, such as views on which some intentional standing states are distinct structures and others are dispositions.[13]

In what follows, I first put pressure on the distinct structures view, arguing that dispositionalism is preferable to it. I then argue that dispositionalism is not quite right either, since the relevant dispositions are not genuinely intentional. I then argue that even if some alleged personal standing states do involve or correspond to distinct structures, these structures should not be characterized as intentional when they are not being used. Any distinct structures we might have do not *continuously* intentionally represent.

One reason to be suspicious of the distinct structures view is that it seems there is no non-arbitrary way of deciding which distinct structures to posit. The occurrent states we are disposed to have form a continuum of cases that differ in whether we have ever had an occurrent version of the state or nearby states before, how likely we are to have the state in various circumstances, and how much thinking or processing is required in order to have the state. This suggests that there is no clear division in

---

[13] On some views, the only concepts and other representations that we have are those involved in our current intentional states, but on other views, it might be correct to say that we "have" concepts and representations even when they are not in use, perhaps because they are capacities or physical structures in our brains. It might seem that, on the latter views, representations have their contents even while not in use, which would make them standing states. However, the sense in which they "have" their contents when not in use is not the same as that in which distinct structures are supposed to have their contents. Representations that are not in use but that we in some sense count as having "have" contents in that when they contribute to occurrent intentional states they contribute those contents. Distinct structures, on the other hand, are supposed to continuously represent their contents even when not in use.

the mind, such as one marked by having a distinct structure, between cases in which we have a personal standing state and those in which we do not.

Schwitzgebel (2001) provides a variety of cases in which he claims it is arbitrary to either ascribe or not ascribe a particular standing belief to an individual. One kind of case involves gradual forgetting:

> When I was in college, I knew the last name of the fellow whose first name was "Konstantin" and who lived across the hall from me in freshman year. I have not been in contact with him since 1987, and my memory of him is slowly fading. When I was twenty-five, if you asked me his last name, I probably but not certainly would have given you the right answer. Reminiscing with college buddies, it might easily have come to mind; in a distracting circumstance alien from my college environment, it might not have come at all, or maybe with effort, or maybe only later as I was driving home and not giving the matter any conscious attention. Now, at thirty-two, I cannot give you the answer with any certainty, and I would probably get it slightly wrong—but maybe if I chanced to see him in San Francisco I would find the correct name coming out of my mouth. I could tell you that his name starts with a 'G', and if you told me what it was I would confidently recognize it—maybe even correct you if you made a little mistake in pronouncing it. I could pick it out on a multiple-choice test with similar-looking alternatives. Ten years from now, I shall not be able to recall it under any circumstances, but I could probably still pick it out on a multiple-choice test, unless the alternatives were very close. As I get older, I could be misled by less and less similar alternatives, until success requires alternatives so divergent as no longer to test my knowledge that his name was such and such, but only my knowledge of whether, for example, his name was a short Chinese name or a mid-length German one. At eighty, I shall have no memory of Konstantin whatsoever. (pp. 76–77)

Schwitzgebel claims that, while it may be clear that in his college days he had the belief that Konstantin's last name was "Guericke" and that when he turns 80 he does not have the belief, there is no determinate time at which he passes from having the belief to not having it. Any choice of such a point would be arbitrary. Instead, Schwitzgebel suggests that for much of the time between his college days and his turning 80, he is in a state of "in-between belief," where he neither believes nor fails to believe that Konstantin's last name is "Guericke." Schwitzgebel provides several more examples of in-between believing, including cases in which a subject's avowed beliefs conflict with her judgments about particular cases, cases of self-deception, and cases of gradual learning (Schwitzgebel 2001, 2002).

Schwitzgebel suggests that such cases are best accommodated by a dispositionalist account of belief on which beliefs are clusters of dispositions to engage in certain behaviors or enter certain mental states, including phenomenal states. In his college days, Schwitzgebel has all or most of the dispositions characteristic of the belief that Konstantin's last name is "Guericke," while at 80, he has none or almost none of them. At the in-between stages, he has some but not all of these dispositions, and that is what it is for him to have the in-between belief. That he has some but not all of the dispositions is all there is to be said about whether he has the belief; there is no further fact of the matter as to whether he *really* has it, as to whether "Konstantin's last name is either recorded somewhere deep in [his] memory or it is not" (Schwitzgebel 2001, p. 82).

Similarly, Searle (1991) suggests that an advantage of his view that all intentional states are at least potentially conscious is that it allows us to say that there is no deep fact of the matter as to whether one has a particular standing belief. For example, he suggests that there is no fact of the matter as to whether he should count as believing that doctors wear underwear or that station wagons are inedible (Searle 1991, p. 62). Searle suggests that rather than think of the mind as "a big filing cabinet in which we store a whole lot of information" (p. 63), we should instead think of what we have as "a whole lot of capacities in the brain for generating conscious thoughts" (p. 63). Like Schwitzgebel, Searle proposes something like a dispositionalist view of standing states, though the dispositions he identifies with standing states are dispositions to have phenomenal intentional states.[14]

Schwitzgebel and Searle's examples tell against the distinct structures view. The problem is that having a distinct structure is roughly an all-or-nothing matter, but having a belief can be a matter of degree. Having a disposition or a cluster of dispositions, on the other hand, is a matter of degree—you can be disposed to engage in certain belief-appropriate behaviors or have certain further belief-related mental states, but not others, in certain circumstances, but not in others, and with a certain likelihood.

The past few decades of psychological research on episodic memory, our memory for events, also suggests against the distinct structures view. The best going view seems to be that recalled episodic memory episodes are largely reconstructed, partly based on cues from the immediate environment and background knowledge, rather than read off a stored representation.[15] In a pioneering study, Loftus and Palmer

---

[14] See also Audi (1972, 1994), who defends a very different kind of dispositionalist view.
[15] See Schacter and Singer 1962 and Schacter and Addis 2007 for a psychological overview and Michaelian 2011 and De Brigard 2014 for philosophical discussion.

(1974) had subjects watch a video of a car accident. They were then asked either "About how fast were the cars going when they smashed into each other?" or similar questions using more neutral language, such as "About how fast were the cars going when they hit each other?" Subjects who were presented with the question using the word "smashed" estimated higher speeds, with a mean estimate of 40.8 miles per hour, compared to those in the "hit" and other neutral conditions, with the mean estimate of 34.0 miles per hour for "hit." Those in the "smashed" condition were also more likely to falsely remember seeing broken glass. This type of effect of new input on memory retrieval is known as the **misinformation effect**.

Many other experiments by Loftus and others have produced similar results. In another study, Braun et al. (2002) had subjects read a Disneyland advertisement asking them to recollect their childhood experiences at Disneyland. Among other things, the ad described shaking hands with Bugs Bunny. After reading the ad, 16% of subjects falsely remembered that they had in fact shaken hands with Bugs Bunny at Disneyland. (We know these are false memories because Bugs Bunny is not a Disney character.)

These and other similar results suggest that memory recollection is largely a constructive process. Events are not simply recorded in one's head and then replayed on demand. Rather, we use whatever resources are available to construct plausible reconstructions of what might have happened. These resources include hints from our current environment, such as the phrasing of certain questions, which is why we are susceptible to the misinformation effect.

The reconstructive nature of memory exacerbates the problem for the distinct structures view concerning which standing states to attribute to people. Should we attribute to a subject in Loftus' original car crash study the belief that the car was going at around 34 miles per hour or the belief that it was going at around 41 miles per hour? What should we say about whether, prior to questioning, the subject believed there was broken glass? The dispositional view can say that the subject, prior to questioning, has, say, the disposition to judge that the car was traveling at around 34 miles per hour in one set of circumstances, the disposition to judge that the car was traveling at around 41 miles per hour in another set of circumstances, and so on. There is no further question about what she *really* believed prior to questioning. The same goes for the broken glass.

All this helps to further erode the picture of the mind as containing a giant receptacle of explicitly encoded beliefs, desires, etc., and instead suggests one on which the mind is a producer of thoughts and experiences. But one might object that even if this shows that in many cases of episodic memory, and perhaps other kinds of standing states, we do not have distinct structures corresponding to the relevant states, this does not mean that there are *no* distinct structures corresponding to any standing states. For example, perhaps there are distinct structures corresponding to my knowledge of my own name and other facts I know by rote. Call this the **rote knowledge objection**.

The dispositionalist might respond that, again, there is a continuum of such cases and any way of drawing a line between cases that are supposed to involve a distinct structure and those that are not would be arbitrary, even if the line is drawn close to one extreme. Further, given that many cases of personal standing states are to be treated as dispositions, it would be more parsimonious to treat them all that way, even those that do not directly tell against the distinct structures view. There is more to say about the rote knowledge objection, but I will set it aside for now and return to it shortly.

So far, we have seen that various considerations militate in favor of dispositionalism and against the distinct structures view. While I am sympathetic to dispositionalism, it is not quite the view I want to adopt. Dispositionalism accepts that there are intentional personal standing states but claims that they are nothing but dispositions. In contrast, while I accept that some cases involve nothing but dispositions, I do not think we should grant them the status of *intentional*. We might say that the dispositional view, as I have presented it, is a **reductive dispositionalism**: it reduces intentional personal standing states to dispositions. A view closer to my preferred view, in contrast, is **eliminative dispositionalism**, which denies the existence of genuinely intentional personal standing states and claims that what we have instead are various dispositions (see, however, §8.3.2, where I suggest we can say a bit more about personal standing states).

The picture of memory and standing states that emerges from the above discussion is more congenial to eliminative dispositionalism than to reductive dispositionalism. The picture that emerges is similar in certain respects to a plausible picture of certain aspects of our perceptual systems, the systems generating occurrent perceptual states. Perceptual systems have the capacity or disposition to generate various kinds of conscious occurrent intentional perceptual states (and various other responses) in various circumstances, but we do not want to say that they continuously intentionally represent the contents they are disposed to generate or that they sort of or "in-between" intentionally represent these contents. For example, my visual system is disposed to generate a conscious occurrent state representing a red square (and various other responses) in various circumstances, but it would be incorrect to say that I intentionally represent a red square when this disposition is not manifested. In the case of perceptual systems, the disposition to generate conscious occurrent states (and perhaps other responses) is not sufficient for representing the content of those occurrent states when the disposition is not being manifested. If all we have in the case of the non-perceptual systems underlying belief, desire, memory, and other alleged standing states are dispositions to generate occurrent states (or other responses), we should also say that this is not sufficient for continuously intentionally representing the contents of those occurrent states. In other words, we accept an eliminative dispositionalism for the "standing states" of perceptual systems consisting in the disposition to generate conscious occurrent perceptual representations, so we should similarly accept an eliminative dispositionalism for standing states more generally.

One might object that we are disposed to manifest the relevant dispositions in more circumstances in the case of personal standing states like beliefs and desires than in the perceptual case. But we can imagine cases of perceptual systems being as disposed to manifest the relevant dispositions as the systems generating belief, etc. Suppose that after some trauma involving a red square, I am disposed to hallucinate red squares all over the place. Still, when I am not hallucinating a red square, I do not count as intentionally representing a red square. Likewise, we can imagine cases of the systems underlying belief, etc., being disposed to produce an occurrent state in very rare circumstances (indeed, perhaps most cases are like this). If we do not count as having "standing states" intentionally representing perceptual contents that we are disposed to entertain in equally rare circumstances, we should not count as having personal standing states intentionally representing various contents in the non-perceptual case either. At best, the difference between perceptual systems' dispositions to generate conscious occurrent intentional states and belief, etc., systems' dispositions to generate occurrent intentional states is a matter of degree, not kind. So, we should not grant one set of dispositions the status of being genuinely intentional but not the other. We should grant neither this status.[16]

Strawson (1994, 2004) similarly argues that mere dispositions do not give rise to intentional states:

[I]t is no more true to say that there are states of the brain, or of [a subject,] Louis, that have intrinsic mental content, when Louis is in a dreamless and

---

[16] Declan Smithies has suggested that another potential disanalogy is that personal standing states like beliefs and desires are often supposed to be dispositions to engage in behaviors as well as to have certain occurrent states, whereas it is not clear that the dispositional "standing state" of the visual system that I have in mind are dispositions to behavior. For this reason, it might be more explanatorily useful to ascribe intentionality to personal standing states than to "standing visual states," which motivates ascribing intentionality to the former cases and not to the latter. However, the "standing states" of the visual system are indeed disposed to generate behaviors and various other responses. For example, being disposed to hallucinate red squares comes with a disposition to engage in certain red-square-related behaviors. Additionally, as we will soon see in §8.3.3, we can perfectly well accommodate the usefulness of personal standing states like beliefs and desires in explaining behavior without taking them to be genuinely intentional.

experienceless sleep, than it is true to say that there are states of a CD that have intrinsic musical content as it sits in its box.... It is true of Louis that he believes that water is wet and likes black olives, just as it is true of this CD that it is a CD of Beethoven's fifteenth string quartet. But there are no mental phenomena in the dreamless [portion of reality that consists in Louis], just as there is no music in the room as the CD sits on the shelf. (Strawson 1994, p. 167)

Strawson concludes that "strictly speaking, [there are] no dispositional nonexperiential mental phenomena" (Strawson 1994, p. 167). Just as a CD sitting on the shelf does not play music, and (we might add) the perceptual representations involved in conscious perceptual experience that are not being used do not intentionally represent perceptual contents, so too do dispositional states that are not being manifested fail to intentionally represent their contents.[17]

While I have recommended eliminative dispositionalism over views that accept the existence of intentional personal standing states, I want to suggest that the eliminativist need not deny the existence of distinct structures, so long as these structures do not continuously intentionally represent. Let us return to the rote knowledge objection, the objection to (reductive) dispositionalism that memory research doesn't establish that we fail to have distinct structures corresponding to *all* standing states. One might claim, for example, that memory research does not show that we don't have a distinct internal structure corresponding to our knowledge of our own names, which, presumably, is not very susceptible to the misinformation effect. Earlier, I suggested that the (reductive) dispositionalist has grounds to claim that such standing states should be given a (reductive) dispositionalist treatment.

This objection is also an objection to eliminative dispositionalism, since the eliminative dispositionalist does not accept the existence of genuinely intentional distinct structures corresponding to any personal standing states. The eliminativist about personal intentional standing states can appeal to the same considerations as the reductive dispositionalist to argue that all we really have in the relevant cases are dispositions to have occurrent states (and perhaps other responses). But, interestingly, there is another, more conciliatory, response open to an eliminativist about personal intentional standing states who is not particularly wedded to eliminative *dispositionalism*: Even if we do have distinct structures corresponding to some of our personal standing states, it does not follow that these structures

---

[17] Pitt (MS-a) makes a similar point with an analogy to photographs stored on one's computer. Just as what is stored on your computer's hard drive are encodings or "recipes" for generating photographs, given the appropriate programs and hardware, so too is what's stored in one's head merely an encoding or "recipe" for generating phenomenal intentional states or other responses.

continuously intentionally represent their contents while they are not being used. Suppose that perceptual systems also have distinct structures corresponding to some of the conscious occurrent representations that we are disposed to have, say, of familiar scenes (e.g., your living room, a favorite view). It would still not be right to say that we count as intentionally representing these familiar scenes even when we are not occurrently representing them. The eliminativist can allow for such distinct structures in perceptual systems, so she can likewise allow for such distinct structures in belief, etc., systems. In neither case are they intentional when they are not being used. This view is eliminativist, in that it denies that we have genuinely intentional personal standing states, but it also accepts that we may have distinct structures, which, the view maintains, do not count as intentional when they are not being used. Since my interest is in denying that there are intentional personal standing states, it does not matter to me whether it turns out that eliminative dispositionalism or this more general version of eliminativism is correct.

I have argued that we should treat personal standing states generally in the same way that we treat certain of the "standing states" of our perceptual systems. But why, one might wonder, is it so tempting to treat at least some of them differently, particularly those corresponding to beliefs and desires? Why do we think we continuously intentionally represent our belief and desire contents, even when we do not entertain or otherwise occurrently represent them, whereas we have no such temptation to think we continuously represent perceptual contents we are not occurrently representing? The reason is that, as we will see in the next subsection, we *take* ourselves to have standing states like beliefs and desires, whereas we do not take ourselves to have perceptual "standing states."

8.3.2 SELF-ASCRIPTIVISM ABOUT PERSONAL STANDING STATE CONTENTS

In §7.3, I suggested a self-ascriptivist view of the alleged contents of thought, on which we derivatively represent these contents by taking our immediate contents to represent them. This section examines whether this kind of self-ascriptivism can be extended to the case of at least some personal standing states.

The intuition behind self-ascriptivism is that the only way to target contents that are not phenomenally represented—that are not, as it were, forced upon us by experience—is to ascribe them to ourselves. There are many ways in which we might ascribe contents to ourselves. In §7.3, I proposed a fairly undemanding way in which we might do this in the case of occurrent thoughts and the concepts they involve: Immediate content C (and any representations or intentional mental states with immediate content C) *derivatively represents* C+ (for S) if S takes C to mean C+. S *takes* C to mean C+ if S has a set of dispositions to have cashing out thoughts that together specify that C cashes out into C+. *Cashing out thoughts* are thoughts stating that one content is an elucidation, unpacking, precisification, or in some other way a "better" version of another.

I want to suggest that we can expand our notion of derived mental representation to capture at least some standing state contents, particularly those corresponding to beliefs, desires, and other personal standing states that we accept largely on intuitive grounds. Just as we might self-ascribe contents to our immediate contents, so too can we self-ascribe contents to ourselves independently of any particular immediate contents. This simply involves taking *ourselves* to represent various contents. As in the case of self-ascriptivism about the alleged contents of thoughts, this might involve being disposed to accept that we represent various contents. For example, suppose I am disposed to accept that I represent that the Acropolis is in Athens. Simply in virtue of this, I count as derivatively representing that the Acropolis is in Athens. This is true even though I may have no distinct structure that derivatively represents this content.

This kind of self-ascriptivism involves ascribing contents to ourselves rather than to our immediate contents. We might specify the resulting kind of derived mental representation as follows:

(Taking-standing) Subject S **takes** herself **to have a state** with content C+ if
(1) S is disposed to accept that she has a state with content C (upon sufficient reflection), and (2) either C is identical to C+ or S takes C to mean C+.
(DMR-standing) Subject S **derivatively represents** C+ (for S) if S takes herself to have a state with content C+.

Self-ascriptivism about personal standing states combines nicely with self-ascriptivism about the alleged contents of thoughts. If a subject is disposed to accept that she has a state with a particular content, C, and C derivatively represents C+ for her, then she counts as taking herself to represent C+ and, hence, as derivatively representing C+ (for herself). For example, suppose I am disposed to accept that I have a state representing the phenomenal content <the Acropolis is in Athens>, and I also take the phenomenal content <the Acropolis is in Athens> to mean some more complex content <the Acropolis is in Athens+>. Then I count as derivatively representing <the Acropolis is in Athens+>.[18,19]

---

[18] As in the case of (Taking), defined in §7.3.1, the relevant dispositions doing the work in (Taking-standing) must be dispositions to have phenomenal intentional states. See §7.3.3.

[19] One might wonder whether we have to take ourselves to have takings in order for these takings to do their work, i.e., whether takings have to themselves be self-ascribed. The answer is "no" (see also n. 22 of Chapter 7). One might object that if takings can do their work without being self-ascribed, then mere

So far, this offers a theoretical home for the *contents* of beliefs, desires, and any other personal standing states we are disposed to ascribe to ourselves, but it doesn't provide an account of their attitudes. It doesn't, for instance, tell us what makes a standing belief a *belief* rather than a hope, a desire, or an intention. But many of the same options that are available for accounting for the attitudes of occurrent thoughts are open to us here. Appendix E of Chapter 7 argued that my picture of thought is compatible with views that take attitudes to be a matter of functional roles (attitude functionalism), phenomenal characters (attitude phenomenalism), or represented contents (attitude representationalism) but that it is particularly congenial to a version of attitude representationalism that takes the contents special to each attitude to be derived contents. On this version of attitude representationalism, a thought is a desire, say, rather than a belief because it has a phenomenal content that we take to mean a further content, like <good>.

Attitude representationalism also allows us to say that at least some personal standing states in their entirety, and not just their contents, are derivatively represented. On this combined view, we might count as having a standing desire that P simply because we take ourselves to represent, say, that P is good.

This depends, of course, on attitude representationalism being true. If attitude representationalism is false, then the view that personal standing states derivatively represent their contents only offers a theoretical home for the alleged contents of personal standing states and not the attitudes they allegedly involve. This is a fallback position for those who reject attitude representationalism.

---

dispositions to occurrently represent should qualify as derivatively representing without having to be self-ascribed. It seems the bar is lower for takings than for other kinds of states.

I want to suggest that takings have a special status in virtue of their self-ascriptive contents, which allows them to do their work without our having to take ourselves to have them. We can think of takings as providing a kind of endorsement, a seal of approval, on our dispositions, sorting the ones that determine the contents we in some sense target or intend from the others. Requiring takings to themselves be self-ascribed would lead to a regress, where endorsements would have to themselves be endorsed in order to do any endorsing.

The only other alternative is to take our present phenomenal states to endorse our takings. While I think that something like this might be going on (see n. 21 of Chapter 7), requiring this for a content to be in some sense targeted by us would be quite demanding. In order for a content to be in some sense targeted or "ours," we would have to either phenomenally represent it or point to it in some way in our phenomenal consciousness at all times. But we are temporal beings, existing over time. We do not need to constantly be clinging onto all our contents in this way in order for them to count as "ours." The less demanding alternative, then, is to let takings do the endorsing and to allow them to do so without themselves having to be endorsed. However, a nearby alternative position requires our phenomenal states to in some sense defer to or target our cashing out dispositions and dispositions to accept ourselves as having various states in order for those dispositions to result in derived mental representation.

As we've seen, there are derivativist and eliminativist versions of self-ascriptivism (§7.4 and §8.2). However, the arguments in §7.4 and §8.2 suggest against derivativism, and the arguments in §8.3.1 support eliminativism. This leaves us with my preferred view, eliminativist self-ascriptivism, but a derivativist self-ascriptivism is a fallback position for those who endorse self-ascriptivism but are not convinced by my arguments against derivativism and for eliminativism.

8.3.3 FOLK PSYCHOLOGY

In §1.3.1, I considered an approach to fixing reference on intentionality that takes intentionality to be a posit in our folk psychological theory of mind and behavior. On this approach, folk psychology is a theory that attributes beliefs, desires, and other states to subjects, and intentionality is a feature such states are taken to have. The reason I rejected this approach is that it could end up picking out something other than the core phenomenon we are interested in when we are interested in the "aboutness" or "directedness" of mental states, or nothing at all.

I want to suggest that the folk psychological approach does not in fact end up picking out intentionality. Exactly what notion of "intentionality" folk psychology is committed to is an open empirical question, as far as what we've said so far is concerned. However, it is clear that the "intentional" states that folk psychology attributes to us are not limited to those that happen to be phenomenal intentional states. Rather, these states include personal standing and personal occurrent states representing many of the non-phenomenal contents described in Chapter 7, such as rich descriptive contents and object-involving contents, many of which are broad contents. Insofar as the contents assigned by folk psychology are supposed to be in some sense targeted, endorsed, or accepted by the representing subject, or to in some sense capture the representing subject's point of view, the only available options are phenomenal contents and derived contents. So, in the best-case scenario, folk psychology attributes to subjects phenomenal and derived contents, and the notion of "intentionality" implicit in folk psychology picks out the disjunctive kind of phenomenal intentionality or derived mental representation. In the worst-case scenario, the folk psychological notion of "intentionality" includes various assumptions about intentionality that phenomenal intentionality and derived mental representation do not satisfy and, so, ends up picking out nothing at all.

Supposing that the best-case scenario obtains, we can see why folk psychology is so predictively accurate, even though it does not limit itself to positing intentional states, and even though it may not even distinguish between intentional states and derived mental representational states. Folk psychological content attributions lump together phenomenal contents with derived contents, which can be either directly or indirectly derivatively represented. Phenomenal contents and derived contents are the contents we in some sense target or accept as our own, so they serve as something like attractors for our rationally guided behaviors. Even though we may not always be occurrently thinking most of these targeted contents, we tend to home in on them as we acquire relevant information and as they become relevant to our inferences and behaviors.

Recall that, roughly, we directly derivatively represent a content when we are disposed to have cashing out thoughts that specify the content by literally containing the content in their immediate contents. For example, BACHELOR might directly derivatively represent <unmarried man> for a subject thanks to her disposition to have a cashing out thought with the content <by <bachelor>, I mean <unmarried man>>. Such a subject's concept BACHELOR in some sense targets the content <unmarried man>. As a result, when it is relevant, and when she is being sufficiently reflective, she is likely to infer that bachelors are unmarried and to use this information to guide her bachelor-related inferences and behavior. For example, she is likely not to apply her concept to John, who she believes to be married. Importantly, we cannot predict such inferences and behaviors based solely on her moment-by-moment phenomenal contents. We also need to know something about which further intentional states involving the concept BACHELOR she is likely to endorse. Attributing to her bachelor-related standing and occurrent states with rich direct derived contents is one way of keeping track of this information.

Similarly, attributing to subjects various indirect derived contents can be predictively useful. Indirect derived representation involves being disposed to have cashing out thoughts that specify an immediate content's derived content by referring to it, rather than by containing it. Although a subject may not know what she refers to, and hence which indirect derived contents she derivatively represents, she in some sense has a "path" to her content. She is in principle able to figure out what it is that she indirectly derivatively represents by finding out relevant facts about the world. For example, if a subject indirectly derivatively represents water by being disposed to have cashing out thoughts that specify that <water> cashes out into the clear watery stuff around here, then she in some sense knows how her indirect derived contents depend on facts about the world and which parts of the world she needs to investigate to find out what <water> means for her, namely, the parts containing the clear watery stuff around here. We might expect her to progressively home in on her targeted indirect derived content as she finds out more relevant facts about the world. As she does so, her <water>-related behaviors will also progressively come to converge on her target, H_2O. Knowing her indirect derived contents can help us predict her inferences and behaviors in circumstances in which she learns relevant information about her environment that helps her home in on the self-ascribed targets of her water-related thoughts.[20,21]

In short, it is not implausible that the folk psychological notion of "intentionality" bundles together information about the phenomenal and derived contents of occurrent and standing states, yielding a picture of our mental life that includes not just our moment-by-moment intentional contents but also the phenomenal and derived contents that we in some sense target and that our inferences and behaviors tend to converge on.

8.3.4 SUBPERSONAL STANDING STATES

The discussion in this section has focused on personal standing states, such as the beliefs and desires we take ourselves to have on intuitive grounds. Some, but not all, of the points made above apply to subpersonal standing states like the "assumptions" of the visual system, the states of edge-detecting neurons that are not in use, and our standing knowledge of the grammar of our own language.

As in the case of personal standing states, we can distinguish between two views of intentional subpersonal standing states: they might be distinct internal structures, or they might be dispositions, which might include dispositions to have occurrent states with the same or similar contents, to engage in various behaviors, or to have various related internal states. Mixed views are also possible.

The arguments for preferring dispositionalism over the distinct structures view do not clearly extend to subpersonal standing states, since these arguments apply

---

[20] Burge's (1979) well-known example of the concept ARTHRITIS nicely illustrates these claims. Bert and his intrinsic duplicate, who we can call Twin Bert, are members of different linguistic communities. In Bert's linguistic community, "arthritis" refers to an inflammation of the joints, while in Twin Bert's linguistic community, "arthritis" refers to an inflammation of the joints or thighs, a condition that we might call "tharthritis" in English. Bert and Twin Bert's histories coincide up until they visit their doctors complaining about their suspected "arthritis" in their thighs. Bert is corrected by his doctor, while Twin Bert is not, and their histories diverge, with Bert's arthritis-related behaviors becoming directed toward arthritis and Twin Bert's becoming directed toward tharthritis. Importantly, Bert and Twin Bert's behaviors are related toward their different targets precisely because Bert and Twin Bert in some important sense were targeting different diseases with their respective concepts all along, a sense that is captured by the notion of indirect derived mental representation. Knowing the indirect derived contents of their concepts helps us predict their behaviors in circumstances in which they learn relevant information about what they were targeting.

[21] All this presupposes that we have some understanding of the conditions that need to be satisfied in order for a given content to refer to something. We might have such an understanding because we generally refer by description and we know the relevant descriptions (see n. 31 of Chapter 7), because we refer by having an internal criterion for reference (see Appendix H of Chapter 9), or because we have a priori or intuitive insight on what determines conditions of reference.

most directly to the case of episodic memory and cases that might be thought to be relevantly similar, like those of belief and desire. In some cases of subpersonal standing states, such as the case of edge-detecting neurons that are not in use, there might be good reason to think that there are distinct structures underlying our dispositions (e.g., the neurons themselves). In other cases it might be less plausible, such as in the case of our standing knowledge of our grammar. As far as what we've said, it is an open empirical question which, if any, subpersonal standing states are or involve distinct structures.

However, the reasons for thinking that any distinct structures or dispositions corresponding to personal standing states are not genuinely intentional also apply to subpersonal states. The argument against reductive dispositionalism about personal standing states was an argument by analogy. Perceptual systems have dispositions to generate conscious occurrent intentional states (and other responses), but these dispositions are best thought of as *mere* dispositions to have intentional states, not genuinely intentional states themselves. Similarly, any dispositions corresponding to beliefs, desires, and other personal standing states are nothing more than mere dispositions. In the same way, even if subpersonal standing states are or involve dispositions to have occurrent intentional states (or other responses), we should take them to be mere dispositions rather than genuinely intentional mental states.

Similarly, the argument against taking any distinct structures corresponding to personal standing states to be intentional was an argument by analogy. If we have distinct structures corresponding to the dispositions to have conscious perceptual states, we should not say that they continuously intentionally represent the contents that they are used to consciously represent. Likewise, we should not say that any distinct structures corresponding to personal standing states like beliefs and desires continuously represent the contents of any related occurrent states. For the same reason, we should not take any distinct structures corresponding to subpersonal standing states to be genuinely intentional either. Even if such structures play a role in intentionally representing various contents when they are in use, they do not continuously represent them when they are not.

Although, as I have suggested, we derivatively represent many of the contents of personal standing states, and perhaps even some personal standing states in their entirety, the same does not apply to most subpersonal standing states. Since we do not in most cases ascribe such states or their alleged contents to ourselves, we do not in most cases derivatively represent them or their contents. In the next section, however, I argue that even though nonconscious occurrent states do not have intentional or derived contents, they might be said to represent in some other extended sense that requires no more than tracking relations and functional roles. As we will see, subpersonal standing states (as well as personal standing states and practically any other kind of internal state) can also be said to represent in this extended sense, and this might be all we need in order to satisfy our needs with respect to such states.

8.4 Allegedly Nonconscious Occurrent States

There are many different kinds of allegedly nonconscious personal and subpersonal occurrent states that we might want to treat as representational in some way, such as states of individual neurons, synapses, or other neural states, computational states, distributed states of a neural network, states involved in nonconscious priming and implicit bias, and nonconscious thoughts. Many have raised doubts as to whether we should really think of such states as representational.[22] If not, then there is no objection to PIT from nonconscious occurrent states. I will sidestep this issue and grant, for the sake of argument, that there is at least a loose or extended sense in which all of the states mentioned above qualify as "representational," whether or not it is explanatorily useful to think of them in this way. The worry, then, is that these states are intentional but not phenomenal and, so, that it is not clear how PIT can accommodate them.

This section argues that, in most cases, the correct view of allegedly nonconscious occurrent states is eliminativist: most of these states are not intentional, even though they might carry information or "represent" in some sense. However, I also want to suggest that in some cases inflationism might be correct: some of these states might in fact be phenomenal intentional states.

8.4.1 ELIMINATIVISM ABOUT MOST NONCONSCIOUS OCCURRENT STATES

The eliminativist strategy about a mental state says that either the state does not exist or it is not intentional. I want to suggest that, with a few exceptions, eliminativism is the correct view about most of the above-mentioned (allegedly) nonconscious occurrent states. These states include the subpersonal occurrent states posited by neuroscience and computational and connectionist models of the mind. For example, the eliminativism I want to accept maintains that edge-detecting neurons

---

[22] For example, Piccinini (2008) argues that computational states are not individuated by representational features. Egan (2010) similarly argues that computation should be understood non-representationally and that representational descriptions of computational systems only provide a pragmatic "gloss." Ramsey (2007) argues that states of neural networks are not representational. Chomsky (1995) and Orlandi (2014) argue that subpersonal visual states should not be understood as representational. Cao (2012) suggests that individual neurons or even groups of neurons are not clear cases of representation; see also Sullivan (2010) for discussion.

firing in V1 do not intentionally represent edges and the occurrent states involved in nonconscious linguistic processing do not intentionally represent rules of grammar or other contents.

I will argue for the eliminativist strategy by showing that it is very much in line with what we might call the **Standard View** of nonconscious occurrent states. Here are some claims that I take to be part of the Standard View and that the advocate of PIT who is an eliminativist about nonconscious occurrent states can accept:

(SV1) Allegedly nonconscious occurrent states track various items, e.g., edges. For example, they might be causally sensitive to the relevant items, or they might correspond to them in a particular way when functioning properly.

(SV2) Allegedly nonconscious occurrent states play various functional roles. For example, they might cause or be caused by other states, or they might be connected in various ways to behavior.

(SV3) Most, if not all, allegedly nonconscious occurrent states are not phenomenally conscious.

This much we can all agree on. We can agree that allegedly nonconscious occurrent states bear various tracking relations and play various functional roles and, further, that most of them are not phenomenally conscious. Now, if all we mean by "representation" is something that is assumed to amount to some construction out of tracking relations and functional roles, including computational roles, then we can also agree that allegedly nonconscious occurrent states "represent" in this somewhat extended sense. Let us call representation in this sense **TR-representation** (for "representation assumed to amount to no more than TRacking relations and functional roles"). So, we can also agree on this claim:

(SV4) Allegedly nonconscious occurrent states TR-represent various contents.

Note that (SV4) leaves open the question of whether the notion of TR-representation is explanatorily useful and, if so, for which purposes. It also leaves open the question of whether there is a single privileged notion of this sort or whether there are multiple interesting notions of this sort that might be useful for different purposes. The advocate of PIT who is an eliminativist about nonconscious occurrent states does not think TR-representation is intentionality, but she need not deny that it exists or that it is explanatorily useful.

So far, we have seen that there is much agreement between the advocate of PIT who takes an eliminativist approach to allegedly nonconscious occurrent states and the Standard View. Indeed, the advocate of PIT can also accept the further claim, which I assume is part of the Standard View, that, like allegedly nonconscious occurrent states, phenomenally conscious states TR-represent:

(SV5) Phenomenally conscious states TR-represent.

The advocate of PIT who takes an eliminativist approach to allegedly nonconscious occurrent states can agree that phenomenally conscious states, states that involve phenomenal consciousness, bear various tracking relations to various items and play various functional roles and, when they bear the right tracking relations and play the right functional roles, they TR-represent. Indeed, this is also a plausible thing to say about standing states, including subpersonal standing states.

Where, then, one might wonder, is the disagreement between the Standard View and the advocate of PIT who is an eliminativist about allegedly nonconscious occurrent states? The main disagreement, I want to suggest, lies over this final claim that I will take, for the sake of argument,[23] to be part of the Standard View:

(SV6) The intentionality of phenomenally conscious states is a kind of TR-representation.

According to (SV6), the intentionality of our phenomenally conscious states is nothing over and above the TR-representation that we find in, say, nonconscious early visual processing. Of course, conscious TR-representation may be more complex and sophisticated in various ways than nonconscious TR-representation, and its being conscious might involve some additional ingredients, such as that of playing a special functional role. But, at bottom, according to (SV6), the intentionality of phenomenally conscious states is just more of the same of what gives us the TR-representational features of nonconscious occurrent states. This, of course, is precisely where the defender of PIT disagrees, since she takes intentionality to require phenomenal consciousness.

Now, (SV6) might suggest a somewhat deflationary view of the intentionality of phenomenally conscious states—their intentionality is *nothing more* than

---

[23] If (SV6) is not taken to be part of the Standard View, then there is no disagreement between the Standard View and the version of PIT that is eliminativist about allegedly nonconscious standing states, and my proposal is even more conciliatory than advertised.

TR-representation. But there is another reading of (SV6) as committing the Standard View to a somewhat *inflationary* picture of TR-representation: TR-representation is the Real Deal when it comes to intentionality, the only interesting notion in the area to be had. Such an inflationary picture is likely to lead us to expect quite a lot from TR-representation. For instance, it might lead us to expect that TR-represented contents are not massively disjunctive or indeterminate, or that they correspond to the contents we intuitively ascribe. In contrast, the advocate of the deflationary reading of the Standard View (and the advocate of PIT) is likely to relax the requirements on TR-representation, allowing TR-represented contents to be massively disjunctive, indeterminate, and quite foreign to intuitive content ascriptions.[24]

Regardless of which of the above two readings we give to (SV6), the disagreement over (SV6) is not over the core nature of allegedly nonconscious occurrent states—everyone agrees that all relevant aspects of their core nature are fully characterized by (SV1) through (SV4). Even an advocate of the inflationary reading of (SV6) agrees here: even though she believes that TR-representation is the Real Deal when it comes to intentionality, she still believes that this Real Deal is nothing over and above tracking and functional roles. So even she believes that (SV1) through (SV4) provide a full specification of the relevant aspects of the nature of nonconscious states.

Where does this leave us? Recall that my aim is to defend PIT against the objection that it cannot accommodate allegedly nonconscious occurrent states. We can now see that it can say all the same things about the nature of such states as the Standard View: it can accept (SV1) through (SV4). So, it can accommodate them perfectly well.

Further, accommodating allegedly nonconscious occurrent states does not require PIT to adopt an inflationist or derivativist strategy, on which these states are intentional. Indeed, such strategies arguably represent a further departure from the Standard View, since they would claim that, say, states in early visual processing require a connection to consciousness in order to represent in the sense that the Standard View takes them to represent, a claim that not only fails to be part of the Standard View but also is arguably at odds with it. So, not only is an eliminativist strategy defensible, but it is also arguably more conciliatory to the Standard View than the inflationist and derivativist alternatives.

---

[24] See especially Cummins (1994), who develops a notion of representation for computational theories of cognition that does not yield determinate contents, (correctly) maintaining that this is not a problem given his purposes.

What should we say about the remaining point of disagreement, the disagreement over (SV6)? This disagreement does not concern the core nature of allegedly nonconscious states, so it does not affect my claim here that PIT can satisfactorily accommodate allegedly nonconscious occurrent states. It does, nevertheless, affect the truth of PIT, since if (SV6) is true, then PIT is presumably false. But I have already addressed (SV6): Chapters 3 through 5 argued that intentionality, the feature we introspectively notice in paradigm cases, including phenomenally conscious paradigm cases, is not a matter of tracking relations and functional roles but rather a matter of phenomenal consciousness. If those arguments are sound, then (SV6) is false, and PIT's departure from the Standard View is well supported.

8.4.2 INFLATIONISM ABOUT SOME ALLEGEDLY NONCONSCIOUS OCCURRENT STATES

I have argued for eliminativism about some allegedly nonconscious occurrent states. Another option would be an inflationist strategy that takes these states to have phenomenal intentionality. This kind of strategy accepts much of the Standard View, but it rejects (SV3), the claim that allegedly nonconscious occurrent states are not phenomenally conscious. Bourget (2010a, 2015), Mendelovici (2010), and Pitt (MS-b, MS-a) suggest a strategy of this sort, arguing that many allegedly nonconscious occurrent states are in fact phenomenally conscious.

There are two reasons for not taking this strategy in the case of most allegedly nonconscious occurrent states: First, it is far from clear that these states are phenomenally conscious, and, second, even if they are phenomenally conscious, it is far from clear that their phenomenal contents line up with their alleged contents. For example, it is far from clear that edge-detecting neurons are phenomenally conscious, and even if they are, it is unlikely that their phenomenal contents are something like <edge> (rather than, say, some phenomenal content that they share with all other neurons of the same type).

However, there might be some cases in which these reasons do not apply. There might be cases in which the relevant states are plausibly phenomenally conscious and, further, their phenomenal contents correspond to at least some of the contents we have reason to ascribe to them. Consider the case of Armstrong's (1968) absent-minded driver, who suddenly "comes to" and realizes that he has been driving on "autopilot" for some time. One might suggest that, although he was not aware of it, he was representing the road, the signs, and the cars before him. What are we to say about this kind of case?

One thing we can say that should be fairly uncontroversial is that, while on autopilot, the driver has occurrent internal states that TR-represent his surroundings. Eliminativism about this kind of case would end it at that. But it might not be implausible to add to the story the inflationist claim that the driver has phenomenal states he is not aware of, which allows that he has phenomenal intentional states representing his surroundings that he is not aware of.

That our brains house phenomenal states that we are not aware of may seem bizarre, but it should not trouble us. There are many phenomenal states that we are not aware of, most notably the phenomenal states of others. Just as there are phenomenal states that I am not aware of in others, so too might there be phenomenal states I am not aware of in my own brain.[25]

Inflationism is attractive in the case of the absent-minded driver because the states we want to ascribe to him are very much like the phenomenal intentional states we would want to ascribe to an attentive driver in a similar situation. For example, suppose the absent-minded driver "sees" a red light. Recall that the case of conscious perceptual color representations is a mismatch case for tracking and long-arm functional role theories (§3.4 and §4.3): perceptual color representations represent one thing (something like <edenic red>) and track another (something like a particular surface reflectance profile). An eliminativist strategy applied to the absent-minded driver's state of "seeing" a red light would maintain that, at best, the driver has an internal state that TR-represents a particular surface reflectance profile. But we might want to say that the absent-minded driver represents some of the same contents that the attentive driver represents while driving on the same route, such as <edenic red>. If the arguments in Chapters 3 and 4 are sound, we cannot TR-represent <edenic red>, since we do not track and are not functionally related to any matching item in the world. So, if we want to say that the absent-minded driver represents <edenic red>, we should say that he *phenomenally* represents it, which involves adopting an inflationist strategy about his state.

This sort of inflationist strategy might also be attractive in other cases where we want to ascribe to subjects contents that they are not aware of, especially when such contents cannot be TR-represented. For instance, this might be an attractive way to deal with some cases of subliminal stimuli.

---

[25] It does not matter, for our purposes, whether these phenomenal states count as *mine*. If we adopt a notion of subjects on which subjects are organisms, then these states are mine. If, instead, we adopt a notion of subjects on which subjects are sets of unified phenomenal states, then these phenomenal states are not mine, since they are not unified with my other phenomenal states. Instead, they belong to other subjects, perhaps subjects comprised of single experiences. On either picture, though, the phenomenal states exist, which is all we really need. For simplicity, I will say that the driver has phenomenal states that he is not aware of, but nothing hangs on this choice.

Many studies have shown that subliminal stimuli, stimuli that are presented in such a way that subjects do not report conscious awareness of them, are in some sense processed, affecting subsequent mental states and behaviors. For example, Krosnick et al. (1992) presented subjects with nine slides of a target person engaging in normal daily activities, such as getting into a car. These slides were immediately preceded by 13ms subliminal exposures of either positive-affect-arousing slides (e.g., two kittens) or negative-affect-arousing slides (e.g., a bucket of snakes). Subjects who had been exposed to the positive-affect-arousing slides tended to evaluate the target person more positively than those who had been exposed to the negative-affect-arousing slides.

An eliminativist view might maintain that Krosnick et al.'s subjects did not intentionally represent the subliminally presented images, though they may have TR-represented them or related contents. An inflationist view, however, can say that they had phenomenal intentional states that they were simply unaware of.

Something similar might be said of the relevant blindsight states of blindsight patients. These are patients with early visual cortical damage who claim not to see anything in a portion of their visual field but nonetheless can answer questions about what is presented in that area better than chance (Weiskrantz 1986, 1997). An eliminativist view would claim that, at best, blindsight states represent various contents in the sense of tracking or playing characteristic functional roles. In contrast, an inflationist view might take blindsight states to have phenomenal intentionality that blindsight subjects are not aware of. This position is congenial to the view that blindsight states are phenomenally conscious states that we are not aware of (Gertler 2001a).[26]

It is not my aim to settle the case for or against inflationism about any particular type of nonconscious state. My aim, rather, is to show that PIT quite plausibly has the resources to adequately handle various types of nonconscious states, using either an eliminativist or an inflationist strategy.[27]

---

[26] See also Phillips (2015), who argues that allegedly nonconscious states, including blindsight states, might be phenomenally conscious states that we are unaware of, and Pitt (MS-b), who argues that blindsight states might be phenomenally conscious without being conscious in another sense.

[27] Inflationism might also help strong PIT respond to a challenge that comes from the arguments in Block 2013 together with an additional assumption. Block argues that nonconscious seeing and conscious seeing are the same type of thing. One reason he cites for thinking this is that conscious and nonconscious seeing can be integrated. For instance, we can experience conscious visual illusions that are partly triggered by nonconscious states. Block's view that conscious and nonconscious seeing are the same kind of thing, when combined with the assumption that conscious seeing is essentially intentional (rather than being merely representational in some other sense), suggests that there are nonconscious states of seeing that are intentional, which contradicts strong PIT (and my eliminativist/inflationist position on allegedly nonconscious states). Phillips (2015) argues that the empirical evidence does

8.5 Conclusion

PIT is arguably most plausible in the case of conscious perceptual states, which are rich in phenomenal characters matching much of the content we want to ascribe to them. This and the previous chapter considered various states that are more challenging for PIT: thoughts, standing states, and nonconscious occurrent states. The trouble with these states is that they do not appear to have phenomenal contents, so it is not clear how PIT can accommodate them.

I have suggested a largely eliminativist strategy for dealing with them. Thoughts don't intentionally represent their alleged contents, there are no genuinely intentional standing states, and nonconscious occurrent states either have phenomenal characters or are not genuinely intentional. The resulting view is compatible with strong PIT, the view that all intentionality is phenomenal intentionality.

The overall view might seem quite extreme, rejecting many contents we might want to say we represent, but it is conciliatory to both our intuitive, empirical, and theoretical reasons for positing many of the rejected contents. Although most nonconscious occurrent states and subpersonal standing states do not exhibit genuine intentionality, they can be said to TR-represent, where TR-representation requires nothing more than tracking relations and functional roles. We can say something similar about thoughts and many personal standing states, but we can also say something more in these cases: Although we don't really intentionally represent the alleged contents of thoughts and personal standing states, in many cases we do the next best thing: We *derivatively* represent them.

One might wonder what justifies the differential treatment of nonconscious occurrent states and subpersonal standing states, on the one hand, and thoughts and many personal standing states, on the other. Why do the latter but not the former involve derived representation?

The, admittedly fuzzy, reason for seeking a derivativist-in-spirit treatment of the alleged contents of thoughts and personal standing states is that they form an integral part of our conceptions of ourselves as thinking, perceiving, and generally representing subjects. Their alleged contents are among the contents that we in some

---

not show that seeing and consciousness can be dissociated because it is not clear that the allegedly nonconscious states are not phenomenally conscious. If they are phenomenally conscious, as Phillips suggests, then we can agree with Block that they are cases of seeing and that nonconscious and conscious seeing are the same type of thing. On this suggestion, at least some instances of nonconscious seeing are phenomenally conscious and intentional, which partly explains why they integrate with conscious states of seeing. Careful consideration of these issues and debates takes us too far afield, but, for our purposes, it suffices to say that there might be good reason to adopt an inflationist strategy in a surprisingly wide range of allegedly nonconscious states.

sense target, that we take ourselves and others to be committed to, and that we hold each other accountable for. These are the contents that we have some kind of ownership over. In contrast, most of our nonconscious occurrent states do not figure in our self-conception in this way.[28] And, fortunately, the reason for wanting to accommodate the alleged contents we take ourselves to represent is precisely what makes it the case that we derivatively represent them: We *take* ourselves to represent them.

In conclusion, all intentionality is phenomenal intentionality, and this is, perhaps surprisingly, quite compatible with our scientific understanding of nonconscious states and our everyday understanding of ourselves as representing subjects.

---

[28] This is related, but not equivalent, to the fact that most thoughts and standing states are supposed to be personal states (states that can be said to be had by entire persons, like beliefs, desires, and occurrent thoughts), while most of the nonconscious occurrent states under consideration are supposed to be subpersonal states.

V   The Aspect View

I HAVE ARGUED for strong identity PIT, which is, roughly, the view that intentionality is identical to phenomenal consciousness. This view leaves open an important question about the nature of intentionality: Is intentionality a relation to distinctly existing items that play the role of contents, such as objects, properties, and propositions, or is it a matter of having intentional states with certain integral aspects? This part further fleshes out my picture of intentionality by arguing against a relational view of intentionality and for the alternative aspect view. We will see that the relation view faces two important worries, and that the aspect view can do everything the relation view can do but without a commitment to reified contents.

9   Is Intentionality a Relation to a Content?

OUR AIM IS to provide a theory of intentionality, a theory that describes its nature. I have argued for strong identity PIT, the view that every intentional property is a phenomenal property, every intentional state is a phenomenal state, and every intentional state's content is its phenomenal character. This view tells us that all intentionality is in some sense "felt," that what is represented is simply what is felt, and, more generally, that the nature of intentionality is that of being identical to phenomenal consciousness.

All this, however, leaves open one important question about the nature of intentionality: Is intentionality a relation to distinctly existing contents, or is it a matter of having intentional states with certain integral aspects? This is a question about contents (Are contents distinctly existing entities or are they aspects of intentional states?), as well as a question about how we represent them (Do we have contents by being related to them or by having intentional states with certain aspects?).

The relational view of intentionality is arguably the common sense view. On the face of it, intentionality appears to be a relation to items that exist in their own right and that are represented. For example, the belief that grass is green might seem to be a relation to the very fact that grass is green, a fact that obtains whether or not we represent it, and a perceptual experience of Eleni might seem to be a relation to

Eleni herself, who also exists whether or not we represent her. However, as we will soon see, there are reasons to reject the commonsense relation view and to accept the alternative aspect view, on which intentionality is an integral aspect of subjects and their mental states.

It might seem that the arguments I've presented so far have already settled the issue in favor of the aspect view. Identity PIT, together with the prima facie plausible claim that phenomenal states are not relations to distinctly existing phenomenal characters, entails the claim that intentional states are not relations to distinctly existing contents. This is true, but one might worry that this does not provide a compelling argument for the aspect view, since, consistent with most of my arguments so far, we might reject identity PIT in favor of a version of PIT that takes original intentionality to arise from phenomenal consciousness without being identical to it. Such versions of PIT put some distance between phenomenal consciousness and original intentionality, potentially allowing intentionality to be relational in the relevant way while phenomenal consciousness is not. Indeed, §5.3 considered the commonsense relation view as the basis of an *objection* to identity PIT, and deferred to this chapter for a response. So, while the arguments so far, combined with the assumption that consciousness is non-relational, support the aspect view, there are nearby views that avoid this commitment and that would be very well motivated if the relation view was shown to be true.[1]

My aim in this chapter is to argue for the aspect view on grounds independent of PIT and to show how it might be developed. This will help complete our picture of the nature of intentionality, as well as our defense of identity PIT. I will proceed as follows: Section 9.1 describes the relation view and the aspect view; §9.2 raises some doubts with the relation view; and §9.3 considers some challenges for the aspect view and argues that it fares no worse than the relation view. I close with a brief discussion of the overall theory of intentionality that results from combining the aspect view with strong identity PIT (§9.4).

9.1 The Relation View and the Aspect View

The relation view and the aspect view are views about the deep nature of intentionality, where an intentional state's deep nature is what it *is*, metaphysically

---

[1] I have also not argued for a non-relational view of phenomenal consciousness. Like many others, I will assume this view without explicit argument (but see Gertler 2001a for an explicit defense). For our purposes, it suffices to note that most defenders of relational views of consciousness also defend relational views of intentionality (see, e.g., Bourget 2010a, forthcoming-b, Pautz 2010a, Lycan 2001, and Tye 2015), which is indicative of the fact that the combination of a non-relational view of intentionality with a relational view of consciousness has little appeal.

speaking. An intentional state's deep nature can be contrasted with its superficial character, the set of features that characterize it as the kind of state that it is (§2.2.1). Since the relation view and the aspect view are views about the deep nature of intentional states, they might agree on the superficial character of some intentional state, while disagreeing on its deep nature. For example, they might agree that the thought that grass is green represents the content <grass is green>, rather than <snow is white>, while disagreeing on whether the state is a relation to a distinctly existing entity playing the role of its content.

9.1.1 THE RELATION VIEW

The **relation view** states that to intentionally represent C is to bear a certain relation (other than instantiation) to C, where C is an item existing distinctly from the representing of C in that it is not merely a part, component, or aspect of the representing of C. On the relation view, contents are items that exist in their own right (or, at least, not simply because they are parts, components, or aspects of intentional states), and we represent them by getting appropriately related to them. For simplicity of exposition, unless otherwise specified, I will use the term "relation" for any relation other than instantiation, so we can simply say that the relation view claims that intentionality is a relation to distinctly existing contents. For example, the relation view might claim that intentionally representing that grass is green is a matter of bearing a relation to the fact or proposition that grass is green, which exists distinctly from our intentionally representing that grass is green.[2,3]

The distinctly existing items that are to be identified with contents might be ordinary concrete items (like cats, mats, and states of affairs), properties, propositions, sense data, combinations of these items, or something else. The relevant relation might be a tracking relation, a similarity relation, or an irreducibly mental relation, like an awareness, acquaintance, or grasping relation. Note that the relation view not only claims that intentionality involves being appropriately related to distinctly existing items but also further claims that these items are *what we represent*. They are quite literally what we think, judge, and perceptually represent. In the case of occurrent intentional states, they are what we *entertain*.

---

[2] The relation view is often assumed without argument, but see Pautz 2007 and Bourget forthcoming-b for explicit defenses.

[3] As before, I will simply assume that the subject-side bearers of intentional properties are mental representations. On the relation view, then, intentionality is a relation between mental representations and distinctly existing items that are identified with contents.

An example of a relation view is the tracking theory of intentionality, on which contents might be taken to be abstract properties or propositions, perhaps in addition to concrete objects, and the relevant relation is a species of causal, co-variation, or other tracking relation. It is also possible to construe the naïve realist theory of perception as a relation view of perceptual intentionality on which contents are ordinary, usually concrete, objects and their properties, with the relevant relation being a potentially unanalyzable perception relation. We can also think of the sense data view as a theory of perceptual intentionality on which perceptual intentionality is an awareness relation to mind-dependent mental particulars, or sense data. Despite being mind-dependent, sense data exist *distinctly* (but perhaps not independently) from us and our relations to them, which is why the sense data view, at least on the present construal, qualifies as a relation view. It is also possible to have a primitivist relation view, on which the relevant relation is a primitive representation relation and contents are either concrete items, abstract properties, abstract property clusters, or propositions.

9.1.2 THE ASPECT VIEW

The **aspect view** states that to intentionally represent the content C is to have a state with a particular aspect, where this aspect is identical to C.[4] An **aspect** of an intentional state is the intentional state itself, the intentional property the state is an instantiation of, a property of this property, or an instantiation of the latter kind of property.[5] Intuitively, the idea is that aspects are integral features of intentional states, having no existence distinct from intentional states or properties. The aspect view has roots in adverbialism about perceptual experience (Chisholm 1957b, Ducasse 1942, Sellars 1975), though it differs from adverbialism in its target and central aims, and well-known objections to adverbialism do not apply to it (see Appendix F of this chapter).[6]

---

[4] Thanks to Adam Pautz for suggesting the name "aspect view" for this view.

[5] See Appendix G of this chapter for discussion of these options.

[6] Versions of the aspect view, or something nearby, have recently been defended by Pitt (2009), Kriegel (2007, 2011), Crane (2006, 2013), and Mendelovici (2010) and were arguably the views of Brentano (1874), Husserl (1900), and Anscombe (1965).

  Pitt (2009) claims that intentional contents are psychological types, Kriegel (2007, 2011) claims that intentional contents are ways of representing, or second-order intentional properties, and Crane (2013) claims that intentionality is a primitive non-relational phenomenon. Tye (1989) also provides a notable defense of an aspect view, though he has come to reject the view in later work (e.g., Tye 2000). See also Kriegel (forthcoming) for relevant discussion of Brentano's views.

The aspect view provides us with a very different picture of content than the relation view: While the relation view takes contents to be *things* that exist distinctly of our representing them, the aspect view takes contents to be nothing more than aspects of our intentional states. These aspects are *what* we intentionally represent. In the case of occurrent states, they are what we entertain. Note that this does not require that we represent contents *as* aspects of intentional states but only that the deep nature of contents is that of being aspects of intentional states (see §2.2.1).

For ease of exposition, it is useful to have a naming scheme for the relevant aspects. Let us call the aspect of an intentional state representing C that is identical to its content—i.e., to C—a **C-aspect**.[7] For example, representing the content <blue> is a matter of being in an intentional state with a blue-aspect. Note that an intentional state having a blue-aspect needn't itself be blue or involve blueness in any way, where blueness is a property that blue objects do or can have. The "C" in "C-aspect" is a placeholder for a specification of precisely which aspect of an intentional state plays the role of content. Indeed, a central question for the aspect view is that of whether C-aspects involve **C-ness**, the property that the content C (allegedly) picks out. As we will see in §9.3.4, there are views on which C-aspects involve C-ness and views on which they do not, and these views interact in important ways with theories of truth and reference.

Some possible variants of the aspect view include versions of the mind-brain identity theory, versions of the functional role theory, and versions of PIT. An aspect version of the mind-brain identity theory might take intentional states to be neural states and contents to be aspects of neural states; aspect versions of functional role theories might take intentional states to be functional states and contents to be functional properties; and aspect versions of PIT might take intentional states to be phenomenal states and contents to be phenomenal characters. It is also possible to hold a primitivist aspect theory (this is, roughly, Crane's (2013) view).

9.1.3 INTERNALISM AND EXTERNALISM

The debate between the relation view and the aspect view does not directly map onto the debate between internalism and externalism. According to externalism, at least some of a subject's intentional states are at least partly determined by environmental factors, while according to internalism, a subject's intentional states are fully determined by her intrinsic properties. It is possible to hold an internalist

---

[7] Thanks to Chang Liu for suggesting this way of naming aspects.

relation view, on which intentionality is a relation to distinctly existing contents and the contents a subject is related to are fully determined by her intrinsic properties (see, e.g., Jackson 1998a, Bourget 2010b, forthcoming-b, and Pautz 2010a). Although less common, it is also possible to hold an externalist aspect view. Such a view might take the aspects of intentional states that are identical to contents to be extrinsic properties of subjects. On the externalist aspect view, intentionality is a relation to items outside the head, but these items are not taken to be contents.[8]

9.2 Two Worries with the Relation View

This section raises two worries with the relation view that help motivate the alternative aspect view: The first worry is an extension of the mismatch problem for tracking and functional role theories (§3.2): Many relation views cannot plausibly accommodate all the diverse intentional states that we can manifestly enjoy. Relation views that avoid this problem are driven to ontological extremes, which suggests that the relation view is wrongheaded.

The second worry is a generalization of the Real Problem for tracking and functional role theories (§4.4): No relation we can bear to the items that are supposed to be identified with contents can make those items entertained or otherwise represented by us.

9.2.1 THE INVENTORY PROBLEM

The relation view might seem innocent and intuitive enough in many everyday cases. For example, it seems fine to say that Evangelia's thoughts about George involve a relation to George himself, who forms part of her thought content. However, once we consider the wide and diverse range of contents we can entertain, it seems that the relation view must posit uninstantiated properties, existing sets of abstract or concrete possible worlds, or other "exotic" (Sainsbury 2010) or "peculiar" (Schellenberg 2011) entities. This, I will argue, is problematic for reasons beyond the mere fact that we arguably have no independent reasons to think they exist.[9]

---

[8]   Adam Pautz has suggested to me that there are possible versions of the tracking theory that take intentionality to consist in causal or other tracking relations to property instantiations, which are not identified with contents. Such a view is an example of an externalist aspect view.

[9]   See especially Crane 2001, Thau 2002, Kriegel 2007, Schellenberg 2011 and Papineau 2014 for objections to the relation view or related views on such grounds.

This problem arises in the case of intentional states about objects that do not exist, like Santa Claus (see, e.g., Thau 2002, Kriegel 2007, and Crane 2001). When Evangelia thinks about Santa Claus, there is no Santa Claus to figure in the content of her thought. What the relation view must take to play the role of content in her Santa Claus state, then, is something other than a concrete flesh-and-blood Santa Claus, such as a merely possible object, an abstract object, or a cluster of properties. The worry is that any entities that can plausibly be identified with the content <Santa Claus> will be exotic or peculiar entities that we should not be committed to.

I don't think it is clear that accommodating the case of <Santa Claus> commits the relation view to problematic entities. One view of <Santa Claus> that arguably doesn't appeal to problematic entities takes it to be a cluster or other combination of properties, such as the properties that we think of Santa Claus as having. Properties might be taken to be **tropes**, which are particular ways that individual objects are; **Aristotelian universals**, which are abstract properties that can be instantiated in multiple items and exist only in their instances; or **Platonic universals**, which are abstract properties that can be instantiated in multiple items and that exist *independently* of their instances. While Platonic universals might be exotic or peculiar, tropes and Aristotelian universals presumably are not, and it is far from obvious that the content <Santa Claus> cannot be constructed out of them. If so, then the case of the content <Santa Claus> does not commit the relation view to problematic entities.[10]

The worry, however, arises in a more acute form in certain mismatch cases for the tracking theory, like that of perceptual color representations (§3.4). If my claims in Chapter 3 are correct, perceptual color representations represent primitive color contents, like $<blue_{21}>$, that do not match any instantiated properties. Since perceptual color contents do not match any instantiated properties, we cannot identify them with tropes or Aristotelian universals. Since they are presumably internally unstructured, in that they do not include other contents as constituent parts,[11] we also cannot identify them with combinations of instantiated properties, as we did <Santa Claus>. We are left to identify perceptual color contents with Platonic universals or other peculiar entities. Other

---

[10] Tye (2000), Byrne (2001), Pautz (2007), and Bourget (forthcoming-b) take at least perceptual experiences to be relations to property clusters, and the view is very much in line with descriptivist views of reference (Jackson 1998a, Kroon 1987).

[11] They might, nonetheless, be externally structured. See §9.3.3 and §7.2.4.

mismatch cases in which we represent internally unstructured contents pose similar problems.[12,13]

I have focused on objectual and proprietal[14] contents, like <Santa Claus> and <blue$_{21}$>, but the same points apply in the case of propositional contents, so a commitment to **propositionalism**, the view that all intentional states represent propositional contents, cannot help us avoid the problem.[15] The relation theorist presumably wants to identify propositional contents, like <grass is green>, with matching proposition-like entities, like facts, sets of concrete or abstract possible worlds, structured propositions consisting in objects and properties, or structured existentially quantified propositions. In the case of false propositional contents, like <Santa Claus gave Eleni a trampoline>, the view that this content is a fact is immediately off the table, since there exists no fact that matches it, and hence no fact that can plausibly be identified with it. One might worry, as in the case of <Santa Claus>, that the remaining options commit us to exotic or peculiar entities.

Now, as in the case of the objectual content <Santa Claus>, it is not clear that accommodating <Santa Claus gave Eleni a trampoline> commits the relation view to problematic entities. The relation view might identify this content with an existentially quantified structured proposition, which is constructed out of unproblematic tropes or Aristotelian universals.

However, such a strategy does not work in cases of propositional contents involving internally unstructured proprietal elements that don't match instantiated

---

[12] Schellenberg (2011) similarly argues that views of perception taking us to be related to abstract property clusters require peculiar entities to accommodate certain kinds of color hallucinations, such as hallucinations of Hume's missing shade of blue.

[13] The view that contents are **intensions**, which are functions from possible worlds (and perhaps contextual factors) to extensions, also has trouble accommodating the content <blue$_{21}$>—or any other content—without commitment to questionable entities. If functions are sets of ordered pairs of inputs and outputs, then intensions are sets of ordered pairs of possible worlds and extensions. If an ordered pair exists only if its elements exist, then the intensions view is committed to existing abstract or concrete possible worlds and existing extensions. But, again, it is questionable whether the required items exist. It is unclear that alternative conceptions of intensions, functions, or ordered pairs can avoid commitment to problematic entities. For example, a view allowing functions to exist independently of the existence of the relevant ordered pairs of inputs and outputs would be committed to something like "Platonic" functions, which would themselves be exotic or peculiar. Perhaps, instead, the intensions view can analyze away talk of intensions or functions, perhaps in terms of subjects' dispositions or something else. Such a view may well end up being a relation view of a different sort, or even an aspect view, and would have to be considered in its own right. (None of this, of course, suggests that there is anything problematic with using intensions to *model* contents.)

[14] I borrow the term "proprietal contents" from Kriegel (MS), who uses the term to describe my view of the contents of moods (in Mendelovici 2013a and 2014).

[15] See Grzankowski 2013, Montague 2007, and Mendelovici 2018. The kind of propositionalism at issue here is what I call "shallow propositionalism" in Mendelovici 2018.

properties. Consider the visually represented content <there is a red square in front of me>. Since there are no instantiated color properties, this content cannot be identified with a matching existentially quantified structured proposition consisting only of tropes or Aristotelian universals. The only existentially quantified structured proposition that can plausibly be identified with it involves Platonic universals. Similarly, any matching set of abstract or concrete possible worlds or structured proposition consisting in objects and properties will arguably have to involve Platonic elements matching the "red" bit of the content: since there are no instantiated color properties, no such matching candidate contents can be plausibly constructed out of existing ingredients found in the concrete world.

In summary, the problem is that it is not clear that the items that the relation view takes us to be related to in fact exist. We can call this the **inventory problem** for the relation view, since the inventory of the mind threatens to outrun any inventory of items we have independent reason to accept. The relation view must posit items specially tailored to play the roles of contents, such as Platonic universals. While these items might be recruited to play other roles as well, it is far from clear that they are *needed* elsewhere.

There are a few points to make from all this. First, a commitment to items of questionable existence such as Platonic abstracta takes the intuitive wind out of the relation view's sails. While the relation view can offer an intuitive treatment of Evangelia's thoughts representing George, this intuitive treatment does not extend to her perceptual color states and many other intentional states she can enjoy. Above, I suggested that the relation view might be taken to be supported by commonsense intuition. Whether or not commonsense intuition can support claims about the deep nature of intentionality, any such support is arguably undercut by the relation view's unintuitive treatment of mismatch cases. (I will say more about whether common sense supports the relation view in §9.3.1.)

Second, the relation view's questionable ontological commitments are themselves reasons to doubt the view. If independent considerations suggest against accepting such commitments, they are a cost to the theory (see especially Kriegel 2011 for an argument from ontological parsimony against relation views committed to Platonic universals). Of course, if there are strong reasons to believe the relation view, then this might be reason to accept the view together with its ontological commitments. But if the aspect view can do everything the relation view can do, as I argue in §9.3, then we can make an argument in favor of the aspect view from ontological parsimony. (Notice that the aspect view does not similarly take on questionable ontological commitments. Even if it takes contents to be properties (such as intentional properties or properties of intentional properties—see Appendix G of this chapter), it need not accept that unrepresented contents really exist, so it can take contents to be tropes or Aristotelian universals.)

Third, and I think most importantly, the extremes[16] to which the relation view is pushed in order to accommodate the vast inventory of representable contents suggests that the whole approach is wrongheaded. On the relation view, what we can represent is limited by a pre-set inventory of distinctly existing items, and representing is a matter of getting appropriately related to these items. However, the inventory of the mind shows no sign of being limited in this way. This is why the only relation views that can accommodate all the intentional states we can enjoy are those that push us to otherwise unwarranted ontological extremes. The world of concrete objects, instantiated properties, and obtaining states of affairs is simply not enough to capture the vast inventory of the mind. But if the relation view is right, then it is surprising that the only version of the view that can accommodate the inventory of the mind is one that posits a virtually unlimited inventory of ontologically dubious items. The picture this situation suggests is not that there exists a vast inventory of items that can form the contents of our intentional states but rather that our minds have the ability to create their own contents. The represented world is composed not of pre-existing things that our minds somehow manage to grab hold of but rather of aspects of our own internal states.

9.2.2 THE REAL PROBLEM

The Real Problem with the relation view is that it's hard to see how any relation to distinctly existing items can make them entertained or otherwise intentionally represented.

Let us first consider a relation view that takes contents to be concretely existing objects, their properties, and obtaining states of affairs. On this view, we literally intentionally represent—and, in the case of occurrent states, *entertain*—tables, chairs, and states of affairs, e.g., consisting of tables being next to chairs. The Real Problem with this relation view is that no ordinary relation can behave like this. No ordinary relation can allow us to literally entertain tables and chairs, to take hold of objects existing in the concrete world and bring them into our minds to make them available to our cognitive systems.

---

[16] One might suggest that the relation view's commitments are not all that extreme: it need only accept *some* Platonic universals or other questionable entities, those needed to accommodate cases in which we represent internally unstructured contents for which there are no matching instantiated properties. But such a view, of course, would be quite ad hoc. If some internally unstructured proprietal contents are Platonic universals, then presumably they all are. In any case, even if we only had to accept *some* questionable entities, this would still commit us to an inappropriately inflated ontology and cast doubt on the relation view.

We can put the point in terms of psychological involvement. Recall that psychological involvement is a matter of playing a role in mental life, such as that of being introspectively accessible, affecting further cognition or behavior, or merely partly constituting our representational perspective on the world; in short, psychological involvement is a matter of contents behaving as if they're there (see §2.2.3). The problem is that, except in cases where we think about parts of ourselves, concretely existing objects, properties, and states of affairs exist distinctly and usually independently of us, our cognitive systems, and our intentional states. So, it's hard to see how any relation we can bear to these distinctly and independently existing items can make them psychologically involved. So, contents can't be such items. Tables, chairs, and obtaining states of affairs are not thinkables, experienceables, entertainables, or, more generally, (intentionally) representables. They are not the kinds of things that can play the role of intentional contents.[17]

The same worry afflicts other versions of the relation view that take contents to exist independently of us. Even if there existed the required items (e.g., Platonic universals, sets of possible worlds), it's not clear how we could come to entertain them or make them accessible to our cognitive systems. The problem with the relation view in general, then, is that being related to a distinctly and independently existing thing doesn't make it available to you or in any way psychologically involved.

In §4.4, I argued that the Real Problem with any view that gets its contents from tracking relations is that tracking relations cannot grab hold of externally existing items, bringing them into our minds to make them available to us, or allow us to reach out into the world to somehow cognitively touch them. Tracking relations *just* track. In order for tracking relations to give rise to intentionality, they would have to not only relate us to items in the world but also make these items available to our cognitive systems. They would have to make these items psychologically involved, making them available for use in thought, reasoning, inference, and introspection. The Real Problem with the relation view is a generalization of this problem. It's

---

[17] It does not help to say that the relevant distinctly existing items form constitutive parts of intentional states and thus gain entry into the cognitive economy. In effect, this suggestion draws a line around mental vehicles and the relevant items and calls those items together with some particular way in which they are related "intentional states." But this does not make it any clearer how the items come to play a psychological role in our mental economies despite existing distinctly and independently of our internal states. Compare: We could choose to use the term "intentional state" to refer to mental representations, Quebec City, and some relation obtaining between the mental representations and Quebec City. This would not make Quebec City psychologically involved. In order for the relation between internal states and the distinctly existing items to be identified with contents to make the distinctly existing items psychologically involved, there must be something extra special about it, but it's unclear how any relation can have such a special feature.

hard to see how *any* relation can do what tracking relations cannot, how any relation can grab hold of items that exist distinctly and sometimes independently of us and make them available to us, or allow us to reach out and make some kind of epistemic contact with them.[18,19]

9.3 The Alleged Virtues of the Relation View

The previous section provided two arguments against the relation view. It might be claimed, though, that the relation view should still be preferred to the aspect view

---

[18] There is one relation view that seems to escape this kind of worry, the view that takes the relevant relata to be mind-dependent sense data. Unlike other relation views, the sense data view takes contents to be internal to us, kicking around in our heads, directly available to play various roles in the cognitive economy. So, the sense data view's contents *can* be psychologically involved. But the sense data view is the exception that proves the rule, since the feature of the sense data view in virtue of which it allow contents to be psychologically involved is precisely the feature that it has in common with (most versions of) the aspect view: It takes (at least perceptual) intentionality to only constitutively involve one's internal states, allowing contents to be psychologically involved by taking them to literally be in our heads, with the fact that we are related to them in a special way doing nothing to contribute to their psychological involvement. If we had sense data but were not related to them by the relevant relation, they would still be able to be psychologically involved. So, the sense data view still faces the Real Problem: The alleged intentionality relation, even on this view, cannot *make* contents entertained or otherwise represented in a psychologically involved way.

[19] BonJour (1998) raises a similar worry with what he calls the "symbolic conception of thought," on which intentionality involves having tokens of mental symbols whose "content is not fixed by their intrinsic character, but is instead imposed upon them from outside by relations of some sort in which they are involved" (p. 165). The problem is that the symbolic conception cannot make sense of our awareness of the contents of our intentional states:

> If tokens of the mentalese word corresponding to 'triangular' have the representative content that they do entirely by virtue of standing in such an external relation to triangular things (or even to the abstract universal triangularity), then the person having the thought, trapped as it were on one end of this relation and having direct access only to the tokens themselves, would have no way of being aware of what the symbol thus represents, no way of having any inkling at all of what he is thinking about by virtue of the presence of the symbol in his mental economy—a result that is, I submit, plainly absurd. (pp. 167–168; footnote suppressed)

Although BonJour frames his worry as one about how we can be aware of our contents, it is clear that the worry afflicts all aspects of psychological involvement. The problem is that something cannot play a role in the cognitive economy simply by being on the far end of a causal or other kind of relation. See also Pautz (2007, 2010b), who considers a similar objection to his relational representationalist view of phenomenal consciousness.

Somewhat relatedly, Kriegel (2011) argues that relation views that take intentionality to be a relation to abstracta go against the principle that concrete phenomena can only be explained in terms of other concrete phenomena. Since intentionality is a concrete phenomenon, it cannot be explained in terms of a relation to abstracta. Papineau (2014) raises similar worries with relational views of phenomenal states: "My conscious sensory feelings are concrete, here-and-now, replete with causes and effects. How can their metaphysical nature essentially involve relations to entities that lie outside space and time?" (p. 7).

because it has many virtues that the aspect view lacks: It is supported by common sense, allows for public and unrepresented contents, makes sense of structured intentional states, has an easy time accommodating various theories of truth and reference, and is congenial to externalism.

This section argues that the aspect view and the relation view—or at least the only viable versions of the relation view, the ones with excessive ontologies—have all the same truth-indicating virtues. This provides a defense of the aspect view against objections to the effect that it lacks some of the relation view's virtues. It also allows us to complete the argument from ontological parsimony for the aspect view over the relation view that we began in §9.2.1: The aspect view can do everything the relation view can do but without questionable ontological commitments, so it should be preferred.

9.3.1 ACCORDING WITH COMMON SENSE

It might be argued that the relation view is more commonsensical than the aspect view and that this is a reason to prefer it. For example, when Lina thinks about Whiskers, it might intuitively seem correct to describe her as bearing a relation to the real live cat, Whiskers. Likewise, when Marius perceptually represents Whiskers on the mat, it might intuitively seem correct to describe him as bearing a relation to the state of affairs of Whiskers being on the mat.

One reason to think that the common sense view is the relation view is that the language we use to describe intentional states is relational. For example, a sentence like "Marius perceptually experiences Whiskers on the mat" has a relational grammatical form, which suggests that it expresses a relation.[20] However, that sentences describing intentional states have a relational form does not automatically mean that the relation view is the common sense view. Perhaps the language we use to describe intentional states is relational, but it is noncommittal on whether intentionality itself is relational,[21] or perhaps our language is committed to the relation view but we don't fully accept these commitments. Or perhaps we do accept these commitments and our intentional state attributions themselves have a relational form, but they have non-relational truth-makers.[22] Perhaps there isn't even

---

[20] Bourget (2010b, 2017a, forthcoming-b) makes a more sophisticated argument along such lines.

[21] See Crane 2013, ch. 2 and Sainsbury 2010.

[22] See Matthews' (1994, 2007) measurement-theoretic approach to propositional attitudes. Matthews likens attributions of propositional attitudes to subjects to attributions of weights to objects, which have a relational form, relating an object to a number, but whose truth-makers arguably do not involve relations to numbers. Papineau (2014) makes a similar suggestion about phenomenal states.

a clear common sense view at all. For instance, perhaps our common sense beliefs about intentionality are confused, inconsistent, or noncommittal.

Even if there is a common sense view and it is a relation view, it is not clear that this supports the relation view over the aspect view because it is not clear that language and common sense are reliable indicators of truth in this domain. This is arguably supported by the fact that there are plausible explanations of why our language and common sense views might be relational that do not require the truth of the relation view. One such explanation is that we think of intentional states as relational because it is more economical than thinking of them as having specific aspects. If we thought of them as having specific aspects, we would need to use a special set of representations representing these special aspects. Thinking of intentional states as relations to distinctly existing items, on the other hand, allows us to represent them by reusing our pre-existing representations of these distinctly existing items. For example, we can use the same representations that we use to think <The cat is on the mat> to think <Marius believes that the cat is on the mat> (just as we reuse some of the same words to form the two sentences, instead of invoking an entirely new vocabulary specifically for intentional states and their contents). This might be more economical than using a new set of representations to represent intentional states and their contents.

If something along the lines of this (admittedly speculative) story is true, then our best explanation of why our language and common sense view are relational does not require the truth of the relation view. This would debunk any evidence we might have from common sense and everyday language for the relation view. The common sense view would be the relation view whether or not it is true, which means that its being the common sense view is not evidence of its truth. In other words, according with common sense would not be a truth-indicating virtue (p. 118) of the relation view.

Even if we cannot offer a specific story debunking the evidence for the relation view purportedly offered by common sense, we might still be skeptical of common sense's ability to track truth in this domain. In order for common sense to reliably track truth in a domain, it should have some kind of special access to that domain. One might suggest that in the case of intentionality, this special access comes from introspection.

The problem is that, at best, introspection can only tell us about the superficial characters of intentional states; it does not simply reveal to us their deep natures (§2.2.2). But the disagreement between the relation view and the aspect view is not over the superficial characters of intentional states but over their deep natures. In order for introspection to reveal the truth of the relation view, it would have to have a special kind of access to intentional states' deep natures, which it does not.

In any case, even if we grant that according with common sense is a truth-indicating virtue, this would not support any empirically adequate version of the relation view. Insofar as any view of intentionality seems to be suggested by common sense intuitions, it seems to be a naïve referential view, a view on which intentionality directly acquaints us with the referents and truth-makers of our intentional states. This is clearest in perception, where it might seem to us that we are in direct contact with the world before us. But even in thought we seem to be in direct contact with facts and everyday objects. For example, when you think about a loved one, it seems you are directly thinking about *that* flesh-and-blood person.

Something like these intuitions is expressed by Harman (1990) when he argues that the view that seeing red involves a relation to sense data is analogous to the view that Ponce de Leon was searching for the *idea* of the Fountain of Youth: "...[Ponce de Leon] was not looking for an idea of the Fountain of Youth. He already had the idea. What he wanted was a real Fountain of Youth, not just the idea of such a thing" (p. 36). Similarly, one reason Kriegel (2007) gives for rejecting relation views on which contents, such as <Bigfoot>, are or involve Platonic universals or sense data is that "intuitively, Bigfoot seems to be a non-mental concretum, though one that does not exist, rather than an existing abstractum or mental concretum" (p. 310). Harman and Kriegel take the views they target to go against common sense intuition. Intuitively, Ponce de Leon was searching for a real, concrete Fountain of Youth and the Bigfoot we think about is a non-mental concretum.

While Harman and Kriegel take common sense intuitions to tell against certain views, it is noteworthy that the alternative views they suggest also go against common sense intuitions. Harman's alternative view is that we represent intentional objects, which are analyzed away somehow, perhaps in terms of abstract or nonexistent items. Kriegel's alternative view is a version of the aspect view on which contents are ways of representing, or properties of intentional properties. The problem is that it is no more intuitive to say that Ponce de Leon was searching for an *abstract* or *nonexistent* Fountain of Youth than it is to say that he was searching for a mental Fountain of Youth.[23] Likewise, it is no more intuitive to say that when we think of Bigfoot we are thinking of properties of intentional states than it is to say that we are thinking of abstracta.

The bottom line is that *none* of the relation views currently on the table make it the case that intentionality is a relation to real, concrete Fountains of Youth

---

[23] See also Thau 2002 for the very similar point that Ponce de Leon was not searching for a nonexistent Fountain of Youth.

or Bigfoots, since there is no real, concrete Fountain of Youth or Bigfoot to be related to. If common sense tells us that we represent the Fountain of Youth and Bigfoot by being related to them, then we must reject common sense and accept that intentionality is not quite what we believe it to be. If the common sense view is the naïve referential view, then any empirically adequate relation view will have to be a little bit revisionary. So, even *if* according with common sense were a truth-indicating virtue, it would not be one that any viable version of the relation view has, so it gives us no reason to prefer the relation view to the aspect view.[24]

This is all as it should be if we agree that introspection does not reveal to us the deep nature of intentional states and their contents. If introspection does not reveal the deep nature of contents, then it is hard to see how we could come to have veridical common sense intuitions about the deep nature of contents. Where Harman and Kriegel go wrong in their arguments is in taking intuition and introspection to shed light on not just the superficial characters of intentional states—i.e., on *which* contents we represent—but also on their deep natures. For all introspection and intuition can reliably tell us, the content of Ponce de Leon's searching might turn out to be an idea and what we are aware of when we think about dragons might be something abstract or mental. Indeed, all this provides an argument for the claim that introspection does not reveal the deep natures of contents: Insofar as introspection suggests a view of the deep nature of intentionality, it is a view that we know with near certainty to be false.[25]

In summary, it is not clear that the relation view better accords with common sense than the aspect view. But even if it did, it is not clear that this would be a truth-indicating virtue. And even if it were, it would not be a truth-indicating virtue than any viable relation view has. So, common sense does not give us reason to favor the relation view over the aspect view.

9.3.2 ALLOWING FOR INDEPENDENTLY EXISTING CONTENTS

On most versions of the relation view, contents exist independently of intentional states. This might be thought to confer various benefits in allowing for shared and

---

[24] This point, in effect, is another way of making the point in §9.2.1 that the inventory problem undercuts any support the relation view might be thought to receive from common sense.

[25] This argument also blocks other nearby arguments for the relation view that appeal to transparency observations (Harman 1990, Tye 2000) or other introspective observations. Such observations can only reliably tell us about the superficial character of intentional states, not about their deep natures, since insofar as they can be taken to tell us about their deep natures, what they tell us is most certainly false. But in order for introspective observations to support the relation view, they would have to tell us about deep natures.

unrepresented contents and in allowing us to model contents in useful ways.[26] Insofar as we think that there are shared and unrepresented contents and that contents should be able to be modeled in the relevant ways, allowing for such contents is a truth-indicating virtue of the view. I will argue that the aspect view also has this virtue.

Shared Contents

Relation views that take contents to exist independently of intentional states can offer a neat account of how multiple subjects can represent the same contents: Since contents are items that exist independently of representing subjects, multiple subjects can become appropriately related to the very same content. For example, Lina and Marius have a belief with the same content that grass is green because they are both related in the appropriate way to the very same thing, the content <grass is green>. In the same way, the relation view can account for how distinct intentional states in the same subject—for example, a belief and a desire—can have the same contents: They are appropriately related to the same items.

On the aspect view, contents aren't distinctly existing items, and so it is difficult to see how multiple subjects can share them. However, the aspect view has an alternative way of understanding shared contents: Since contents are aspects of intentional states, subjects represent alike when their intentional states are alike with respect to these aspects. How to flesh out this proposal depends on what exactly we take aspects to be. Recall that an aspect of an intentional state is the intentional state itself, the intentional property the state is an instantiation of, a property of this property, or an instantiation of the latter kind of property. For our present purposes, we can isolate two broad options: The relevant aspects are either properties (intentional properties or properties of intentional properties) or states (instantiations of intentional properties or instantiations of properties of intentional properties). (See Appendix G for discussion of these options.)

If aspects are taken to be properties, then two subjects have the same contents when they instantiate the same aspects. In the above example, Lina and Marius represent the same content because they have intentional states with the same

---

[26] Versions of the sense data view that take sense data to be mind-dependent are an exception. These views may not seem to have the purported virtues of the relation view described in this section, though modified versions of the arguments supporting the claim that the aspect view shares in these virtues might apply to them.

aspects. Since Lina and Marius instantiate the very same property, they quite literally share a content.[27]

One might worry that if we instead take contents to be states, they are irredeemably private: Although you and I can have the same properties, we cannot have the same property *instantiations*. But, while it is true that, on this picture, we cannot entertain *numerically* identical contents, we can still entertain *qualitatively* identical contents, and this is enough to say that we can share contents.[28] In other words, on this picture, sharing contents amounts to having aspects that are the instantiations of the same properties. Indeed, on this view, it might make sense to introduce a new term for the properties that contents are instantiations of—e.g., we might call them **content properties**. We can then say that while Lina and Marius, strictly speaking, have numerically different contents, they have the same content properties. Indeed, on the view that contents are states, much of what we want to say about contents might, strictly speaking, only be true of content properties. For example, generalizations over contents, e.g., generalizations concerning the entailment relations of contents, might be best thought of as generalizations over content properties.[29]

Unrepresented Contents

Relation views that take contents to exist independently of intentional states can offer a neat account of unrepresented contents: Contents exist independently of us, and so they can exist without anyone representing them. This allows us to make sense of truths concerning particular contents that no one has ever represented, as well as to make generalizations that hold over all possible contents, whether they are represented or not.

The aspect view takes contents to be aspects of intentional states, which, as mentioned above, are either properties or states. An aspect view that takes contents to be properties takes unrepresented contents to be uninstantiated properties.[30] An aspect view that takes contents to be states instead rejects uninstantiated contents but replaces talk of such contents with talk of uninstantiated content properties.

---

[27] Pitt (2009, p. 122) offers a similar response to a similar objection to his type psychologism, which takes intentional contents to be psychological types.

[28] Of course, we can also have similar, but not qualitatively identical, contents. This might be enough to make sense of some cases of "shared" contents.

[29] Indeed, on this version of the aspect view, much of what *I* have said in previous chapters might only be true when construed as a claim about content properties, but writing with this in mind would have made the exposition unnecessarily complicated with little payoff.

[30] Pitt (2009) makes such a suggestion.

There is a potential problem for both versions of the aspect view: If we reject a Platonic view of properties, we may be compelled to deny that the aspects of uninstantiated intentional states, and hence unrepresented contents (or content properties), exist.[31] The worries facing non-Platonic views of properties in the case of unrepresented contents also arise with uninstantiated properties more generally. For example, we might want to speak of uninstantiated mass properties, masses that no objects happen to have, or to make generalizations holding over all mass properties, whether they are instantiated or not. There are various options for the non-Platonist here: She might say that uninstantiated properties merely possibly exist, that they exist as objects of thought but have no "real" existence, that our claims about them should be understood as counterfactual claims that tell us what *would* happen were they to be instantiated, or that they simply do not exist in any sense. It is not my aim to settle the question of what the non-Platonist should say about uninstantiated properties. My claim, instead, is that whatever she says about uninstantiated properties in general should apply equally well to unrepresented contents.[32]

Note that if accommodating truths about uninstantiated properties requires us to accept Platonic universals, then the relation view and the aspect view are on par with respect to their ontological commitments. The difference is that the aspect view takes us to instantiate the Platonic entities, while the relation view takes us to be related to them in some other way. This would undercut any arguments from parsimony for the aspect view, but it would not undercut the argument from the Real Problem (§9.2.2), so if, as I am in the process of arguing, the aspect view has all the same truth-indicating virtues as the relation view, the aspect view would still come out ahead.

Modeling Contents
It can be useful to model contents as sets of possible worlds, structured propositions, possible states of affairs, or other such items. Such models are useful for

---

[31] An Aristotelian view of properties has room to accept the existence of uninstantiated properties that are in some sense composed of instantiated properties. So, a version of the aspect view combined with this view of properties is only committed to denying the existence of uninstantiated properties that are not composed of instantiated properties.

[32] One might worry that one option is closed to the aspect theorist, that of unrepresented contents existing in the mind as objects of thought. How this option plays out depends on what it is to think about contents. If thinking about a content requires entertaining the content itself, then any content that is *thought of* is also *thought*, and so the relevant aspects will exist. But if we are able to think of contents without entertaining them (perhaps by derivatively representing them), then they can exist *merely* as objects of thought. Neither option raises special worries for the aspect view.

understanding the truth conditions of contents and the relations between various contents. Since the relation view maintains that contents are distinct from the having of contents, it allows us to focus in on contents and to model them in such ways.

However, it should by now be clear that even though, on the aspect view, contents do not exist independently of intentional states, contents can still be *considered* separately from any particular intentional states. There is no reason why these contents (or content properties) can't be modeled using sets of possible worlds (e.g., the sets of possible worlds in which intentional states with those contents are true), structured propositions, and the like. Compare: We can model the phenomenal character of color experiences with a three-dimensional color space even if the phenomenal characters of color experiences have no existence distinct from that of color experiences, and we can model the length of physical objects on a line even if lengths have no independent existence from the physical objects having those lengths. Having a "dependent" existence is no bar to being considered in isolation and modeled in various ways.[33]

9.3.3 INTENTIONAL STRUCTURE

As mentioned earlier, the aspect view bears some resemblance to adverbialism, which faces notorious difficulties in making sense of structured perceptual states (see also Appendix F). One might worry that the aspect view faces similar challenges in accommodating intentional structure.

There are two kinds of items we might want to say are structured: vehicles of intentionality and contents. For example, we might want to say that the vehicle GRASS IS GREEN is structured, and we might want to say that its content, <grass is green>, is structured.

There is a further orthogonal distinction we can make between two kinds of structure that either contents or vehicles might have: Contents or vehicles of intentionality are **internally structured** when they have proper parts that are also contents or representations, respectively. Contents or vehicles of intentionality are **externally structured** when they have properties of having values on certain dimensions.[34] For example, color contents are externally structured in that they have values on the dimensions of hue, saturation, and brightness, but they are not

---

[33] See also Matthews' (1994) account of how a system of propositional contents can be used to model our non-relational propositional attitude states.

[34] All vehicles and contents will be externally structured in lots of ways, but not all of their external structure will be interesting. Presumably, the kind of external structure that is interesting is the kind that pertains to the features that are relevant to individuating contents and vehicles.

internally structured because they do not have proper parts that are also contents. Roughly, internal structure is a matter of having parts, while external structure is a matter of having properties.

So, there are four kinds of intentional structure we might want to accommodate: the internal and external structure of vehicles, and the internal and external structure of intentional contents. Let us now consider in turn how the relation view and the aspect view can accommodate these kinds of structure.

Structured Vehicles

Let us begin by examining the prospects of accommodating internally structured vehicles. Perhaps the most notable view on which vehicles of intentionality are internally structured is the language of thought hypothesis (Fodor 1975), which posits a set of internally unstructured representations that have syntactic features determining how they can combine with one another to form internally structured representations that contain them as parts. For example, representing a red square might involve the internally unstructured representations RED and SQUARE being combined in a particular way to form the internally structured representation RED SQUARE. Fodor combines the language of thought hypothesis with a tracking theory of intentionality, which is a kind of relation view (Fodor 1987, 1990), but this is not obligatory. The story so far makes no specific mention of whether contents are items that representations are related to or aspects of intentional states, so it can equally well be combined with the aspect view. Similar points arguably apply to other views on which vehicles are structured. If so, the aspect view can accommodate internally structured vehicles just as well as the relation view.

Let us now turn to the prospects of accommodating externally structured vehicles of intentionality. We might want to say that different vehicles are similar to and different from one another without literally containing the same vehicles as parts. Such a view might be attractive if we take vehicles to be neural activation patterns. On a view taking vehicles to be externally but not internally structured, representing a red square might involve having a vehicle that is similar in some respects to other vehicles (e.g., one representing a blue square) but different in other respects. Again, this view on which vehicles are externally but not internally structured is equally compatible with the relation view and the aspect view, since it makes no mention of how the externally structured vehicles get to have their contents.

In sum, both the relation view and the aspect view can plausibly accommodate structured vehicles.

Structured Contents

Both the aspect view and the relation view face challenges in accommodating structured *contents*. Now, some views might deny the existence of structured contents. For example, on one version of the language of thought story, all there is to intentional structure is the representation of unstructured contents by structured vehicles. But it really does seem that contents are structured, both internally and externally. It seems there's internal structure because what we entertain or otherwise represent has distinguishable parts or features that arguably qualify as contents. When we think that the cat is on the mat, there is a *cat* bit and a *mat* bit, which can reoccur in other thoughts, such as the thought that the mat is on the cat, and both seem to consist in "saying" something. It also seems that contents can be externally structured, since they can be similar to one another without sharing parts. For example, the content $<red_5>$ can be similar to $<red_6>$ in hue and saturation, though not in brightness. These examples of internal and external structure cannot be explained solely in terms of the structure of vehicles, since the relevant structure seems present in *what is represented*, i.e., in a mental state's content.

Let us first consider the prospects of accommodating externally structured contents on the relation view and the aspect view. If the relation view takes externally structured contents to be items like Platonic universals or abstract sets of possible worlds, then it can say that contents are externally structured when they are similar to or different from other contents in particular respects. For example, the perceptual state representing <square> might involve a relation to the Platonic universal *square*, which is similar to and different from the Platonic universal *triangle* in certain respects.

Like the relation view, the aspect view has little trouble accommodating externally structured contents. There is no reason why aspects cannot vary from one another along various dimensions, yielding a rich network of externally structured contents.

It could very well turn out that many apparent cases of internal structure are in fact cases of external structure. For example, it could be that the content <big dog> does not contain <big> and <dog> as constituent parts but is instead best thought of as an internally unstructured content that is similar to and different from other contents (e.g., <small dog>, <big cat>) in certain ways. If so, then being able to accommodate external structure goes a long way for both the relation view and the aspect view.

Things are more complicated when it comes to internal structure. The kinds of internal structure we might want to account for include predicative structure (e.g., as in <grass is green>), truth-functional logical structure (e.g., as in <grass is green and snow is white>), and other kinds of logical structure (e.g., as in <there is something green>, <gray cat>, <large goldfish>). The central challenge for any view accepting internally structured contents is that of specifying how exactly an internally structured content's constituent contents come together to form a structured whole, e.g., how <red> and <square> combine to form <red square>, and how <grass> and <green> combine to form <grass is green>.

It might seem that the relation view has an easier time accounting for internal structure, since it can say that the distinctly existing entities to be identified with contents are internally structured in the ways required. For example, it might say that the content <grass is green> is the fact that grass is green, which itself has a predicative structure. This won't do, though, since not all propositional contents are true, so not all propositional contents can plausibly be identified with facts. In order to account for internally structured contents, then, it looks like the relation view will need to invoke a new kind of structure, one distinct from the structure of facts.

The problem is that it is not clear how the relation view can make sense of such structure. Suppose some internally structured contents are composed of Platonic universals. The problem is that of explaining how exactly two Platonic universals come together to form a unity that is more than the sum of its parts. For example, how do <brown> and <dog> come together to form <brown dog> rather than just the set consisting of the contents <brown> and <dog>? Or suppose some internally structured contents are composed of Platonic universals and existing concrete objects. The same problem arises in explaining how Platonic universals and existing concrete objects come together to form a unity (recall that the objects needn't instantiate the relevant Platonic universals in order for us to represent the relevant internally structured content). For example, how do <Bumper> and <goldfish> come together to form <Bumper is a goldfish> rather than just the set consisting of <Bumper> and <goldfish>?[35]

There are many sophisticated accounts formally specifying the rules governing the truth conditions of structured contents (see, e.g., Frege 1956, Russell 1937, Soames 2010, King 2007, and Bealer 1982), and one might suggest that a relation theoretic account of how contents come to be internally structured is to be found there. However, insofar as these proposals include accounts of internally structured contents, internal structure is largely posited, not completely explained. For example, and very roughly, Frege (1948) takes it to be part of the nature of contents that some are "saturated" and others are "unsaturated," allowing the saturated ones to fill in the unsaturated ones; Bealer (1982) appeals to "thought-building" operations that mirror, but are not identical to, the relations holding facts together; King (2007) takes complex linguistic facts and mental "ascriptions" to unify contents; and Soames (2010) appeals to a mental act of "predication." Such views may point to the locus of internal structure, whether it be in the mind, in language, or in an abstract Platonic

---

[35] This last example is an instance of the well-known problem of the unity of the proposition, the problem of explaining how the elements of a structured proposition come together to form a unified proposition rather than a mere list or set of elements (see Russell 1937, Gaskin 2008, and King 2007).

realm, but they ultimately appeal to unexplained structure or structure-building ingredients that are specifically posited to give rise to internal structure. This is not to say that such views are false but only that they cannot provide the relation view with a complete and intelligible explanation of internal structure.

Just as the relation view must account for how distinctly existing entities come together to form structured wholes, the aspect view must account for how aspects of intentional states come together to form structured wholes. In the worst case, the aspect view might simply have to say that there are special "predicative" or other ways of combining aspects into structured wholes or appeal to other structure-building elements. If so, the aspect view is arguably no worse off than the relation view. Let us briefly explore, though, the question of whether the aspect view can say a bit more about internal structure. I want to suggest that at least some aspect views can provide an intelligible explanation of at least some kinds of internal structure.

Since aspects are states or properties, internally structured contents would have to be internally structured states or properties. What this looks like depends on whether aspects are intentional states or properties (i.e., "first-order" states or properties—see Appendix G), or if they are properties of such states or properties (i.e., "second-order" states or properties). If aspects are first-order states or properties, then internal structure involves two or more such items coming together to form an experienced unity that is more than the sum of its parts. Note that it would not be enough to simply say that internal structure involves aspects being co-instantiated by the same vehicle, since it is not clear that mere co-instantiation by a vehicle unifies the aspects to form a complex whole. For example, suppose a single vehicle has both a red-aspect and a square-aspect. It is not clear why—absent primitive or unexplained structural relations, of course—this should result in a red-square-aspect rather than *just* a red-aspect co-instantiated with a square-aspect. In other words, it's not clear why it should result in the vehicle having the content <red square> rather than its having two distinct contents, <red> and <square>.

If, instead, aspects are second-order states or properties, then we have a natural way of accommodating at least some kinds of internal structure: Two aspects are unified into a single structured aspect when they are had by the same intentional state or property. For example, representing <red square> might involve having a single intentional state that has two aspects, a red-aspect and a square-aspect. Since the combined aspects are had by the same intentional state, it is more plausible that they form an experienced unity that is more than just the sum of its parts. Whereas in the case of the first-order view, the plausible outcome of the co-instantiation of a red-aspect and a square-aspect is two distinct intentional states (or properties) being had by the same vehicle, in the case of the second-order view, the outcome is a single intentional state (or property) that is two different ways, a red-aspect way and a square-aspect way. In effect, we are accounting for internally structured second-order states and properties in terms of externally structured first-order intentional states and properties, which, as we saw above, are much easier to accommodate.[36]

As it stands, the above account can explain only one kind of internal structure, that of conjunctively composed proprietal contents. Indeed, this is the kind of structure that we might be able to account for in terms of external structure anyways (see above), so we have not made much progress. We still do not have an account of predicative or other kinds of structure. Perhaps there is room to account for predicative or other structure in terms of the *kinds* of aspects that are unified. In line with what we've seen above, however, it seems likely that even such an account will have to take some kinds of internal structure or structure-building ingredients to be primitive or at least unexplained.

The above discussion is far from providing a satisfactory account of how contents can be structured on either the relation view or the aspect view. However, it is worth pointing out that identity PIT, which identifies intentional contents with phenomenal characters (and which is compatible with both the relation view and the aspect view), can *accommodate* structured contents, even if it cannot fully explain them. This is because the phenomenal characters of phenomenal states arguably themselves have both internal and external structure. For example, an experience of a blue and round ball involves both predicative structure and conjunctively composed proprietal structure. The constituent phenomenal characters do not simply co-occur but, instead, modify each other in a certain way, forming an internally structured whole that is more than the sum of its parts.[37] The constituent phenomenal characters, and perhaps also the internally structured whole, are also interestingly externally structured in that they have various properties that make them similar to and different from the phenomenal characters of other experiences. It may be mysterious or even incomprehensible to us just how phenomenal characters come to have this structure, but since we arguably know that they *do* have it, identity PIT can *accommodate* similarly structured contents, whether or not it can fully *explain* them. This may be a consideration in favor of identity PIT, since it correctly predicts that there are structured contents. (But this is not, of course, a consideration in favor

---

[36] This is the basic idea that lies behind Kriegel's (2007) defense of adverbialism from the many property problem. Allowing for internal structure is an important advantage of versions of the aspect view that take contents to be properties of intentional states or instantiations of such properties (such as Kriegel's version) over other versions that take contents to be intentional properties or states. See Appendix G of this chapter.

[37] Some versions of the binding problem (see Revonsuo 1999 and Smythies 1994) can be understood as special cases of the problem of explaining the apparent internal structure of phenomenal consciousness.

of the aspect view over the relation view, since identity PIT can be combined with either view.)[38]

In summary, accounting for intentional structure, particularly the internal structure of contents, is challenging, but the aspect view fares no worse than the relation view when it comes to accommodating internally and externally structured vehicles and contents.[39]

9.3.4 TRUTH AND REFERENCE

It is quite plausible that intentional states have **conditions of truth and reference**, that is, that there are conditions in which intentional states are true or refer to particular items. For example, an intentional state representing <grass is green> is true just in case grass is in fact green. I will take a **theory of truth (or reference)** to be a theory that provides criteria that determine the conditions in which a mental state is true (or what it refers to).

One might think that it is easier to account for truth and reference on the relation view than on the aspect view. Before evaluating this claim, I want to suggest that it is not entirely nonnegotiable that intentional states are true or refer in certain conditions. While we cannot help but be confronted with intentionality through introspection, we are not clearly similarly confronted with truth, reference, and conditions of truth and reference. It is not *clearly* incompatible with our experience that there is no fact of the matter as to what is the "correct" relation between intentional states and other items in the world (however, see below, where I will suggest that conditions of truth and reference might turn out to be introspectively accessible after all). Unless there are other strong reasons to think that there must be such things as truth and reference, facilitating a theory of truth and reference may not be a truth-indicating virtue rather than merely a desire-satisfying virtue, a virtue that makes it more desirable that a theory or claim be true. If it is merely a desire-satisfying virtue, then even if the relation view has it but the aspect view does not, it does not provide a reason to prefer the relation view.

Even if facilitating an account of truth and reference is a truth-indicating virtue, it is not clear that this would suggest in favor of the relation view. In what follows, I

---

[38] One could also make an argument from the minimization of mystery for identity PIT: Structured contents are mysterious, and structured phenomenal characters are mysterious. If we identify the two, then we minimize the mystery.

[39] In Mendelovici forthcoming-b, I argue that there are principled obstacles to understanding how mental things, including intentional contents, combine. If this is right, then it should not be surprising if neither the relation view nor the aspect view can fully explain structured contents.

consider three types of theories of truth and reference—correspondence theories, identity theories, and mixed theories—and suggest that relation view and aspect view versions of them are equally problematic. I then propose a version of the correspondence theory that might seem promising, which is compatible with both the relation and the aspect view.

Correspondence Theories

According to **correspondence theories of truth (or reference)**, a content is true (or refers) if it appropriately corresponds to, but is not identical to, a state of affairs (or an item of another kind, such as an object or property), which is its truth-maker (or referent).

The burden of a correspondence theory is to explain the nature of the relevant correspondence relation. When do two items, which in many cases belong to different ontological categories, "belong" together? For example, why is it that the content <grass is green> is supposed to go with the concrete fact that grass is green and the content <George> is supposed to go with the flesh-and-blood individual George?

It might seem that the relation view is in a better position to offer a correspondence theory of truth and reference because distinctly existing contents often come with a built-in connection to the world. For instance, Platonic universals are the sorts of things that can be **instantiated** by ordinary objects, and propositions are the sorts of things that can **obtain**. On a relation view involving Platonic universals, for example, truth and reference are at least partly a matter of the Platonic universals we represent being instantiated in the appropriate ways. Similarly, if we take contents to be propositions, which might be structures consisting of Platonic universals, sets of possible worlds, scenarios, or some such, then truth is a matter of these propositions obtaining. On a possible worlds view, this might, for instance, be a matter of the actual world being in a represented set of possible worlds.

Where the relation view invokes relations of instantiation and obtaining, the aspect view invokes its own primitive correspondence relation. One might worry that such a primitive correspondence relation is mysterious and brute. However, both instantiation and obtaining are arguably quite mysterious themselves, and perhaps even primitive and brute. Platonic universals and propositions, on the one hand, and property instances and states of affairs or facts, on the other, are very different kinds of things, usually belonging to entirely different ontological categories.[40] Similarly, if we take contents to be sets of abstract possible worlds, then

---

[40] Note that this worry does not affect the Aristotelian universals view of properties, since this view takes universals to be abstracted away from concrete property instances, so there are non-brute facts

there have to be facts of the matter as to when an abstract possible world counts as "the same world as" a concrete actual world, a relation that is arguably brute and mysterious.[41] Indeed, one might worry that the relation view simply kicks the challenge of accounting for truth and reference upstairs: we trade the question of how intentional states are supposed to correspond to the world for that of how propositions or Platonic universals are supposed to correspond to the world.[42]

I will later consider another correspondence theory that I think is more promising than the ones mentioned here and that is available to both the relation view and the aspect view. But for now, we can conclude that it is not clear that the relation view has an easier time facilitating a correspondence theory of truth and reference than the aspect view.

Identity Theories

Perhaps we can avoid any mention of mysterious facts about when items in one ontological category are "supposed to" go with items in another ontological category by adopting an **identity theory of truth (or reference)**, which states that a content is true (or refers) if it is identical to a fact (or other item), which is its truth-maker (or referent).

One might suggest that the relation view has an easier time facilitating an identity theory of truth or reference because the truth-makers and referents of intentional states exist distinctly of those states. Such a view might claim that the contents of true intentional states are simply worldly states of affairs and the referents of referring intentional states are other worldly items.

The problem with such a view is that not all contents have truth-makers or referents, so we cannot identify *all* contents with their truth-makers and referents. Presumably the contents that can't be identified with truth-makers or referents will end up being abstract propositions, Platonic universals, or other such items. But this leads to an unattractive disjunctivism about contents on which there are two indistinguishable but very different ways of having contents with the same superficial characters. For example, on this view, the content <grass is green> is a concrete state of affairs if grass is in fact green, but it is an abstract proposition or other alternative

---

about which universals are related to which concrete property instances. So, it is not the case that we are committed to a mysterious instantiation relation whether or not we accept the relation view. The problem arises for the relation view precisely because if it invokes properties, these properties must be Platonic universals (see §9.2.1).

[41] Lewis (1986) calls such a relation between possible worlds and the actual world the "selection relation" and argues that it is brute and mysterious.

[42] The sense data view faces the same challenges. Sense data are not the same kinds of things as external objects, so it is not clear how they are supposed to correspond to them.

item if grass is not green. Since contents behave similarly whether or not they are true or refer, there is reason to reject such a disjunctivist view.[43]

On the aspect view, an identity theory of truth and reference identifies true and referring contents with aspects of intentional states. While this view avoids disjunctivism, it is effectively a kind of **semantic idealism**, taking referents and truth-makers to be aspects of our own intentional states, which, on many views, will be internal states (but see §9.3.5). When this view is combined with identity PIT, we end up with a view on which referents and truth-makers are aspects of our own phenomenal states. Now, while this may be a deal-breaker for many, unless we have reason to think that avoiding semantic idealism is a truth-indicating virtue, rather than a desire-satisfying virtue, it is not automatically a reason to reject the view.

Mixed Theories

Let us now consider the prospects for the relation view of a mixed theory invoking elements from both the identity and the correspondence theories. Note that the identity theory's problem that not all contents have referents or truth-makers applies most clearly to propositional contents, whose purported referents are obtaining states of affairs, and objectual contents, whose purported referents are particular objects. But one might suggest that, on a relation view accepting Platonic universals, this problem does not afflict proprietal contents, whose purported referents are properties, since the Platonist can accept that all proprietal contents refer. This might motivate a mixed view, on which an identity theory of reference applies to proprietal contents or a subset of such contents (perhaps the internally unstructured ones), which refer to themselves, but truth and other instances of reference are a matter of correspondence. Such a mixed view might take all contents to be constructed out of Platonic universals and logical relations (and perhaps indexical ingredients), with internally structured contents getting their conditions of truth and reference compositionally based on their constituent proprietal contents and their modes of composition (and perhaps indexical ingredients).[44]

While we can grant that this view manages to explain how we can refer to Platonic universals, we do not yet have an account of how some combination of

---

[43] One might suggest that concrete facts and Platonic propositions are really the same kind of item, which in some cases happens to be a Platonic item and in other cases happens to be a concrete fact, but this suggestion just moves the bump around under the rug. One now wonders what makes a Platonic item and a concrete fact count as *the same thing*. What makes the concrete fact that grass is green and the Platonic proposition that grass is green count as the *same* proposition?

[44] Such a view is congenial to descriptivist views of some kinds of reference (see Jackson 1998a and Lewis 1984).

Platonic universals is made true by or refers to something else. For example, consider the content <there is a blue ball>. On the picture under consideration, this is an internally structured content involving <blue> and <ball>, which are identical to their referents, the Platonic universals *blue* and *ball*. So far so good. But what makes the internally structured whole true or false? Presumably, what would make it true would be a concrete state of affairs of a blue ball existing. Since this concrete state of affairs is not *identical* to the internally unstructured content but, instead, something that is supposed to *correspond* in a particular way with it, this identity theory of the reference of (perhaps unstructured) proprietal contents is combined with a correspondence theory of truth and perhaps some kinds of reference. But then we face the shortcomings of the correspondence theory again: we must appeal to facts about the instantiation of Platonic universals or the obtaining of propositions or other items. We are again faced with the problem of explaining why two items of distinct ontological categories—e.g., Platonic universals and (in most cases) concrete items—"belong" together.

BonJour (1998, §6.7) offers what can be construed as an aspect theoretic version of the above-mentioned mixed theory. BonJour takes all intentional states to represent combinations of properties and indexical elements. On his account, intentional states with proprietal contents literally contain the properties they refer to. So, an intentional state with the content <triangle> literally contains the property of triangularity, though it is not itself triangular.[45] This is an identity theory of reference of at least the intentional states representing proprietal contents, since the properties such intentional states refer to are properties that they instantiate. This, in effect, is what the claim that a C-aspect involves C-ness, the property that the content C (allegedly) picks out, amounts to (see §9.1.2). However, since, presumably, the truth-makers of many structured contents are not literally contained in our intentional states, the view is most fruitfully combined with a correspondence theory of truth in the same

---

[45] BonJour (1998) writes:

> ... [T]he universal instantiated by thoughts of triangular things is a more complex universal having the universal triangularity as one of its components, with other components pertaining to other aspects of the content, to the kind of thought in question (belief, desire, intention, contemplation, etc.), and perhaps to further matters as well. Such a complex universal would have to be so structured that a mental act could be an instance of the complex universal without it thereby being literally an instance of triangularity, indeed without anything being such an instance. (p. 184)

BonJour also considers and rejects a nearby view on which there are two ways of instantiating a property, perhaps similar to Aristotle's view on which thinking about something requires the mind to be "capable of receiving the form of an object ... without being the object" (*De Anima* III 4, 429a15-16). Thanks to Sam Baker for helpful discussion on Aristotle.

way that the relation view's identity theory of reference for the representation of properties is best combined with a correspondence theory of truth.[46]

A potential worry with this view is that there is little reason to think that properties of intentional states are or even can be instantiated outside of intentional states. In other words, there is little reason to think that C-aspects involve C-ness if C-ness is assumed to be a property that non-intentional items do or can have. However, this does not automatically give us reason to reject the view, since one might agree with me that the relevant aspects of intentional states are not—or even cannot be—instantiated by non-intentional items but nonetheless maintain that C-aspects refer to C-ness. It's just that nothing does or perhaps even can have these properties outside the mind.[47]

The Matching Theory

I now want to propose a version of the correspondence theory that is compatible with both the aspect view and the relation view, though it is particularly congenial to the aspect view. On this view, the relevant correspondence relation is the matching relation, where a content matches another item when the item has all the features of the content's superficial character.[48] On this **matching theory**, a content is true (or refers) if it matches some other item in the world, which is its truth-maker (or referent).[49]

The main consideration in favor of the matching theory is that it captures what we take to be required for truth and reference by our very own lights. When we entertain a content, we seem to have a clear idea of what it would take for the world

---

[46] Note that this mixed view is compatible with an Aristotelian view of properties, since any represented property is instantiated in the mind. So, it arguably avoids the worry that it must invoke a wholly mysterious instantiation relation. See n. 40.

[47] There are two versions of the resulting view, both of which might seem unattractive in that they paint a stark vision of our abilities to know about the mind-independent world: On the first version, propositional intentional states generally assert the external or mind-independent existence of items having the properties their components refer to. But nothing external has (or perhaps even *can* have) the relevant properties. So, while proprietal contents *always* succeed in referring, propositional contents are systematically (and perhaps necessarily) false.

The second version of this view drops the claim that propositional intentional states generally assert the *external* existence of items having the properties their constituent proprietal contents refer to and merely takes them to assert the *existence* of items having the relevant properties. Since the only items that can have these properties are internal items, this brings us back to semantic idealism, on which the referents and truth-makers of our intentional states are always mental items.

The choice between an all-encompassing error theory and semantic idealism is an unhappy one, but, unless we have independent reason to think that both an error theory and semantic idealism are false, being forced into this choice is not automatically a reason to think the view is false.

[48] See n. 9 of Chapter 5.

[49] The matching theory is similar in name and in spirit, but not in substance, to Montague's (2009, 2013) "matching view" of the perception of objects.

to be as it says it is or to contain what it is about—it would have to be *like that*, where "that" picks out the content that is entertained and "like" expresses a relation of similarity. This suggests a correspondence theory on which the correspondence relation is a kind of similarity relation. In which way are contents supposed to be similar to their referents and truth-makers? My suggestion is that the relevant kind of similarity is matching, which is a matter of the features of a content's superficial characters being had by something in the rest of the world. The reason for this is that it is the superficial characters of contents, not their deep natures, that are discerned in introspection and that we take to characterize the world around us, so it is arguably our contents' superficial characters, and not their deep natures, that form the referent of "that" when we think that in order for our intentional states to be true the world would have to be *like that*. This is why we don't think that the world must be mental when we think it must be *like that*, even if contents are in fact mental items.

Alternative pictures of truth and reference arguably require too much or too little for truth and reference. The correspondence theories that we previously considered don't preserve the idea that truth and reference require that the world be similar to our intentional states (e.g., abstract propositions need to obtain, not be similar to concrete states of affairs, and Platonic universals need to be realized by things in the world, not be similar to them). So, these alternative correspondence theories require too little of true or referring intentional states. In contrast, identity theories require too much. We arguably don't intuitively require the world to have the same deep nature as our contents in order for those contents to be true or refer. When we think the world must be *like that* in order for our intentional states to be true or refer, the way we think the world must be is captured by the superficial character of our contents, the features of our contents that introspection discerns, and not the deep nature of our contents, to which we are oblivious. If this is right, then the requirements for truth and reference are mere matching, not complete similarity, and certainly not numerical identity. This is what counts as truth and reference by our own lights. Alternative theories are too demanding or not demanding enough, but the matching theory is just right.

The matching theory is congenial to the aspect view. It promises to avoid some of the unwanted consequences of aspect theoretic theories of truth and reference that invoke elements from the identity theory. In particular, it avoids saying that truth and reference require that C-aspects be instantiated outside of the mind. Truth and reference require only that C-aspects *match* items outside the mind. Of course, matching involves an identity between a content's superficial character and something else, so it involves the sharing of properties. But, importantly, these properties needn't be contents themselves. They might, for instance, be abstract or structural properties of contents. Still, it is not clear whether anything in the mind-independent world does or can match our contents. But there is more hope than on the aspect theoretic version of the identity and mixed theories, since the requirements are far less demanding, particularly if superficial characters are or include abstract or structural features of contents.[50] Of course, absent reasons to think that our intentional states are sometimes true or refer, this feature of the matching theory is not a truth-indicating virtue but only a desire-satisfying one.

The matching theory of truth and reference is also available to the relation view. On the relation theoretic version, truth and reference are a matter of the relation view's distinctly existing contents, whatever they are, matching the world.

The view's flexibility also allows it to be extended to the derived mental representational states discussed in §7.3 and §8.3.2: derived mental representational states are true or refer if their contents, which are possible phenomenal contents or object-involving contents (which are just objects, properties, and other items), match the world. What it takes for a possible phenomenal content to match the world is for its superficial character to be identical to features of the world. What it takes for an object-involving content to match the world is, arguably, for the very object, property, or other item to exist—after all, when we derivatively represent object-involving contents, we do so because we take ourselves to mean the relevant items in their entirety, so their entire natures are their superficial characters, their features that characterize them as the contents that they are.[51,52]

The upshot of this discussion is that, first, truth and reference are quite mysterious, both on the aspect view and on the relation view. Second, there are at least three views

---

[50] Even if most of the aspects of our mental states fail to match items in the world, there might be room for a notion of partial truth as a kind of partial matching. This is attractive if our superficial characters involve both features that are not instantiated outside the mind (e.g., perhaps, certain qualitative features) and features that are (e.g., perhaps, certain structural features).

[51] Here we are operating with an extended notion of a superficial character, on which contents that aren't intentional contents count as having superficial characters.

[52] Pautz (2007) argues that only the relation view can make sense of our knowledge of the similarities and differences between properties that we obtain solely by having certain experiences, such as our knowledge that $orange_5$ is more similar to red_{15} than it is to $purple_{21}$ that we might obtain solely by having experiences of the relevant colors. The aspect theorist might respond that, insofar as we have such knowledge, it is based on a comparison of the contents of color experiences, which are aspects of intentional states. The matching theory allows us to further say that, since these aspects refer to whatever external world items they match, the relations of similarity and difference between them are likely to reflect the relations of similarity and difference of whatever they refer to, which would be the properties $orange_5$, red_{15}, and $purple_{21}$ (assuming such properties exist—if they do not, what we end up with is conditional knowledge). What makes the knowledge we obtain in this case knowledge of properties and not of mere aspects of our intentional states is that the contents we use to think it refer to properties and are made true by facts about how properties are related. Any other theory of truth and reference that preserves a structural similarity between aspects and their referents and truth-makers can say something similar.

of truth and reference compatible with the aspect view: a correspondence theory that accepts a primitive correspondence relation, a BonJour-style view combining an identity theory of at least some kinds of reference with a correspondence theory of truth and perhaps other kinds of reference, and the matching theory. On the first two, intentionality may only secure conditions of truth and reference with the help of further ingredients, while on the third, conditions of truth and reference might simply fall out of intentional states, given our everyday understanding of truth and reference (but see Appendix H). The same or analogous theories of truth and reference are also available to the relation view, so it is not the case that either view is in a better position to facilitate a theory of truth and reference.

9.3.5 EXTERNALISM

One might suggest that the relation view, but not the aspect view, is compatible with externalism, the view that there are broad contents. If externalism is true, this would be a reason to prefer the relation view.

One quick response to this kind of worry is that the aspect view *is* compatible with externalism. As discussed in §9.1.3, it is possible to hold an externalist aspect view. Such an aspect view might claim that the relevant aspects involve relations to the environment but that none of the environmental relata are themselves properly considered *contents* (see n. 8). However, such a view is arguably somewhat unnatural.

I want to suggest, instead, that we can accommodate externalist intuitions in a way that is compatible with the aspect view by admitting broad derived contents. Chapter 7 presented a self-ascriptivist view of many of the alleged contents of thought and showed how it can capture various types of broad contents, including natural kind contents, deferential contents, and object-involving contents. When combined with an aspect view taking the relevant aspects to be intrinsic properties of individuals, the result is a view that is internalist about original intentionality but externalist about at least some kinds of derived mental representation.[53] Such a view can arguably accommodate externalist intuitions sufficiently well to make externalism about original intentionality unnecessary (see §7.3 and §8.3.2).[54]

---

[53] Horgan and Tienson (2002) also propose a view on which there are narrow phenomenal contents and broad derived contents.

[54] Mendelovici 2010, ch. 12, argues that externalist intuitions, such as Twin Earth intuitions, are best thought of as informing us about derived contents, not original contents, and so that they are adequately accommodated by broad derived contents.

9.3.6 TAKING STOCK

I've considered various alleged virtues of the relation view over the aspect view: It might be claimed that the relation view is better supported by common sense, provides a superior account of public and unrepresented contents, better accommodates intentional structure, is in a better position to account for truth and reference, and is more congenial to externalism. I have argued that the aspect view fares no worse than the relation view with respect to all these alleged virtues. All this helps flesh out the aspect view and ward off potential objections. It also allows us to complete an argument from parsimony for the view: The aspect view can do everything the relation view can do without the relation view's hefty ontological commitments. So, we should prefer it.

9.4 Conclusion

I have argued for the aspect view of intentionality, on which representing C is a matter of having an intentional state with a C-aspect, and against the alternative relation view, on which representing C is a matter of bearing a special relation to a distinctly existing item, C. The relation view reifies and (usually) externalizes contents, taking them out of the mind and endowing them with their own distinct existence. This move might be thought to confer various advantages, allowing for contents that are public, compositionally structured, apt for truth and reference, and broad. But we have seen that moving contents out of the mind confers no such advantages. Instead, it precludes contents from playing their single most important role, that of being entertained or otherwise represented. By taking contents to be integral aspects of intentional states, the aspect view puts contents back in the mind, where they can be thought, entertained, and intentionally represented in a psychologically involved way.

The aspect view helps complete our overall picture of intentionality. Parts III and IV argued for strong identity PIT, the view that, roughly, original intentionality is identical to phenomenal consciousness. If my claims in this chapter are correct, this view is best combined with the aspect view, resulting, roughly, in a non-relational view of phenomenal consciousness/intentionality.

This allows us to respond to the worry raised in §5.3 for identity PIT that original intentionality and phenomenal consciousness cannot be identified because they have different deep natures, with intentional states, but not phenomenal states, being relations to distinctly existing contents. Since, as I argued in this chapter, intentionality is not relational in the way this objection supposes, there is no such barrier to identifying them.

On the resulting view, intentional contents are phenomenal characters, and phenomenal characters are aspects of phenomenal states. Which aspects of phenomenal states phenomenal characters end up being depends on which aspects of phenomenal states are *felt* or *experienced* (see Appendix G). Those aspects, whatever they are, are our contents. They are what we think, perceptually represent, or otherwise entertain. They are our immediate contents (§7.2.1), making up our immediate representational perspective on the world.

Assuming internalism about phenomenal consciousness, the resulting view is radically internalistic. Not only is what determines which intentional contents we represent in the head, but intentional contents themselves are quite literally in the head—they are phenomenal states or properties of phenomenal states. Although there is room on the picture for broad contents, as well as relations of truth and reference, it is the representing subject herself who determines her targeted contents (and perhaps even what is required for truth and reference—see Appendix H). In this way, the overall view respects what is arguably the core internalist idea that we are the authors of our own contents (see also §10.2).

Appendix F: The Aspect View and Adverbialism

Adverbialism is the view that perceptual experiences are modifications of subjects, such as ways of sensing, rather than relations between subjects and objects of experience (Chisholm 1957b, Ducasse 1942, Sellars 1975, Papineau 2014, and Gow MS). Historically, adverbialism was meant to provide an alternative to the sense data theory, on which perceptual experience has an act-object structure and the objects of experience are sense data. The way adverbialism avoids a commitment to sense data, and thus provides an alternative to the sense data theory, is by rejecting a relational conception of experience and instead claiming that experiences are modifications of subjects. Adverbialism is so called due to its commitment to the linguistic project of offering plausible adverbialist paraphrases of perceptual ascriptions, such as (1), in terms of adverbial constructions such as (2):

(1) David sees a red patch.
(2) David senses redly.

Although there are many similarities between adverbialism, as traditionally conceived, and the aspect view, there are some important differences. One difference is in their targets. Traditionally, adverbialism is a view of perceptual experience, while the aspect view is a view of intentionality. Another difference concerns the perceived importance of providing adverbial paraphrases of perceptual ascriptions. The aspect view makes no claims concerning everyday language or even about the most useful way of formulating claims about intentional states. Perhaps our everyday language and our most useful scientific language for describing intentional states are implicitly committed to the relation view and the adverbialist paraphrase project fails. The aspect view is neutral on this point, since it is only concerned with the nature of intentional states, not the language we do or should use to talk about them (see also §9.3.1). The advocate of the aspect view might be happy to continue using everyday language even if it superficially appears to conflict with the nature of intentionality, as long as we do not take seriously the commitments of such language.[55] Finally, adverbialism is only one version of the aspect view, a version that is arguably best interpreted as taking the relevant aspects to be properties of intentional properties. Kriegel (2011), an aspect theorist who takes contents to be properties of intentional properties, calls his view "adverbialism" for this reason. But, as discussed in §9.1 and especially Appendix G, there are other versions of the aspect view as well (on my preferred view, the relevant aspects are states of intentional states).

Jackson's many property problem (1977) is a well-known worry with adverbialism, and one might reasonably wonder whether a similar problem afflicts the aspect view. Briefly, the many property problem is that there is no good way to paraphrase sentences such as (3):

(3) David experiences a red square and a blue triangle.

Here are two candidate paraphrases:

(4) David senses redly and squarely and bluely and triangularly.
(5) David senses red-squarely and blue-triangularly.

(4) won't do because it does not distinguish between the case where David experiences a red square and a blue triangle and the case in which he experiences a blue square and a red triangle. (5) involves introducing a new predicate for every set of properties an experience attributes to the same object. The problem with this paraphrase is that it does not allow us to draw certain apparently valid inferences from (5), such as that David senses redly and that he senses squarely, since "red-squarely" is a primitive linguistic expression and does not decompose into "redly" and "squarely."

---

[55] Papineau (2014) and Gow (MS) make similar points.

The many property problem concerns the adverbialist's paraphrase project, which, as mentioned above, the aspect view need not endorse.[56] But one might still wonder whether the aspect view faces something like this problem. Intentional states compose, but, one might argue, aspects cannot compose; they can only co-occur. If aspects can only co-occur, then representing a blue triangle and a red square will involve, say, the co-occurrence of four aspects: a blue-aspect, a triangle-aspect, a red-aspect, and a square-aspect. But this is also what representing a blue square and a red triangle would involve. Thus, it seems the aspect view cannot distinguish between intentional states with different structures that involve the same basic elements.[57]

As it stands, the same worry might be raised against the relation view that accepts structured contents. Take a relation view on which the state of representing a red square and a blue triangle is an internally structured intentional state involving relations to redness, squareness, blueness, and triangularity. One might complain that these relational properties can only be co-instantiated; all we have are a relation to redness, a relation to squareness, a relation to blueness, and a relation to triangularity. But that is also what representing a blue square and a red triangle would involve. So, it seems that the non-linguistic analogue of the many property problem also afflicts the relation view.

This does not show that no relation or aspect view can make sense of the cases. What is shows is that if we think that there are structured intentional states, then we need a story about intentional structure. Subsection 9.3.3 considers the prospects of providing such a story for both the relation view and the aspect view and argues that the aspect view is no worse off than the relation view.

Appendix G: Contents as First- or Second-Order States or Properties

The aspect view has various broad options as to what exactly are the aspects to be identified with contents. One choice point concerns whether contents are, on the one hand, intentional properties or properties of intentional properties or, on the other hand, *instantiations* of either kind of property. In other words, the choice point concerns whether contents are *properties*, i.e., presumably general or abstract ways things are or might be, or *states*, i.e., instantiations of properties, or particular ways that particular things are. Another choice point concerns whether contents are *first-*

or *second*-order properties/states. These choice points result in four possible views of the relevant aspects.

Two contemporary versions of the aspect view, Kriegel's (2007, 2011) adverbialism and Pitt's (2009) intentional psychologism, take contents to be abstract or general items. On Pitt's intentional psychologism, contents are psychological types, and we represent them by instantiating them. Pitt's view can be roughly understood as an aspect view on which contents are identified with intentional properties.[58] On Kriegel's adverbialism, contents are ways of representing, or properties of intentional properties. So, Kriegel's view also takes contents to be properties.[59]

Alternatively, we might take contents to be not properties but rather *instantiations* of properties, or, in other words, *states*. On such a view, contents are concrete particular property instantiations rather than abstract or general ways things might be.

Our choice between these views will depend on what plays the role of content. Content is what is intentionally represented. In the case of occurrent states, it is what is entertained. So, deciding between these views will depend on which aspect of intentional states is entertained or otherwise intentionally represented. If, as seems plausible, what is entertained or otherwise intentionally represented is, in its deep nature, a concrete particular, not an abstract or general item, then contents are states, not properties.

One might claim that worrying about the question of whether contents are properties or states is splitting hairs. Any aspect theorist will agree that both the relevant properties and the relevant states exist and that we can speak of either. The question of which to call "contents" is of little consequence. The question is indeed one of detail rather than one of the general direction of a theory of intentionality (which is why it is relegated to this appendix). However, how we answer this question makes a difference to the very fundamental question of what exactly it is that we entertain or otherwise represent, where this is to be understood as a question about the deep nature of contents. What exactly is it that is running through our heads when we think and perceive? Are these things general properties? Or are they particular property instantiations? If contents are property instantiations, then what we literally entertain are concrete things, perhaps even physical things, presumably in our heads. If contents are properties, then what we entertain may be something abstract, perhaps even Platonic.

---

[58] Pitt does not equate types with properties, but I will skate over this detail.

[59] Kriegel defines "content" as what individuates intentional properties qua intentional properties, which leads to his taking contents to be properties of intentional properties. So, any disagreement with him here might be merely terminological, unless he also wants to say that contents are what are *entertained* (see below).

This leads us to what I take to be the key reason to think that what we entertain are states, not properties, and hence to the view that the relevant aspects are states: Intentionality is a concrete psychological phenomenon, and intentional states are concrete psychological states of entertaining or otherwise intentionally representing contents. By taking contents to be concrete psychological items, the state view appropriately respects these ideas. Though we can speak of the properties that our contents are instantiations of, and though it may even be natural to call them "contents" when speaking loosely, strictly speaking, what we entertain or otherwise represent is a concrete property instantiation rather than the property it is an instantiation of.[60]

The second choice point concerns whether to take contents to be, on the one hand, *first-order* intentional states or properties (i.e., intentional states or properties themselves) or, on the other hand, *second-order* intentional states or properties (i.e., states of intentional states or properties of intentional properties). Pitt's view, roughly, takes contents to be first-order intentional properties, while Kriegel's view takes contents to be second-order intentional properties.

Our choice between a first- and second-order view of contents will again depend on what plays the role of content. If what is entertained or otherwise intentionally represented is a first-order intentional property (or state) in its entirety, then contents are first-order properties (or states), while if it is only a property (or state) of intentional properties (or states) that is entertained or otherwise intentionally represented—say, the feature that differentiates a given intentional property (or state) from other intentional properties (or states)—then contents are second-order properties (or states).

Subsection 9.3.3 suggests that the second-order view may be in a better position to account for some internally structured contents than the first-order view. This might be a reason to prefer it. However, it is not clear how strong this reason is, since it is not clear what is the best thing to say about internally structured contents. In any case, the choice between a first-order view and a second-order view is far from obvious and has few downstream consequences, so I remain neutral on the issue, with a weak preference for the second-order view.

The four options concerning the aspects with which to identify contents correspond to four general options concerning phenomenal characters: Phenomenal characters might be first- or second-order states or properties. Since phenomenal

---

[60] One might worry that this makes contents problematically private. Subsection 9.3.2 addresses this concern, suggesting that much of what we want to say about shared contents is true of the properties that contents are instantiations of ("content properties") rather than contents themselves.

characters are the specific "what it's like" or felt qualities of phenomenal states, our choice between these options will depend on what we want to say is "felt" in having a phenomenal state. Presumably, what is felt is a concrete particular property instantiation, not a general or abstract property, which suggests in favor of taking phenomenal characters to be states rather than properties.

It is less clear whether phenomenal characters are *first-order* phenomenal properties (or states) or *second-order* phenomenal properties (or states), i.e., whether what is felt is a phenomenal property (or state) in its entirety or a property (or state) of a phenomenal property (or state). If phenomenal properties (or states) are experienced in their entirety, then phenomenal characters are just phenomenal properties (or states). If phenomenal properties (or states) have experienced and unexperienced aspects (e.g., something that is "felt" and a "feeling" of that thing), then phenomenal characters include only the experienced aspects, so they are second-order phenomenal properties (or states).

As in the case of intentional contents, we might have a weak reason to prefer the second-order view if we think it provides a better account of the internal structure of phenomenal characters (§9.3.3). However, the choice is not obvious, and not much hangs on it.

Identity PIT identifies intentional contents with phenomenal characters, so, if we are to combine the aspect view with identity PIT, our views of intentional contents and phenomenal characters must agree. I've suggested that there is independent reason to think that both intentional contents and phenomenal characters are states, not properties, and that it is unclear whether these states are first- or second-order states, though there may be reason to prefer the second-order view in both cases. This, of course, is good news for identity PIT.

Appendix H: An Internal Theory of Truth and Reference

A theory of reference for mental states provides criteria that determine what a mental state refers to in various conditions, and a theory of truth for mental states provides criteria that determine the conditions in which a mental state is true. Correspondence and identity theories, as we have presented them, tell us what these criteria are. For example, a correspondence theory of truth states that a mental state is true if it bears a certain correspondence relation to a fact, and an identity theory of reference states that a mental state refers to an item if its content is identical to that item.

A further question about truth and reference, however, concerns what *determines* these criteria. We can distinguish between two kinds of answers: The first is that *we* determine them, while the second is that the mind-independent world does the work for us. Let us say that an **internal theory of truth (or reference)** is one that takes the criteria determining whether a mental state is true (or what it refers to) to be specified by us, and an **external theory of truth (or reference)** is one that takes the criteria determining whether a mental state is true (or what it refers to) to be determined at least in part by factors other than our specifications.

There are deep problems with internal theories of truth and reference. According to internal theories, we specify the criteria determining the conditions in which a mental state is true or what it refers to in different conditions. But in order for our specifications to have any force, they must determinately refer to the conditions required for truth and reference. The problem is that, on pain of circularity, the criteria that determine the conditions of reference of our specifications can't be determined by the specifications themselves. For example, a theory of reference might state that mental states refer to whatever they bear a particular relation R to. In order for us to internally specify this criterion, our specification of the condition of a mental state's bearing R to something must already refer to the condition of a mental state's bearing R to something. Otherwise, our specification does not manage to fix on the condition that it purports to pick out and that is supposed to matter for reference. Put simply, our specifications cannot specify the criteria by which they refer, so, if conditions of truth and reference are determined by internally specified rules, these specifications must get their referents in some other way.

This, in effect, is the import of Putnam's (1977) model-theoretic argument against metaphysical realism. Putnam, roughly, argues that any consistent theory can be interpreted (i.e., be assigned referents and truth-makers for its terms and sentences) in "deviant" ways such that it comes out true, and there is no way internal to the theory to specify the "intended" interpretation. Any proposed constraint on interpretation is "just more theory"; it is just another sentence to be added to the theory, which itself can be deviantly interpreted. These points are just as true of contents as they are of sentences in a theory. Of course, contents are "interpreted" all on their own in that they are *contents*, but they are not "interpreted" all on their own in the relevant sense of having conditions of truth and reference. In order to have conditions of truth and reference, some further facts must obtain, whether they are put in place by us or the world (see §9.3.4). So, Putnam's worry applies to contents, as well as to theories. As he puts it, "You can't single out a correspondence between two things just by squeezing *one* of them hard" (Putnam 1981, p. 73; emphasis in original). This is true whether the thing you squeeze is a sentence in a theory or an intentionally represented content.

So, perhaps we should consider an external theory of truth and reference. According to an external theory, factors external to our specifications play a role in determining the criteria of truth and reference. For example, the mind-independent world itself might determine that a mental state refers to whatever item it bears a particular causal relation to, whatever item it is similar in a certain respect to, or whatever item it bears some other relation to. This, in effect, is Lewis' (1984) response to Putnam. Lewis claims that external facts about natural kinds constrain the interpretation of our theories. These constraints are not "just more theory" because they are supposed to be external constraints, constraints supplied by the world itself, not by our theory.

Putnam (1983) argues that the problem with such external constraints is that they result in a "magical" theory of truth and reference. Roughly, the idea is that any external constraints on truth and reference would have to involve new, brute, nonphysical, and irreducibly semantic facts. For example, an external constraint might specify that a particular causal relation, R, is the reference relation. The problem is that the fact that it is *this* relation—rather than, say, some other causal or other kind of relation—that has this special status is a further fact about the world, one that is arguably brute, nonphysical, and irreducibly semantic. Putnam argues that this is unacceptable (at least by the lights of his opponent, whom he takes to be committed to physicalism).

While I don't think irreducibly semantic facts are automatically a deal-breaker, I do think there is something right about Putnam's charge. As he notes, there are many candidate criteria of truth and reference, each singling out different candidate reference and truth-making relations. Which one of these is the correct criterion is a further fact about truth and reference. Any such further fact would be primitive and brute. But it is not clear why we should care about any such criteria singled out by such further facts. What we care about when we care about truth and reference is not whether the world conforms to our mental states by some potentially arbitrary standards determined by potentially brute metaphysical facts but rather whether the world conforms to our mental states by *our* standards. Suppose that some brute metaphysical fact determined that C was the criterion for reference. If we do not in some sense intend or accept C as the criterion for reference, then, insofar as we are interested in reference, we have no reason to care about whether our mental states satisfy C. For example, suppose that, according to C, my content <the longest goldfish alive> referred to a ham sandwich. Even though my content and the ham sandwich satisfy C, my content does not refer to the ham sandwich in any sense of "reference" that I care about. Even if C coincided with my concept of reference, in that, according to C, my concept of reference referred to C, that would not be enough, because my concept of reference might refer to some other standard, C′, according to C′. What would make C matter is for my concept of reference to refer to it *by my own standards*. But then it's my standards that make

C matter, that single it out as the relation to identify with reference, not the world's.

In short, what we care about is whether our mental states relate to the world as measured by our own standards, in the ways that we intend, whatever they are, not in ways measured by some external standard. The only theory of truth and reference that can deliver is an internal theory. Nothing else will do.

I want to suggest that the matching theory introduced in §9.3.4 can be construed as an internal theory that avoids the difficulties mentioned above for internal theories. For the matching theory to avoid these difficulties, its criteria of truth and reference must be specified by us using contents that refer to these criteria independently of whether they satisfy them. In Putnam's terms, we need an internal constraint that is not "just more theory," one that is already interpreted.

It is not implausible that there are some items that we can refer to without the help of the criteria specified by the matching theory. These might include items we can "directly" refer to, such as our own mental states, their features, our minds, and ourselves. Perhaps we can directly refer to these items by simply having them and attending to them in the right way so as to set them apart in thought, or perhaps, in some cases, we refer to them by having higher-order thoughts that embed them. Unlike in the case of reference to mind-independent objects, we *have* these items in our minds, available to be singled out. In this case, we are not singling out a correspondence between two items by squeezing one of them really hard; we can squeeze our intended targets directly.

Other items we might be able to refer to without the help of the matching criteria are abstractions from or constructions out of the items we can directly refer to. These items might include certain properties and relations that are exemplified by items we can directly refer to, such as the relation of similarity, the property of being mental, and the property of being identical, all of which are arguably exemplified by mental states. They might also include logical constructions of these items, such as the conditions of one mental state being similar to another, the condition of a mental state not being mine, or the condition of not being mental.

If the matching theory can be specified using contents that only refer to items of the above-mentioned kinds, then perhaps it can serve as an internally specified criterion for truth and reference. The matching theory states that a content is true if it matches the world and that a content refers to an item if it matches that item. More explicitly, the matching theory specifies criteria along the following lines:

(True) A content C is true if there is some item x such that x is wholly distinct from C and x has the features of (or is similar to) C's superficial character.

(Refers) A content C refers to some item x if x is wholly distinct from C and x has the features of (or is similar to) C's superficial character.

The conditions specified by (True) and (Refers) are logical constructions out of identity, similarity, and superficial character, which are abstractions from items we can directly refer to. So, we can arguably specify the relevant conditions out of contents that refer to them without needing their help. Of course, in order for the matching theory to provide an internal constraint on truth and reference for any given subject, she must in some sense represent the truth and reference rules herself.

This is far from providing a satisfactory internal theory of reference, but I think it's a start. Many questions remain, such as those concerning the sense in which we can be said to represent the matching criteria (do we phenomenally or derivatively represent them?), whether different truth and reference rules apply to different kinds of contents (do we have different reference rules for contents about mental and non-mental states?), whether the criteria by which contents that refer without the help of our matching rules can be properly considered internal (can we properly be said to specify them and is it a problem if not?), how many different ways of referring there are (can we refer directly, through abstraction and construction of directly referring contents, through matching, and through description?), and how the different ways of referring that we want to accept can interact with each other (can we refer by descriptions composed of contents that directly refer or refer by matching, as well as contents that refer by matching?). But, if such a theory can be made to work, then we arrive at a truly internalist conception of the mind, one on which any phenomenal contents, derived contents, or criteria of truth and reference that we have are fully determined by non-relational, intrinsic, and accessible aspects of our own minds.

VI Conclusion

10 Conclusion: Intentionality and Other Related Phenomena

WE STARTED OFF by noticing that we have visual experiences, auditory experiences, thoughts, and other mental states that we describe as presenting, representing, or "saying something." We took intentionality to be this phenomenon that we at least sometimes notice introspectively in ourselves (Chapter 1). I then argued that intentionality, this "saying something" that we introspectively observe, is not a matter of our tracking external items or having internal states that play certain functional roles (Chapters 3–4). Instead, it is a matter of phenomenal consciousness, the subjective, felt, or qualitative aspect of mental life (Chapters 5–6). This is, roughly, the phenomenal intentionality theory, on which there is a central type of intentionality, phenomenal intentionality, that arises from phenomenal consciousness alone, and all other kinds of intentionality at least partly derive from it. On my specific version of PIT, strong identity PIT, phenomenal intentionality is the only kind of intentionality (strong PIT), and phenomenal consciousness gives rise to phenomenal intentionality simply by being identical to it (identity PIT). In Chapter 9, I further argued that intentionality is non-relational, in that intentional states are not relations to distinctly existing items that play the roles of contents. Instead, intentional states are modifications of subjects, and contents are aspects of intentional states.

On my picture, intentionality is scarcer than we may have previously thought. Unlike many other versions of PIT, my version takes a hard line when it comes to the alleged contents of thoughts, standing states, and nonconscious occurrent states. Thoughts derivatively represent the contents we might have antecedently taken them to represent, but this derived mental representation is not a kind of intentionality (Chapter 7). Standing states also have derived contents that do not qualify as intentional, and nonconscious occurrent states neither intentionally nor derivatively represent (Chapter 8).

In §6.1, I suggested that what makes my version of strong identity PIT a theory of *intentionality* in terms of phenomenal consciousness rather than a theory of *phenomenal consciousness* in terms of intentionality is that it "fits" intentionality to consciousness rather than consciousness to intentionality. In other words, it attributes to consciousness/intentionality the features we might want to attribute to consciousness rather than the features we might want to attribute to intentionality. We are now in a position to see how this is true. Phenomenal consciousness is often thought to be relatively scarce (compared to the supposed abundance of intentionality), internalistic, non-relational, and resistant to naturalization. Chapters 7–8 argued that intentionality is as scarce as phenomenal consciousness is thought to be and that externalist intuitions best motivate externalism about derived mental representation, not intentionality; Chapter 9 argued for a non-relational and probably internalistic conception of intentionality; and one upshot of Chapters 3–4 is that intentionality is fairly resistant to naturalization. If all this is right, then intentionality fits phenomenal consciousness, not the other way around, and my version of strong identity PIT is properly thought of as a theory of intentionality in terms of phenomenal consciousness.

10.1 Return to Other Ways of Fixing Reference on Intentionality

Although my focus has been on intentionality, the discussion has shed light on related phenomena along the way. A theme that emerges is that intentionality does not play all the roles it is sometimes thought to play. Chapter 1 briefly overviewed various possible ways of fixing reference on intentionality and argued that, if what we are interested in is the phenomenon gestured at by "aboutness" and "directedness" talk, there is reason to prefer my fairly minimal ostensive definition, since this phenomenon of "aboutness" or "directedness" might fail to have the features deemed essential by alternative definitions. Let us consider these approaches again to see what has become of these other features.

10.1.1 FOLK PSYCHOLOGY

We attribute to ourselves and others contentful states, such as beliefs, desires, and perceptual experiences, which help us make sense of and predict each other's behavior. One approach to intentionality, then, is to take our target to be a posit in such a folk psychological theory of mind. We rejected this approach to intentionality, but we can still ask what, if anything, plays the relevant role in folk psychological theory. In Chapter 1, I argued that this way of fixing on intentionality might not pick out the same thing as my ostensive definition. In §8.3.3, I argued that our folk psychological notions keep track of much more than our moment-by-moment phenomenal contents; they arguably keep track of a combination of phenomenal contents, direct derived contents, indirect derived contents, and derivatively representational standing states. I also suggested that this is a particularly useful combination of things to keep track of if what we want to do is predict behavior. Folk psychology has conflated various distinct factors, only some of which are genuinely intentional, to yield a notion of content that helps us navigate our complex social world.

10.1.2 THE MIND-BRAIN SCIENCES

Another way of fixing reference on intentionality is via its alleged role in scientific theorizing about the mind and brain. Although we dismissed this approach, we might still ask what answers to the representation-like notions invoked in the mind-brain sciences. In Chapter 8, I argued that the nonconscious states posited by various scientific approaches do not intentionally represent. I emphasized the points of agreement between this view and what I take to be the standard view on the matter: Nonconscious states might track various items in the environment, play various functional roles, and fail to have phenomenal features. They might even be fruitfully described as "representing" various contents, where this notion of representation ("TR-representation") is understood as involving no more than tracking and functional roles. Like nonconscious states, phenomenally conscious states and standing states might also have such TR-representational features in addition to their intentional features, although they needn't in any way match the states' phenomenal contents or derived contents. While the mind-brain sciences might invoke representational notions that pick out intentionality or derived mental representation, many of the representation-like notions at play arguably pick out something along the lines of TR-representation.

10.1.3 GETTING AROUND IN THE WORLD

Another approach to intentionality that I initially rejected takes it to be a matter of having an internal representation of the world that we use for the purposes of getting by. We might be moved toward such an approach by consideration of our impressive ability to get what we need, avoid the things that are harmful to us, plan sophisticated actions well in advance of the time for action, and in general survive in the world. Again, we dismissed this approach, but we can still ask what plays the relevant roles in helping us get around in the world. From what we've seen, we can conclude that, apart from intentionality itself, one important factor in the generation of successful behavior is bearing tracking relations to items in the world. We manage to get by not only by intentionally representing things but also by tracking things that are important to us. The importance of tracking is underscored in mismatch cases for the tracking theory, cases where intentionality and tracking come apart. I have argued that there are several cases like this and that the kind of reliable misrepresentation they often involve might be quite useful for getting around in the world. We often gain no additional benefit when it comes to the successful generation of behavior by representing the same thing that we track rather than representing something else with the very same tracking relations in place. And in certain cases, it might be cheaper, easier, or more efficient to represent something other than what we track.

10.1.4 TRUTH AND REFERENCE

Another way of approaching intentionality is from the perspective of truth and reference. We can take intentionality to be the having of conditions of truth or reference, or that which gives rise to conditions of truth or reference. I decided against this approach as a way of fixing on intentionality because it is not entirely clear that intentionality gives rise to conditions of truth or reference without the help of further ingredients, or even that it gives rise to conditions of truth or reference at all. But we can still ask what accounts for conditions of truth and reference, if anything.

In §9.3.4, we saw that truth and reference pose a special challenge to any theory of intentionality and that my overall view is compatible with various theories of truth and reference. One view takes truth and reference to be a primitive correspondence relation. If this view is correct, then intentionality all on its own does not secure conditions of truth and reference, and an approach to intentionality in terms of truth and reference will pick out a combination of intentionality and this correspondence relation. Another view, which is my preferred view, takes truth and reference to be a matter of our represented contents matching the world. What plays the role of determining conditions of truth and reference according to such a view is an open question, depending on whether the fact that truth and reference are a matter of matching falls out of the nature of intentionality or is a further fact.[1]

10.1.5 TAKING STOCK

In Chapter 1, I argued that definitions of "intentionality" in terms of folk psychology, notions used in the mind-brain sciences, getting around in the world, and truth and reference *might not* pick out the same thing as my preferred ostensive definition. We are now in a position to see that, for the most part, they probably in fact do not. What answers to the folk psychological definition is probably, at best, a combination of intentionality and derived mental representation; what answers to the mind-brain scientific definition is arguably various notions of TR-representation; what answers to the definition in terms of getting around in the world at least involves a combination of both tracking and intentionality; and what answers to the definition in terms of truth and reference is an open question, with my preferred answer being intentionality in combination with particular intentional states specifying how we are to be interpreted (see n. 1). It turns out, then, that intentionality, in our sense, does not in fact play many of the roles that it is sometimes thought to play. Despite this, it plays a central role in the mind, constituting the very stuff of thought and perceptual experience, and allowing us to derivatively represent a plethora of contents beyond the confines of our own consciousness.

10.2 Radical Internalism

The overall view I have presented is a sketch of a radically internalist picture of the mind, one that places the mind firmly within the representing subject. I do not simply mean that it is internalist in that intrinsic duplicates represent alike (in fact, there are important ways in which they need not represent alike). Rather, I mean that it takes the power to target or mean a content to stem entirely from within, making our contents *ours* in the fullest sense. Intentional contents are not items existing on their own that we happen to get related to. Instead, they are aspects of our very

---

[1] Appendix H of Chapter 9 argued that it is possible to understand the matching theory as an internal theory of truth and reference, on which what determine the criteria of truth and reference are our own stipulations. If this view is correct, what is required for having conditions of truth and reference is particular intentional (or perhaps derivatively representational) states. So, what plays the role of determining conditions of truth and reference is intentionality together with the having of these particular intentional or derived representational states.

own minds, belonging entirely to our own consciousness, and any non-phenomenal contents that we count as representing, including any broad or object-involving contents, are specifically welcomed by us, targeted by our self-ascriptions, and never forced upon us by semantic powers beyond our control. If the claims of Appendix H are correct, our mental states' conditions of truth and reference are fully ours too, in that *we* determine the criteria of truth and reference against which our mental states are assessed.

The general outlook can be contrasted with radically externalist and relationalist conceptions of the mind on which our contents are determined by forces wholly beyond our control, lying at the far end of a causal or other kind of relation. Any semantic properties we might have of this sort are inaccessible and irrelevant to phenomenological and epistemological concerns and, more generally, to our conceptions of ourselves as representing and knowing subjects. The subject who wonders whether she is a brain in a vat or whether her premises support her conclusion is not concerned with such inaccessible contents, but with whether the contents *she* intends are true or false or support each other. It is the contents that *we* target that figure in our conceptions of ourselves as representing subjects. Any other semantic features we might be said to have are in an important sense not really *ours*.

In short, on the radically internalist picture, *we* are the authors of our own contents, either because they are parts of our very own consciousness, or because we specifically intend them by self-ascribing them. They are fully welcome, fully endorsed, and fully *ours*.

Glossary

Adverbialism The view that perceptual experiences are modifications of subjects, such as ways of sensing, rather than relations between subjects and objects of experience.

Alleged contents (of a state or representation) The contents that a state or representation is often thought to have, usually on the basis of intuition or philosophical or psychological theory.

Arising B *arises* from A (or, equivalently, A *gives rise* to B) when B is nothing over and above A, e.g., because B is identical to, fully grounded in, constituted by, or realized by A.

Aspect (of an intentional state) The intentional state itself, the intentional property the state is an instantiation of, a property of this property, or an instantiation of the latter kind of property.

Aspect view The view that to intentionally represent the content C is to have a state with a particular aspect, where this aspect is identical to C.

Attitude functionalism The view that an intentional mental state's attitude is a matter of its functional role.

Attitude phenomenalism The view that an intentional mental state's attitude is a matter of its having certain characteristic phenomenal characters.

Attitude representationalism The view that an intentional mental state's attitude is a matter of its having certain characteristic contents.

Attitudes The attitude component of thoughts and standing states.

Broad content An intentional state's content is *broad* just in case it is at least partly determined by environmental factors.

Cashing out thoughts Thoughts that state that an immediate content at least partly cashes out into another content.

C-aspect The aspect of an intentional state representing C that is identical to its content.

C-ness The property that the content C (allegedly) picks out.

Cognitive phenomenal characters Non-sensory phenomenal characters that are special to thoughts in that they do not generally occur in other types of mental states, such as perceptual states, bodily sensations, or emotional states.

Concepts The subpropositional representations involved primarily in thoughts.

Conditions of truth (or reference) (of an intentional state or content) The conditions in which an intentional state or content is true (or refers to particular items).

Conservatism (about the phenomenal character of thought) The view that there are no phenomenal characters beyond sensory phenomenal characters, which might include perceptual, imagistic, verbal, and emotional phenomenal characters.

Content See (Intentional) content, Derived content, and Represent.

Content-character identity view The view that the intentional contents of originally intentional states are identical to their phenomenal characters.

Correspondence theory of truth (or reference) The view that a content is true (or refers) if it appropriately corresponds to, but is not identical to, a state of affairs (or an item of another kind, such as an object or property), which is its truth-maker (or referent).

(Deep) nature (of an intentional content/state/property) What an intentional content/state/property really *is*, metaphysically speaking.

Derivatively intentional property A way things are or might be with respect to their derived intentionality, or a derivatively intentional way things are or might be.

Derivatively intentional state An instantiation of a derivatively intentional property.

Derivatively (intentionally) representing Something *derivatively (intentionally) represents* a content when it instantiates a derivatively intentional property representing that content.

Derivativism (about an allegedly nonconscious intentional state) The view that the relevant contents are derivatively intentionally represented.

Derivativist self-ascriptivism The view that we derivatively intentionally represent various contents by ascribing them to ourselves or our mental states.

Derived content Content that is derivatively represented. See also (DMR) and (DMR-standing).

Derived intentionality Intentionality that derives from other instances of intentionality.

Desire-satisfying virtue A feature of a theory or claim that makes it more desirable that it be true.

Direct derived representation Derived representation in which a vehicle of derived representation represents a content that our takings, stipulations, etc. directly specify.

Dispositionalism (about personal standing states) The view that personal standing states are dispositions to have occurrent states with the same or similar contents or other relevant dispositions, such as dispositions to behave in particular ways. Also called **reductive dispositionalism**.

Distinct (internal) structures Distinct, fairly localizable, and persistent structures in our heads.

Distinct structures view The view that personal standing states are distinct internal structures that continuously intentionally represent their contents.

(DMR) Immediate content C (and any state or vehicle with immediate content C) *derivatively represents* C+ (for S) if S takes C to mean C+.

(DMR-standing) Subject S *derivatively represents* C+ (for S) if S takes herself to have a state with content C+.

Edenic colors Colors exactly as they appear to be, i.e., simple, primitive, sui generis, non-dispositional, non-relational, and non-mental color properties.

Eliminative dispositionalism (about personal standing states) The view that there are no personal intentional standing states but only dispositions to have occurrent states with the same or similar contents or other dispositions, such as dispositions to behave in particular ways.

Eliminativism (about an allegedly nonconscious intentional mental state) The view that the mental state does not exist or does not intentionally represent the relevant contents.

Entertaining (Consciously or nonconsciously) thinking, experiencing, or otherwise occurrently representing a content.

Error of commission The error a theory of intentionality makes when the content it assigns to a representation has a superficial character with features that its represented content does not have.

Error of omission The error a theory of intentionality makes when the content it assigns to a representation lacks features that its represented content's superficial character has.

Experience See (Phenomenal) experience.

Externalism (about mental content) The view that there are broad contents.

Externally structured contents, phenomenal characters, or representations Contents, phenomenal characters, or representations that have properties of having values on certain dimensions.

External theory of truth (or reference) A theory of truth (or reference) that takes the criteria determining whether a mental state is true (or what it refers to) to be determined at least in part by factors other than our specifications.

Functionalist derivativism The view that nonconscious states are derivatively intentional because they bear the right kinds of functional relations to actual and potential occurrent states, including phenomenal intentional states.

Functional role theory The view that all (actual) originally intentional states arise from mental representations' functional roles.

Giving rise to See Arising.

Identity PIT The version of PIT that combines the state identity view, the property identity view, and the content-character identity view, i.e., the view that every originally intentional state is identical to some phenomenal state, every originally intentional property is identical to some phenomenal property, and every originally intentional state's content is identical to its phenomenal character.

Identity theory of truth (or reference) The view that a content is true (or refers) if it is identical to a fact (or other item), which is its truth-maker (or referent).

Immediate content An intentional state or representation's *immediate content* is the content that "runs through our minds" or that is immediately available to us when we are in the intentional state or use the representation.

Indirect derived representation Derived representation in which we take a vehicle of derived representation to represent a content that our takings, stipulations, etc. do not directly specify.

Inflationism (about an allegedly nonconscious intentional mental state) The view that the mental state has phenomenal contents.

(Intentional) content Things of the same kind as what we are tempted to describe as *what* our mental states are "directed at" or what they "say" when we introspect on paradigm cases of intentionality.

Intentionality The feature that in paradigm cases we sometimes both (i) notice introspectively in ourselves and (ii) are tempted to describe using representational terms, such as "about," "of," "represent," "present," or "saying something."

(Intentionally) representing Something *intentionally* represents a content when it instantiates an intentional property with that content.

Intentional mental state A mental state that includes, but may not be exhausted by, the instantiation of intentional properties.

Intentional property A way things are or might be with respect to their intentionality, or an intentional way things are or might be.

Intentional state An instantiation of an intentional property.

Internalism (about mental content) The view that there are no broad contents.

Internally structured contents, phenomenal characters, or representations Contents, phenomenal characters, or representations that have proper parts that are also contents, phenomenal characters, or representations, respectively.

Internal theory of truth (or reference) A theory of truth (or reference) that takes the criteria determining whether a mental state is true (or what it refers to) to be specified by us.

Interpretivist derivativism The view that nonconscious states derivatively intentionally represent the contents that a possible ideal interpreter would ascribe to them using intentional systems theory.

Liberalism (about the phenomenal character of thought) The view that thoughts have cognitive phenomenal characters.

Long-arm functional role theory A functional role theory that takes the relevant roles to include both internal functional roles and long-arm functional roles, which are functional roles with respect to items in the external environment.

Matching 1. Content A *matches* content B when they are exactly alike in superficial character. 2. Content A *matches* item B (which may or may not be a content) when all the features of A's superficial character are had by B.

Matching theory of truth (and reference) The view that a content is true (or refers) if it matches some other item in the world, which is its truth-maker (or referent).

(Mental) representations Internal items that are the vehicles of intentionality.

Mismatch case (for a theory of intentionality) A case in which a theory of intentionality makes false predictions regarding the superficial character of represented contents.

Mode of presentation A guise under which a content is represented.

Multiple arisability An intentional property is *multiply arisable* just in case instantiations of this property can arise in different ways.

Naturalistic items Fundamental physical items lacking mentality and items arising from them.

Naturalistic theories of intentionality Theories of intentionality that appeal only to naturalistic items.

Nonconceptual representation A way of representing a content that does not involve or otherwise require having the concepts required to describe it.

Nonconscious occurrent state An occurrent state that is not phenomenally conscious.

Non-phenomenal intentional state An intentional state that is not a phenomenal intentional state.

Non-propositional content A content that does not have a propositional form, e.g., <blue> and <George>.

Non-propositional representation A representation with a non-propositional content, i.e., a content that does not have a propositional form.

Object-involving content A content that constitutively involves a particular object, property, kind, or other worldly item.

Occurrent state A mental state that is used, entertained, or otherwise active at the time at which it is had.

Original intentionality Intentionality that does not derive from other instances of intentionality.

Originally intentional property A way things are or might be with respect to their original intentionality, or an originally intentional way things are or might be.

Originally intentional state An instantiation of an originally intentional property.

Originally representing Something *originally represents* a content when it instantiates an originally intentional property representing that content.

Paradigm cases of intentionality Mundane, everyday cases of mental states like those described in §1.2.

Personal state A state that can be said to be had by an entire person.

Phenomenal character The specific "what it's like" or felt quality of a phenomenal state.

(Phenomenal) consciousness The subjective, experiential, felt, or "what it's like" feature of mental life.

Phenomenal content The content of a phenomenal intentional state.

(Phenomenal) experience See (Phenomenally) conscious (mental) state.

Phenomenal intentionality theory (PIT) The view that all actual originally intentional states arise from phenomenal states.

Phenomenal intentionality Intentionality that arises from phenomenal consciousness.

Phenomenal intentional property A way things are or might be with respect to their phenomenal intentionality, or a phenomenal intentional way things are or might be.

Phenomenal intentional state An instantiation of a phenomenal intentional property.

Phenomenally represented content See Phenomenal content.

Phenomenal property A way things are or might be with respect to phenomenal consciousness, or a phenomenal way things are or might be.

(Phenomenally) conscious (mental) state A mental state that includes but may not be exhausted by, the instantiation of phenomenal properties. Also called a **(phenomenal) experience**.

Phenomenal state An instantiation of a phenomenal property.

Potentialist derivativism The view that potentially conscious states derivatively represent the contents they would originally represent if they were phenomenally conscious.

Primitivism (about original intentionality) The view that original intentionality is primitive.

Property identity view The view that every originally intentional property is identical to some phenomenal property.

Propositional content A content with a propositional form, e.g., <grass is green>.

Propositionalism The view that all intentional states represent propositional contents.

Psychological involvement An intentional state is *psychologically involved* when it plays a psychological role appropriate to its superficial character.

Qualia Felt, subjective, sensational, qualitative, or phenomenal mental items that are not represented contents.

Reductive dispositionalism (about standing states) See Dispositionalism (about standing states).

Relation view The view that to intentionally represent C is to bear a particular relation (other than instantiation) to C, where C is an item existing distinctly from the representing of C.

Represent R *represents* C when C is R's intentional content, C is R's derived content, or C is R's content on some everyday, scientific, or other notion of representation, which need not be that of intentionality.

Representation A mental representation or other item that represents.

Representationalism The view that all actual cases of phenomenal consciousness arise from intentionality, perhaps together with some further ingredients.

Self-ascriptivism The view that we derivatively represent various contents by ascribing them to ourselves or our mental states.

Sensory phenomenal characters The phenomenal characters characteristic of sensory states, such as perceptual and emotional states.

Short-arm functional role theory A functional role theory that takes the relevant functional roles to be internal functional roles, which are functional roles that representations have in relation to other representations or other internal items.

Standing state A mental state that need not be used, entertained, or otherwise active at the time at which it is had.

State identity view The view that every originally intentional state is identical to some phenomenal state.

Strong identity PIT The view that every intentional state, property, and content is identical to some phenomenal state, property, and content, respectively.

Strong identity PIT* Strong identity PIT together with the view that every phenomenal state is identical to some intentional state.

Strong identity PIT+ Strong identity PIT together with the view that intentionality has the features normally attributed to phenomenal consciousness.

Strong PIT   The view that all (actual) intentional states arise from phenomenal states.

Subpersonal state   A state that is had by a subsystem of a person, rather than the person herself.

Subpropositional representation   A representation whose content does not have a propositional form but that can form a part of a propositional content, e.g., <cat> and <blue>.

Superficial character   The features of an intentional state or intentional content that characterize it as the content that it is.

(Taking)   Subject S *takes* a representation's immediate content C *to mean* C+ if S has a set of dispositions to have cashing out thoughts that together specify that C cashes out into C+ (upon sufficient reflection).

(Taking-standing)   Subject S *takes* herself *to have a state* with content C+ if (1) S is disposed to accept that she has a state with content C (upon sufficient reflection), and (2) either C+ is identical to C or S takes C to mean C+.

Theory of intentionality   A theory that describes the deep nature of intentionality.

Theory of truth and reference   A theory that provides criteria that determine the conditions in which a mental state is true or what it refers to.

Thoughts   Occurrent mental states that we are in when we do what we commonly call "thinking."

Tracking   Detecting, carrying information or having the function of carrying information about, or otherwise appropriately corresponding to items in the environment.

Tracking theory   The view that all (actual) originally intentional states arise from tracking.

Tracking representationalism   Representationalism combined with a tracking theory of intentionality.

TR-representation   Representation that is assumed to amount to nothing more than tracking relations and functional roles.

Truth-indicating virtue   A feature of a theory or claim that provides evidence of its truth.

Vehicle of intentionality   A bearer of intentional properties, e.g., a mental representation.

Weak PIT   The view that there is phenomenal intentionality.

Bibliography

Akins, K. (1996). Of sensory systems and the "aboutness" of mental states. *Journal of Philosophy*, 93(7):337–372.

Anscombe, G. E. M. (1965). The intentionality of sensation: A grammatical feature. In Butler, R. J., ed., *Analytic Philosophy*, pp. 158–180. Blackwell, Oxford.

Armstrong, D. M. (1968). *A Materialist Theory of Mind*. Routledge, London.

Audi, R. (1972). The concept of "believing." *Personalist*, 53(1):43–52.

Audi, R. N. (1994). Dispositional beliefs and dispositions to believe. *Noûs*, 28(4): 419–434.

Averill, E. W. (1992). The relational nature of color. *Philosophical Review*, 101(3):551–588.

Bailey, A. R., and Richards, B. (2014). Horgan and Tienson on phenomenology and intentionality. *Philosophical Studies*, 167(2):313–326.

Bain, D. (2003). Intentionalism and pain. *Philosophical Quarterly*, 53(213):502–523.

Baker, L. R. (1985). A farewell to functionalism. *Philosophical Studies*, 48(July):1–14.

Baker, L. R. (1989). On a causal theory of content. *Philosophical Perspectives*, 3:165–186.

Barnes, J. (ed.) (1984). *The Complete Works of Aristotle*, vols. 1–2. Translated by J. A. Smith. Princeton University Press, Princeton, NJ.

Barsalou, L. (1993). Flexibility, structure, and linguistic vagary in concepts: Manifestations of a compositional system of perceptual symbols. In Collins, A., Gathercole, S., Conway, M., and Morris, P., eds., *Theories of Memory*, pp. 29–101. Lawrence Erlbaum, Hillsdale, NJ.

Barsalou, L. W. (1999). Perceptual symbol systems. *Behavioral and Brain Sciences*, 22:577–660.

Bayne, T., and Montague, M. (2011). *Cognitive Phenomenology*. Oxford University Press, New York.

Bayne, T., and Spener, M. (2010). Introspective humility. *Philosophical Issues*, 20(1):1–22.

Bealer, G. (1982). *Quality and Concept*. Oxford University Press, Oxford.

Bermúdez, J. L. (1999). Naturalism and conceptual norms. *Philosophical Quarterly*, 50(194): 77–85.

Block, N. (1986). Advertisement for a semantics for psychology. *Midwest Studies in Philosophy*, 10(1):615–678.

Block, N. (1996). Mental paint and mental latex. *Philosophical Issues*, 7:19–49.

Block, N. (1998). Conceptual role semantics. In Craig, E., ed., *Routledge Encyclopedia of Philosophy*, pp. 242–256. Routledge, London and New York.

Block, N. (2010). Attention and mental paint. *Philosophical Issues*, 20(1):23–63.

Block, N. (2013). The grain of vision and the grain of attention. *Thought: A Journal of Philosophy*, 1(2):170–184.

Boghossian, P., and Velleman, D. (1989). Color as a secondary quality. *Mind*, 98:81–103.

Boghossian, P. A. (1997). What the externalist can know a priori. *Proceedings of the Aristotelian Society*, 97(2):161–175.

BonJour, L. (1998). *In Defense of Pure Reason*. Cambridge University Press, Cambridge, MA.

Bourget, D. (2010a). Consciousness is underived intentionality. *Noûs*, 44(1):32–58.

Bourget, D. (2010b). The representational theory of consciousness. PhD thesis, Australian National University.

Bourget, D. (2015). Representationalism, perceptual distortion and the limits of phenomenal concepts. *Canadian Journal of Philosophy*, 45(1):16–36.

Bourget, D. (2017a). The role of consciousness in grasping and understanding. *Philosophy and Phenomenological Research*, 95(2):285–318.

Bourget, D. (2017b). Representationalism and sensory modalities: An argument for intermodal representationalism. *American Philosophical Quarterly*, 54(3):251–268.

Bourget, D. (2017c). Intensional perceptual ascriptions. *Erkenntnis*, 82(3):513–530.

Bourget, D. (2017d). Why are some phenomenal experiences "vivid" and others "faint"? Representationalism, imagery, and cognitive phenomenology. *Australasian Journal of Philosophy*, 95(4):673–687.

Bourget, D. (forthcoming-a). Anomalous dualism: A new approach to the mind-body problem. In Seager, W., ed., *The Handbook of Panpsychism*.

Bourget, D. (forthcoming-b). Implications of intensional perceptual ascriptions for relationalism, disjunctivism, and representationalism about perceptual experience. *Erkenntnis*.

Bourget, D. (forthcoming-c). The rational role of experience. *Inquiry*.

Bourget, D. (MS). The underdetermination problem for conceptual role semantics and phenomenal functionalism.

Bourget, D., and Chalmers, D. J. (2014). What do philosophers believe? *Philosophical Studies*, 170(3):465–500.

Bourget, D., and Mendelovici, A. (2014). Tracking representationalism. In Bailey, A., ed., *Philosophy of Mind: The Key Thinkers*, pp. 209–235. Continuum, London.

Bourget, D., and Mendelovici, A. (2016). Phenomenal intentionality. In Zalta, E. N., ed., *The Stanford Encyclopedia of Philosophy*. Metaphysics Research Lab, Stanford University, Stanford.

Braddon-Mitchell, D., and Jackson, F. (1996). *Philosophy of Mind and Cognition*. Blackwell, Oxford.

Braun, K. A., Ellis, R., and Loftus, E. F. (2002). Make my memory: How advertising can change our memories of the past. *Psychology and Marketing*, 19(1):1–23.

Brentano, F. (1973/1874). *Psychology from an Empirical Standpoint*. Routledge and Kegan Paul, London.

Buckner, C. (2011). Learning from mistakes: Error-correction and the nature of cognition. PhD thesis, Indiana University, Bloomington.

Buckner, C. (2014). The semantic problem(s) with research on animal mindreading. *Mind and Language*, 29(5):566–589.

Burge, T. (1979). Individualism and the mental. *Midwest Studies in Philosophy*, 4(1):73–122.

Burge, T. (1988). Individualism and self-knowledge. *Journal of Philosophy*, 85:649–663.

Byrne, A. (2001). Intentionalism defended. *Philosophical Review*, 110(2):199–240.

Byrne, A. (2006). Intentionality. In Pfeifer, J., and Sarkar, S., eds., *The Philosophy of Science: An Encyclopedia*, pp. 405–409. Routledge, London and New York.

Byrne, A. (2009). Experience and content. *Philosophical Quarterly*, 59(236):429–451.

Byrne, A. (2010). Recollection, perception, imagination. *Philosophical Studies*, 148(1):15–26.

Byrne, A., and Hilbert, D. R. (2003). Color realism and color science. *Behavioral and Brain Sciences*, 26(1):3–21.

Byrne, A., and Hilbert, D. R. (2006). Color primitivism. *Erkenntnis*, 66:73–105.

Campbell, J. (1993). A simple view of colour. In Haldane, J., and Wright, C., eds., *Reality, Representation, and Projection*, pp. 257–268. Oxford University Press, New York.

Cao, R. (2012). A teleosemantic approach to information in the brain. *Biology and Philosophy*, 27(1):49–71.

Chalmers, D. (1996). *The Conscious Mind*. Oxford University Press, Oxford.

Chalmers, D. (2004). The representational character of experience. In Leiter, B., ed., *The Future of Philosophy*, pp. 153–181. Oxford University Press, Oxford.

Chalmers, D. J. (2002). On sense and intension. *Philosophical Perspectives*, 16(s16):135–182.

Chalmers, D. J. (2006). Perception and the fall from Eden. In Gendler, T. S., and Hawthorne, J., eds., *Perceptual Experience*, pp. 49–125. Oxford University Press, Oxford.

Chalmers, D. J. (2010). *The Character of Consciousness*. Oxford University Press, Oxford.

Chalmers, D. J. (2012). *Constructing the World*. Oxford University Press, Oxford.

Chalmers, D. J. (2016). The combination problem for panpsychism. In Jaskolla, L., and Bruntrup, G., eds., *Panpsychism*, pp. 179–214. Oxford University Press, New York.

Chisholm, R. (1957a). Intentional inexistence. In Chalmers, D., ed., *Philosophy of Mind: Classical and Contemporary Readings*, pp. 484–491. Oxford University Press, Oxford.

Chisholm, R. (1957b). *Perceiving: A Philosophical Study*. Cornell University Press, Ithaca, NY.

Chomsky, N. (1965). *Aspects of the Theory of Syntax*. MIT Press, Cambridge, MA.

Chomsky, N. (1995). Language and nature. *Mind*, 104(413):1–61.

Chomsky, N. (2000). *New Horizons in the Study of Language and Mind*. Cambridge University Press, Cambridge.

Chudnoff, E. (2013). Intellectual gestalts. In Kriegel, U., ed., *Phenomenal Intentionality*. Oxford University Press, New York.

Chudnoff, E. (2015a). *Cognitive Phenomenology*. Routledge, London & New York.

Chudnoff, E. (2015b). Phenomenal contrast arguments for cognitive phenomenology. *Philosophy and Phenomenological Research*, 90(2):82–104.

Churchland, P. (1981). Eliminative materialism and the propositional attitudes. *Journal of Philosophy*, 78:67–90.

Churchland, P. M. (1989a). *A Neurocomputational Perspective: The Nature of Mind and the Structure of Science*. MIT Press, Cambridge, MA.

Churchland, P. M. (1989b). On the nature of theories: A neurocomputational perspective. In Savage, W., ed., *Scientific Theories: Minnesota Studies in the Philosophy of Science*, vol. 14, pp. 59–101. University of Minnesota Press, Minneapolis.

Churchland, P. M. (1995). *The Engine of Reason, the Seat of the Soul: A Philosophical Journey into the Brain*. MIT Press, Cambridge, MA.

Churchland, P. M. (2005). Chimerical colors: Some phenomenological predictions from cognitive neuroscience. *Philosophical Psychology*, 18(5):527–560.

Cohen, J. (2009). *The Red and the Real: An Essay on Color Ontology*. Oxford University Press, Oxford.

Cornman, J. W. (1971). *Materialism and Sensations*. Yale University Press, New Haven, CT.

Cornman, J. W. (1975). *Perception, Common Sense and Science*. Yale University Press, New Haven, CT.

Crane, T. (2001). Intentional objects. *Ratio*, 14(4):298–317.

Crane, T. (2003). The intentional structure of consciousness. In Smith, Q., and Jokic, A., eds., *Consciousness: New Philosophical Perspectives*, pp. 33–56. Oxford University Press, Oxford.

Crane, T. (2006). Is there a perceptual relation? In Gendler, T. S., and Hawthorne, J., eds., *Perceptual Experiences*, pp. 126–146. Oxford University Press, Oxford.

Crane, T. (2013). *The Objects of Thought*. Oxford University Press, Oxford.

Cummins, R. (1994). Interpretational semantics. In Steven, P. S., and Ted, A. W., eds., *Mental Representation: A Reader*, pp. 278–301. Blackwell, Oxford.

Davidson, D. (1968). On saying that. *Synthese*, 19(1–2):130–146.

De Brigard, F. (2014). Is memory for remembering? Recollection as a form of episodic hypothetical thinking. *Synthese*, 191(2):1–31.

Drayson, Z. (2014). The personal/subpersonal distinction. *Philosophy Compass*, 9(5):338–346.

Dretske, F. (1981). *Knowledge and the flow of information*. MIT Press, Cambridge, MA.

Dretske, F. (1986). *Misrepresentation*. Blackwell, Oxford.

Dretske, F. (1988). *Explaining Behavior: Reasons in a World of Causes*. MIT Press, Cambridge, MA.

Dretske, F. (1995). *Naturalizing the Mind*. MIT Press, Cambridge, MA.

Dretske, F. (1996). Phenomenal externalism or if meanings ain't in the head, where are qualia? *Philosophical Issues*, 7:143–158

Ducasse, C. J. (1942). Moore's refutation of idealism. In Schilpp, P. A., ed., *The Philosophy of G. E. Moore*, pp. 225–251. Tudor, New York.

Egan, F. (2010). Computational models: A modest role for content. *Studies in History and Philosophy of Science*, Part A, 41(3):253–259.

Eliasmith, C. (2013). *How to Build a Brain: A Neural Architecture for Biological Cognition*. Oxford University Press, New York.

Farkas, K. (2008a). Phenomenal intentionality without compromise. *Monist*, 91(2):273–293.

Farkas, K. (2008b). *The Subject's Point of View*. Oxford University Press, Oxford.

Farkas, K. (2013). Constructing a world for the senses. In Kriegel, U., ed., *Phenomenal Intentionality*, p. 99–115. Oxford University Press, New York.

Field, H. (1977a). Logic, meaning, and conceptual role. *Journal of Philosophy*, 74:379–409.

Field, H. (1977b). Probabilistic semantics. *Journal of Philosophy*, 74:379–409.

Fodor, J. A. (1975). *The Language of Thought*. Harvard University Press, Cambridge, MA.

Fodor, J. A. (1978). Tom Swift and his procedural grandmother. *Cognition*, 6(September):229–247.

Fodor, J. A. (1987). *Psychosemantics*. MIT Press, Cambridge, MA.

Fodor, J. A. (1990). A theory of content II. In *A Theory of Content and Other Essays*, pp. 89–136. MIT Press, Cambridge, MA.

Frege, G. (1892/1948). Sense and reference. *Philosophical Review*, 57(3):209–230.

Frege, G. (1956). The thought: A logical inquiry. *Mind*, 65(259):289–311.

Gaskin, R. (2008). *The Unity of the Proposition*. Oxford University Press, Oxford.

Gertler, B. (2001a). Introspecting phenomenal states. *Philosophy and Phenomenological Research*, 63(2):305–328.

Gertler, B. (2001b). The relationship between phenomenality and intentionality: Comments on Siewert's *The Significance of Consciousness*. *Psyche*, 7(17).

Goff, P. (2017). *Consciousness and Fundamental Reality*. Oxford University Press, New York.

Goldman, A. (1993). The psychology of folk psychology. *Behavioral and Brain Sciences*, 16:15–28.

Gow, L. (2014). Colour. *Philosophy Compass*, 9(11):803–813.

Gow, L. (MS). Perceptual experience: Non-relationalism without adverbialism.

Graham, G., Horgan, T. E., and Tienson, J. L. (2007). Consciousness and intentionality. In Schneider S., and Velmans, M., eds., *The Blackwell Companion to Consciousness*, pp. 468–484. Blackwell, Oxford.

Grice, H. P. (1989). *Studies in the Way of Words*. Harvard University Press, Cambridge, MA.

Grzankowski, A. (2013). Non-propositional attitudes. *Philosophy Compass*, 8(12):1123–1137.

Hacker, P. M. S. (1987). *Appearance and Reality: A Philosophical Investigation into Perception and Perceptual Qualities*. Blackwell, Cambridge, MA.

Hardin, C. L. (1988). *Color for Philosophers*. Hackett, Cambridge, MA.

Hardin, C. L. (1992). The virtues of illusion. *Philosophical Studies: An International Journal for Philosophy in the Analytic Tradition*, 68(3):371–382.

Harman, G. (1982). Conceptual role semantics. *Notre Dame Journal of Formal Logic*, 28:242–256.

Harman, G. (1987). (Non-solipsistic) conceptual role semantics. In LePore, E., ed., *New Directions in Semantics*, pp. 55–81. Academic Press, London.

Harman, G. (1990). The intrinsic quality of experience. *Philosophical Perspectives*, 4:31–52.

Harnad, S. (1990). The symbol grounding problem. *Philosophical Explorations*, 42:335–346.

Hebb, D. O. (1949). *The Organization of Behavior*. Wiley, New York.

Hilbert, D. R., and Byrne, A. (2007). Color primitivism. *Erkenntnis*, 66(1/2):73–105.

Holman, E. L. (2002). Color eliminativism and color experience. *Pacific Philosophical Quarterly*, 83(1):38–56.

Horgan, T., and Graham, G. (2009). Phenomenal intentionality and content determinacy. In Schantz, R., ed., *Prospects for Meaning*, pp. 321–344. De Gruyter, Amsterdam.

Horgan, T., and Tienson, J. (2002). The intentionality of phenomenology and the phenomenology of intentionality. In Chalmers, D. J., ed., *Philosophy of Mind: Classical and Contemporary Readings*, pp. 520–533. Oxford University Press, Oxford.

Horowitz, A. (1992). Functional role and intentionality. *Theoria*, 58(2–3):197–218.

Horst, S. (2009). Naturalisms in philosophy of mind. *Philosophy Compass*, 4(1):219–254.

Hume, D. (2000/1739). *A Treatise of Human Nature*. Oxford University Press, Oxford.

Husserl, E. (2001/1900). *Logical Investigations*. Routledge, London.

Ivanowich, M. (2015). Representationalism about sensory phenomenology. PhD thesis, University of Western Ontario.

Jackson, F. (1977). *Perception: A Representative Theory*. Cambridge University Press, Cambridge.

Jackson, F. (1998a). *From Metaphysics to Ethics: A Defense of Conceptual Analysis*. Oxford University Press, Oxford.

Jackson, F. (1998b). Reference and description revisited. *Philosophical Perspectives*, 12:201–218.

Jackson, F. (2001). Locke-ing onto content. In Walsh, D., ed., *Royal Institute of Philosophy Supplement*, vol. 49, pp. 127–143. Cambridge University Press, Cambridge.

Jackson, F. (2004). Representation and experience. In Clapin, H., ed., *Representation in Mind: New Approaches to Mental Representation*, pp. 107–124. Elsevier, Oxford.

Jackson, F., and Pargetter, R. (1987). An objectivist's guide to subjectivism about color. *Revue Internationale de Philosophie*, 41(1):127–141.

Jacob, P. (2003). Intentionality. In Zalta, E., ed., *The Stanford Encyclopedia of Philosophy*. Metaphysics Research Lab, Stanford University, Stanford.

Johnston, M. (2007). Objective mind and the objectivity of our minds. *Philosophy and Phenomenological Research*, 75(2):233–268.

Jorba, M. (2016). Attitudinal cognitive phenomenology and the horizon of possibilities. In Gutland, T. B. C., ed., *The Phenomenology of Thinking. Philosophical Investigations into the Character of Cognitive Experiences*, pp. 77–96. Routledge, New York and London.

Kim, J. (1998). *Philosophy of Mind*. Westview Press, Boulder, Colorado.

Kind, A. (2003). What's so transparent about transparency? *Philosophical Studies*, 115(3):225–244.

Kind, A. (2013). The case against representationalism about moods. In Kriegel, U., ed., *Current Controversies in Philosophy of Mind*, pp. 113–134. Routledge, New York.

King, J. C. (2007). *The Nature and Structure of Content*. Oxford University Press, Oxford.

Koralus, P. (2014). The erotetic theory of attention: Questions, focus and distraction. *Mind and Language*, 29(1):26–50.

Kriegel, U. (2003). Is intentionality dependent upon consciousness? *Philosophical Studies*, 116:271–307.

Kriegel, U. (2007). Intentional inexistence and phenomenal intentionality. *Philosophical Perspectives*, 21(1):307–340.

Kriegel, U. (2011). *The Sources of Intentionality*. Oxford University Press, New York.

Kriegel, U. (2013a). Phenomenal intentionality past and present: Introduction. *Phenomenology and the Cognitive Sciences*, 12(3):437–444.

Kriegel, U. (2013b). The phenomenal intentionality research program. In Kriegel, U., ed., *Phenomenal Intentionality*, pp. 1–26. Oxford University Press, New York.

Kriegel, U. (2015a). Perception and imagination. In Miguens, S., Preyer, G., and Morando, C. B., eds., *Prereflective Consciousness: Sartre and Contemporary Philosophy of Mind*, pp. 245–276. Routledge, New York and London.

Kriegel, U. (2015b). *The Varieties of Consciousness*. Oxford University Press, Oxford, UK.

Kriegel, U. (forthcoming). Brentano's concept of mind: Underlying nature, reference-fixing, and the mark of the mental. In Lapointe, S., and Pincock, C., eds., *Innovations in the History of Analytical Philosophy*. Palgrave Macmillan, New York.

Kriegel, U. (MS). The phenomenal intentionality of moods.

Kripke, S. (1972). *Naming and Necessity*. Harvard University Press, Cambridge, MA.

Kripke, S. A. (1982). *Wittgenstein on Rules and Private Language*. Harvard University Press, Cambridge, MA.

Kroon, F. W. (1987). Causal descriptivism. *Australasian Journal of Philosophy*, 65(1):1–17.

Krosnick, J. A., Betz, A. L., Jussim, L. J., and Lynn, A. R. (1992). Subliminal conditioning of attitudes. *Personality and Social Psychology Bulletin*, 18:152–162.

Levin, J. (2000). Dispositional theories of color and the claims of common sense. *Philosophical Studies*, 100(2):151–174.

Lewis, D. (1974). Radical interpretation. *Synthese*, 23:331–344.

Lewis, D. (1984). Putnam's paradox. *Australasian Journal of Philosophy*, 62:221–236.

Lewis, D. (1997). Naming the colours. *Australasian Journal of Philosophy*, 75(3):325–342.

Lewis, D. (1986). *On the Plurality of Worlds*. Blackwell, Oxford.

Loar, B. (2003). Phenomenal intentionality as the basis of mental content. In Hahn, M., and Ramberg, B., eds., *Reflections and Replies: Essays on the Philosophy of Tyler Burge*, pp. 229–258. MIT Press, Cambridge, MA.

Loftus, E., and Palmer, J. (1974). Reconstruction of automobile destruction: An example of the interaction between language and memory. *Journal of Verbal Learning and Behavior*, 13:585–589.

Lowe, E. J. (1996). *Subjects of Experience*. Cambridge University Press, New York.

Lycan, W. (1996). *Consciousness and Experience*. MIT Press, Cambridge, MA.

Lycan, W. (2001). The case for phenomenal externalism. *Philosophical Perspectives*, 15: 17–35.

Mack, A., and Rock, I. (1998). *Inattentional Blindness*. MIT Press, Cambridge, MA.

Mackie, J. L. (1976). *Problems from Locke*, vol. 27. Clarendon Press, Oxford.

Mackie, J. L. (1977). *Ethics: Inventing Right and Wrong*. Harmondsworth: Penguin Books.

Maddy, P. (2001). Naturalism: Friends and foes. *Philosophical Perspectives*, 15:37–67.

Marr, D. (1982). *Vision*. MIT Press, Cambridge, MA.

Masrour, F. (2013). Phenomenal objectivity and phenomenal intentionality: In defense of a Kantian account. In Kriegel, U., ed., *Phenomenal Intentionality*, p. 116–136. Oxford University Press, New York.

Matthews, R. J. (1994). The measure of mind. *Mind*, 103(410):131–146.

Matthews, R. J. (2007). *The Measure of Mind: Propositional Attitudes and Their Attribution*. Oxford University Press, Oxford.

Maturana, H. R., and Varela, F. J. (1992). *The tree of knowledge: The biological roots of human understanding*. Shambhala Publications, Boston.

Maund, B. (1995). *Colours: Their Nature and Representation*. Cambridge University Press, Cambridge.

McGinn, C. (1996). Another look at color. *Journal of Philosophy*, 93(11):537–553.

Mendelovici, A. (2010). Mental representation and closely conflated topics. PhD thesis, Princeton University.

Mendelovici, A. (2013a). Intentionalism about moods. *Thought: A Journal of Philosophy*, 2(1):126–136.

Mendelovici, A. (2013b). Reliable misrepresentation and tracking theories of mental representation. *Philosophical Studies*, 165(2):421–443.

Mendelovici, A. (2014). Pure intentionalism about moods and emotions. In Kriegel, U., ed., *Current Controversies in Philosophy of Mind*, pp. 135–157. Routledge, New York.

Mendelovici, A. (2016). Why tracking theories should allow for clean cases of reliable misrepresentation. *Disputatio*, 8(42):57–92.

Mendelovici, A. (2018). Propositionalism without propositions, objectualism without objects. In Grzankowski, A., and Montague, M., eds., *Non-propositional intentionality*. Oxford University Press, Oxford.

Mendelovici, A. (forthcoming-a). How reliably misrepresenting olfactory experiences justify true beliefs. In Brogaard, B., and Gatzia, D., eds., *The Rational Roles of Perceptual Experience: Beyond Vision*. Oxford University Press, Oxford.

Mendelovici, A. (forthcoming-b). Panpsychism's combination problem is a problem for everyone. In Seager, W., ed., *Handbook of Panpsychism*. Routledge, New York and London.

Mendelovici, A. (MS). The objects of olfactory experience.

Mendelovici, A., and Bourget, D. (2013). Review of Tim Bayne and Michelle Montague's *Cognitive Phenomenology. Australasian Journal of Philosophy*, 91(3):601–604.

Mendelovici, A., and Bourget, D. (2014). Naturalizing intentionality: Tracking theories versus phenomenal intentionality theories. *Philosophy Compass*, 9(5): 325–337.

Mendelovici, A., and Bourget, D. (forthcoming). Consciousness and intentionality. In Kriegel, U., ed., *Oxford Handbook of the Philosophy of Consciousness*. Oxford University Press.

Michaelian, K. (2011). Generative memory. *Philosophical Psychology*, 24(3):323–342.

Miller, G. A. (1956). The magical number seven, plus or minus two: Some limits on our capacity for processing information. *Psychological Review*, 63:81–97.

Millikan, R. G. (1984). *Language, Thought and Other Biological Categories*. MIT Press, Cambridge, MA.

Millikan, R. G. (1989). Biosemantics. *Journal of Philosophy*, 86:281–297.

Montague, M. (2007). Against propositionalism. *Noûs*, 41(3):503–518.

Montague, M. (2009). The content of perceptual experience. In McLaughlin, B., and Beckermann, A., eds., *Oxford Handbook of Philosophy of Mind*, pp. 494–511. Oxford University Press, Oxford.

Montague, M. (2010). Recent work on intentionality. *Analysis*, 70(4):765–782.

Montague, M. (2013). The access problem. In Kriegel, U., ed., *Phenomenal Intentionality*, pp. 27–49. Oxford University Press, New York.

Montague, M. (2016). Cognitive phenomenology and conscious thought. *Phenomenology and the Cognitive Sciences*, 15 (2):167–181.

Nagel, T. (1974). What is it like to be a bat? *Philosophical Review*, 83(4):435–450.

Nanay, B. (2010). Attention and perceptual content. *Analysis*, 70(2):263–270.

Neander, K. (2013). Toward an informational teleosemantics. In Ryder, D., Kingsbury, and J., Williford, K., eds., *Millikan and Her Critics*, pp. 21–40. Wiley-Blackwell, Chichester.

Nickel, B. (2007). Against intentionalism. *Philosophical Studies*, 136(3):279–304.

Nisbett, R. E., and Wilson, T. D. (1977). Telling more than we can know: Verbal reports on mental processes. *Psychological Review*, 84.

Orlandi, N. (2014). *The Innocent Eye: Why Vision Is not a Cognitive Process*. Oxford University Press, New York.

O'Madagain, C. (2014). Intentionality. In *Internet Encyclopedia of Philosophy*.

Palmer, S. (1999). Color, consciousness, and the isomorphism constraint. *Behavioral and Brain Sciences*, 22(6):923–943.

Papineau, D. (1987). *Reality and Representation*. Blackwell, Oxford.

Papineau, D. (2010). Naturalism. In Zalta, E., ed., *The Stanford Encyclopedia of Philosophy*. Metaphysics Research Lab, Stanford University, Stanford.

Papineau, D. (2014). I—The presidential address: Sensory experience and representational properties. *Proceedings of the Aristotelian Society*, 114:1–33.

Parfit, D. (1984). *Reasons and Persons*. Clarendon Press, Oxford.

Pautz, A. (2006). Sensory awareness is not a wide physical relation: An empirical argument against externalist intentionalism. *Noûs*, 40(2):205–240.

Pautz, A. (2007). Intentionalism and perceptual presence. *Philosophical Perspectives*, 21(1):495–530.

Pautz, A. (2008). The interdependence of phenomenology and intentionality. *Monist*, 91(2):250–272.

Pautz, A. (2010a). A simple view of consciousness. In Kroon, F. and Bealer, G., eds., *The Waning of Materialism*, pp. 25–66. Oxford University Press, Oxford.

Pautz, A. (2010b). Why explain visual experience in terms of content? In Nanay B., ed., *Perceiving the World*, pp. 254–309. Oxford University Press, Oxford.

Pautz, A. (2013a). Does phenomenology ground mental content? In Kriegel, U., ed., *Phenomenal Intentionality*, pp. 194–234. Oxford University Press, New York.

Pautz, A. (2013b). The real trouble for phenomenal externalists: New empirical evidence for a brain-based theory of consciousness. In Brown, R., ed., *Consciousness Inside and Out: Phenomenology, Neuroscience, and the Nature of Experience*, pp. 237–298. Springer, Dordrecht.

Pautz, A. (MS). Color eliminativism.

Peacocke, C. (1984). Colour concepts and colour experience. *Synthese*, 58(March):365–382.

Peacocke, C. (1992). *A Study of Concepts*. MIT Press, Cambridge, MA.

Pearce, S. (2016). A pure representationalist account of the attitudes. PhD Thesis, The University of Western Ontario.

Phillips, I. (2015). Consciousness and criterion: On Block's case for unconscious seeing. *Philosophy and Phenomenological Research*, 92(3).

Piccinini, G. (2008). Computation without representation. *Philosophical Studies*, 137(2):205–241.

Pitt, D. (1999). In defense of definitions. *Philosophical Psychology*, 12(2):139–156.

Pitt, D. (2004). The phenomenology of cognition or what is it like to think that *P*? *Philosophy and Phenomenological Research*, 69(1):1–36.

Pitt, D. (2009). Intentional psychologism. *Philosophical Studies*, 146(1):117–138.

Pitt, D. (MS-a). Unconscious thought. In *The Quality of Thought*.

Pitt, D. (MS-b). Unconscious intentionality.

Prinz, J. (2002). *Furnishing the Mind: Concepts and their Perceptual Basis*. MIT Press, Cambridge, MA.

Putnam, H. (1975). *The Meaning of "Meaning."* Cambridge University Press, Cambridge.

Putnam, H. (1977). Realism and reason. *Proceedings and Addresses of the American Philosophical Association*, 50(6):483–498.

Putnam, H. (1981). *Two Philosophical Perspectives*. Cambridge University Press, Cambridge.

Putnam, H. (1983). *Why There Isn't a Ready-Made World*. Cambridge University Press, Cambridge.

Ramsey, W. (2007). *Representation Reconsidered*. Cambridge University Press, Cambridge, UK.

Rensink, R. A., O'Regan, J. K., and Clark, J. J. (1997). To see or not to see: The need for attention to perceive changes in scenes. *Psychological Science*, 8:368–373.

Revonsuo, A. (1999). Binding and the phenomenal unity of consciousness. *Consciousness and Cognition*, 8(2):173–185.

Rey, G. (1980). The formal and the opaque. *Behavioral and Brain Sciences*, 3(1):90.

Rosch, E. (1975). Cognitive representations of semantic categories. *Journal of Experimental Psychology: General*, 104(3):192–233.

Rosenthal, D. (2010). How to think about mental qualities. *Philosophical Issues*, 20(1):368–393.

Russell, B. (1937). *Principles of Mathematics*. Routledge, New York and London.

Ryder, D. (2009). Problems of representation. I: Nature and role. In Calvo, J. S. P., ed., *The Routledge Companion to Philosophy of Psychology*, p. 233–250. Routledge, New York and London.

Sainsbury, R. M. (2010). Intentionality without exotica. In Jeshion, R., ed., *New Essays on Singular Thought*, pp. 300–318. Oxford University Press, New York.

Schacter, D. L., and Addis, D. R. (2007). The cognitive neuroscience of constructive memory: Remembering the past and imagining the future. *Philosophical Transactions of the Royal Society B: Biological Sciences*, 362(1481):773–786.

Schacter, S., and Singer, J. (1962). Cognitive, social and physiological determinants of emotional states. *Psychological Review*, 69:379–399.

Schellenberg, S. (2010). The particularity and phenomenology of perceptual experience. *Philosophical Studies*, 149(1):19–48.

Schellenberg, S. (2011). Ontological minimalism about phenomenology. *Philosophy and Phenomenological Research*, 83(1):1–40.

Schwitzgebel, E. (2001). In-between believing. *Philosophical Quarterly*, 51(202):76–82.

Schwitzgebel, E. (2002). A phenomenal, dispositional account of belief. *Noûs*, 36(2):249–275.

Seager, W. E., and Bourget, D. (2007). Representationalism about consciousness. In Schneider, S., and Velmans, M., eds., *The Blackwell Companion to Consciousness*, pp. 261–276. Blackwell, Oxford.

Searle, J. R. (1980). Minds, brains and programs. *Behavioral and Brain Sciences*, 3:417–457.

Searle, J. R. (1990). Consciousness, explanatory inversion and cognitive science. *Behavioral and Brain Sciences*, 13:585–642.

Searle, J. R. (1991). Consciousness, unconsciousness and intentionality. *Philosophical Issues*, 1(1):45–66.

Searle, J. R. (1992). *The Rediscovery of Mind*. MIT Press, Cambridge, MA.

Searle, J. R. (2004). *Mind: A Brief Introduction*. Oxford University Press, New York.

Sellars, W. S. (1956). Empiricism and the philosophy of mind. *Minnesota Studies in the Philosophy of Science*, 1:253–329.

Sellars, W. S. (1975). The adverbial theory of the objects of sensation. *Metaphilosophy*, 6(April):144–160.

Shapiro, L. A. (1997). The nature of nature: Rethinking naturalistic theories of intentionality. *Philosophical Psychology*, 10(3):309–323.

Shoemaker, S. (2003). Content, character and color. *Philosophical Issues*, 13:253–278.

Siegel, S. (2005). Which properties are represented in perception? In Szabo Gendler, T., and Hawthorne, J., eds., *Perceptual Experience*, pp. 481–403. Oxford University Press, Oxford.

Siegel, S. (2010). *The Contents of Visual Experience*. Oxford University Press, Oxford.

Siewert, C. (1998). *The Significance of Consciousness*. Princeton University Press, Princeton, NJ.

Siewert, C. (2004). Phenomenality and intentionality—Which explains which? Reply to Gertler. *Psyche*, 10(2).

Siewert, C. (2006). Consciousness and intentionality. In Zalta, E., ed., *The Stanford Encyclopedia of Philosophy*. Metaphysics Research Lab, Stanford University, Stanford.

Siewert, C. (2011). Phenomenal thought. In Bayne, T., and Montague, M., eds., *Cognitive Phenomenology*, pp. 231–267. Oxford University Press, Oxford.

Smart, J. J. C. (1975). On some criticisms of a physicalist theory of colors. In Cheng, Charles L. Y., ed., *Philosophical Aspects of the Mind-Body Problem*, pp. 54–63. University Press of Hawaii, Honolulu.

Smithies, D. (2012). The mental lives of zombies. *Philosophical Perspectives*, 26(1):343–372.

Smithies, D. (MS). *The Epistemic Role of Consciousness*.

Smythies, J. R. (1994). Requiem for the identity theory. *Inquiry*, 37(3):311–329.

Soames, S. (2010). *What Is Meaning?* Princeton University Press, Princeton, NJ.

Sosa, D. (2007). The inference that leaves something to chance. In Goldberg, S., ed., *Internalism and Externalism in Semantics and Epistemology*, pp. 219–234. Oxford University Press, Oxford.

Speaks, J. (2010a). Attention and intentionalism. *Philosophical Quarterly*, 60(239):325–342.

Speaks, J. (2010b). Intentionality. In Hogan, P. C., ed., *The Cambridge Encyclopedia of the Language Sciences*, pp. 398–401. Cambridge University Press, Cambridge, UK.

Speaks, J. (2015). *The Phenomenal and the Representational*. Oxford University Press, Oxford.

Stich, S. (1983). *From Folk Psychology to Cognitive Science: The Case against Belief*. MIT Press, Cambridge, MA.

Strawson, G. (1994). *Mental Reality*. MIT Press, Cambridge, MA.

Strawson, G. (2004). Real intentionality. *Phenomenology and the Cognitive Sciences*, 3(3):287–313.

Strawson, G. (2008). Real intentionality 3: Why intentionality entails consciousness. In *Real Materialism and Other Essays*, pp. 281–305. Oxford University Press, Oxford.

Strawson, G. (2011). Real naturalism. *Proceedings of the American Philosophical Association*, 86(2):125–154.

Sullivan, J. A. (2010). A role for representation in cognitive neurobiology. *Philosophy of Science (Supplement)*, 77(5):875–887.

Thau, M. (2002). *Consciousness and Cognition*. Oxford University Press, New York.

Travis, C. S. (2004). The Silence of the Senses. *Mind*, 113(449):57–94.

Tye, M. (1989). *The Metaphysics of Mind*. Cambridge University Press, Cambridge, UK.

Tye, M. (1995a). A representational theory of pains and their phenomenal character. *Philosophical Perspectives*, 9:223–239.

Tye, M. (1995b). *Ten Problems of Consciousness: A Representational Theory of the Phenomenal Mind*. MIT Press, Cambridge, MA.

Tye, M. (2000). *Consciousness, Color, and Content*. MIT Press, Cambridge, MA.

Tye, M. (2008). The experience of emotion: An intentionalist theory. *Revue Internationale de Philosophie*, 62:25–50.

Tye, M. (2009). *Consciousness Revisited: Materialism without Phenomenal Concepts*. MIT Press, Cambridge, MA.

Tye, M. (2015). Phenomenal externalism, Lolita and the planet Xenon. In Sabates, M., Sosa, D., and Horgan, T., eds., *Collection on the Philosophy of Jaegwon Kim*, pp. 190–208. MIT Press, Cambridge, MA.

Tye, M., and Wright, B. (2011). Is there a phenomenology of thought? In Bayne, T., and Montague, M., eds., *Cognitive Phenomenology*, pp. 326–344. Oxford University Press, Oxford.

Viger, C. D. (2006). Is the aim of perception to provide accurate representations? A case for the "no" side. In Stainton, R., ed., *Contemporary Debates in Cognitive Science*, pp. 275–288. Blackwell, Malden MA.

Weiskrantz, L. (1986). *Blindsight: A Case Study and Implications*. Oxford University Press, Oxford.

Weiskrantz, L. (1997). *Consciousness Lost and Found*. Oxford University Press, Oxford.

Wickelgren, W. A. (1979). Chunking and consolidation: A theoretical synthesis of semantic networks, configuring in conditioning, S-R versus cognitive learning, normal forgetting, the amnesic syndrome, and the hippocampal arousal system. *Psychological Review*, 86(1):44–60.

Wickelgren, W. A. (1992). Webs, cell assemblies, and chunking in neural nets. *Concepts in Neuroscience*, 3(1):1–53.

Williamson, T. (2000). *Knowledge and Its Limits*. Oxford University Press, Oxford.

Wright, W. (2003). Projectivist representationalism and color. *Philosophical Psychology*, 16(4):515–529.

Young, C. A. (2015). Phenomenal intentionality and the problem of cognitive contact. PhD thesis, The University of Western Ontario.

Index

aboutness, xv, xvi, 3–5, 7, 7n5, 9, 13–15, 18, 19, 35n5, 153n41, 180, 244

adverbialism, 198, 214, 230–232, 233
   definition of, 230
   and the many property problem, 219n36, 231–232
   See also aspect view

Akins, Kathleen, 36n6, 44n15

argument from commission, 38–43, 46, 53, 54, 66, 68, 68n48, 87–88
   in standard form, 41

argument from omission, 42–44, 46, 51–54, 66, 68–69, 87–88
   in standard form, 43

arising, 33–34, 71, 72–74, 84, 89n12, 93–97, 102, 110
   definition of, 22
   multiple arisability, 96, 105–108
   and the Real Problem with tracking and functional role theories (*see* Real Problem)
   and the Real Reason to accept the phenomenal intentionality theory (*see* phenomenal intentionality theory: arguments for)

aspect
   C-aspect, 199, 223–224, 226–227
   definition of, 198
   as first- or second-order states or properties, 211–212, 218–219, 232–235

phenomenal characters as aspects, 84n1
   See also aspect view

aspect view, xviii, 112, 115, 193–239, 243–244
   the argument from parsimony for, 203, 206–229
   and contents as first- or second-order states or properties, 211–212, 218–219, 232–235
   as a defense of identity PIT (*see* relation view: as an objection to identity PIT)
   definition of, 198

asymmetric dependence theories of intentionality. *See* tracking theories of intentionality: asymmetric dependence tracking theories

attitudes, 102n22, 124n1, 156–159, 179
   attitude functionalism, 157–158, 179
   attitude phenomenalism, 102n22, 157–159, 179
   attitude representationalism, 157–159, 179
   self-ascriptivism about, 157–159, 177–180, 191–192, 245, 247

Barsalou, Lawrence, 133–135, 137

beliefs. *See* standing states; thoughts

binding problem, 219n37

blindsight, xvii, 161, 190

Block, Ned, xvi, 102n23, 108n29, 190–191n27